Deterritorialized Youth

STUDIES IN FORCED MIGRATION

General Editor: Roger Zetter, *Refugee Studies Centre, University of Oxford.*

Deterritorialized Youth

SAHRAWI AND AFGHAN REFUGEES AT THE MARGINS OF THE MIDDLE EAST

Edited by
Dawn Chatty

Berghahn Books
New York • Oxford

Published in 2010 by

Berghahn Books
www.berghahnbooks.com

©2010 Dawn Chatty

Library of Congress Cataloging-in-Publication Data
Deterritorialized youth : Sahrawi and Afghan refugees at the margins of the Middle
East / edited by Dawn Chatty.
 p. cm. -- (Studies in forced migration)
 Includes bibliographical references and index.
 ISBN 978-1-84545-653-5 (hardback : alk. paper)
 1. Refugee children--Afghanistan--Relocation. 2. Sahrawi (African people)--
Relocation. 3. Refugee children--Middle East--Social conditions. I. Chatty, Dawn.
 HV640.5.A28D47 2010
 362.870835'0956--dc22

                                                                    2010006546

British Library Cataloguing in Publication Data
A catalogue record for this book is available from the British Library

Printed in the United States on acid-free paper.

ISBN: 978-1-84545-653-5 (hardback)

Contents

List of Figures

List of Tables

List of Appendices

Introduction: Deterritorialized Youth: Sahrawi and Afghan Refugees at the Margins of the Middle East

Dawn Chatty

Studies of refugee youth in the Middle East have largely focused on Palestinians, while the situation of Afghan and Sahrawi refugee youth at the margins of the Middle East has attracted little attention. The resilience of Palestinian youth has come to be a contemporary theme in numerous academic and practitioner studies (Barber 2001, 2008; Chatty and Hundt 2001, 2005; Hart 2007). Their 'right of return' to their original homeland continues to be hotly debated and discussed internationally. However, Israel, the government occupying their historic homeland, does not allow them back. Sahrawi and Afghan refugee youth, unlike their Palestinian contemporaries, are encouraged to return both by international agencies and the powers occupying their traditional homelands. Some Sahrawi and Afghan refugee youth do return, but largely they remain in transnational 'exile'. For Afghan refugees the reasons for not returning are numerous. In the early years they revolved around a fear that education might not be sustainable – especially for their daughters and sisters – once they return to Afghanistan. This position has now largely reversed itself with some Afghan refugees returning to Afghanistan because educational opportunities in Iran have been curtailed. For Sahrawi youth, education is seen as an important individual and national tool to prepare themselves for reintegration into their temporary 'nation state' in the refugee camps established by the United Nations near the border town of Tindouf in south-western Algeria.

This book is the outcome of three years of research among Afghan refugee youth in Tehran and Mashhad, Iran and Sahrawi refugee youth in Algeria and Spain. It emerged out of an earlier research programme on children and adolescents in prolonged armed conflict and forced migration. The earlier study focused on Palestinian refugee youth in Lebanon, Syria, Jordan, the West Bank and the Gaza Strip (Chatty and Hundt 2005). That research sought to examine what happened in older children's lives when they and the households they belonged to were uprooted and forced to move. It studied children and young people's lives in the context of the family group, the community and the wider social, economic and political arena, and also looked into the ways in which children and young people within households were changed by past and current episodes of forced migration. It considered the alterations to individual rites of passage from childhood to adult status, changes in informal, formal and non-formal education, and access to labour markets, and transformations in community cohesion and social institutions such as marriage, employment and care of the elderly. This focus on the individual in the context of the family and community, and of the specific contributory influence of the economic, social and political arena, was a direct response to what was regarded as a monopoly of two disciplinary approaches to the study of children and youth: developmental psychology and medicine that tended to pathologize situations of individual and community stress.

Research on children and adolescents, in general, was until very recently primarily based on Western models of childhood and child development (Scheper-Hughes and Sargent 1999; Boyden 1994; Chatty et al. 2005). Perhaps the most fundamental principle which grounded these models was the belief that all children throughout the world had the same basic needs, passed through the same developmental stages, reacted in a like manner to armed conflict and forced migration, employed similar coping strategies, and exhibited common resiliencies. What seemed to be overlooked with this predominantly Western model was that in many cultures, the category of adolescent was not recognized and individuals as young as twelve or thirteen were sometimes expected to take on the roles and responsibilities of adults – marrying, raising families, seeking gainful employment and caring for the elderly in the households. How individuals in such cultures reacted to and coped with forced migration was bound to be different from individuals in cultures where adolescence was recognized as a transitional category from childhood to adult responsibility. Only in recent years has research begun to show that our Western-based assumptions of child development are not universal and that children do not automatically progress through the same sequence of developmental states (Rogoff 2003; Dawes and Tredoux 1989). The work of the social psychologist, Rogoff, has been particularly important in bringing to the fore the cultural nature of much child development. However, research findings take time to become part of the practitioner's portfolio. Although the rhetoric is changing, many international aid agencies involved with refugee children and youth continue to implement programmes – relevant to such institutions as child labour, early marriage and early school-leaving – best suited to the Western assumptions of child development. The effort to understand the cultural, social, political and economic contexts within which these phenomena occur does not find its way into the majority of pre-programming planning initiatives. In addition, many international agencies dealing with children and youth are obliged to work within the international legal understandings of these categories such as those of the United Nations Convention on the Rights of the Child which define 'children' as those under the age of eighteen.

Furthermore, much of the research undertaken on the effects of forced migration has been in the domain of psychology and psychiatry. These disciplines prioritize the trauma and coping strategies of the individual victim and survivor (Ahern and Athey 1991; El Bedour et al. 1993; Rousseau et al. 1998). This disciplinary approach raises two fundamental concerns. First, nearly all psychiatric and psychological research among forced migrants uses concepts that are based on Western ideas of illness and pathology. These concepts often do not correspond to local categories and definitions of illness (Young 1982; Ennis-McMillan 2001). In many cultures, illnesses are regarded as originating variously in the intervention of malevolent spirits, or *jinn*, the inappropriate ingestion of cold or hot foods or other natural or supernatural aetiologies. The use of Western diagnostic criteria and scales, developed using professional disease classification, may not, therefore, be appropriate to understanding local and indigenous classifications. Second, the methods used in much of this research focuses solely on the individual patient. This approach limits the extent to which mental health can be conceptualized in the surrounding culture and society. The egocentric focus of concerns common in much Western psychiatry is thus often at odds with the community-centric focus of the lives of many youth in other cultures. Although recent research in Western psychiatry is beginning to recognize the limitations of 'Enlightenment preoccupations' (Bracken, et al. 1995; Bracken and Thomas 2005) and is successfully beginning to problematize much of the trauma focus in the discipline of psychology and psychiatry, still more needs to be done. Within applied psychology an effort is clearly underway to incorporate qualitative methods in much of its research design (Ager 2002; MacMullin and Odeh 1999; Wessells 1998). In the case of the Palestinian refugee children, where the developmental psychology approach has held sway, our research effort was an attempt to effectively contextualize and thus validate research findings. This book has emerged as an effort to create a greater body of data and thus overcome the initial resistance we found among practitioner and policy-making circles when trying to generalize from our Palestinian material.

Understanding how older children and young people managed their lives in the context of prolonged forced migration and armed conflict was the principle aim of the research programme established at the Refugee Studies Centre in 1999. For the following three years, five research teams, headed by Palestinian researchers, collected anthropological data and engaged in participatory 'action-oriented' research with Palestinian refugee youth in Lebanon, Syria, Jordan, the West Bank and the Gaza Strip. In 2002, after it became clear that the Palestinian data and findings were being treated by policymakers and practitioners as exceptional and thus of little practical value or applicability to refugee youth in other parts of the world, we undertook to carry out a second study of refugee youth in the Middle East, in a search for a wider range of comparative material. This new study was launched in 2002 and focused on Sahrawi refugee youth in Algeria and Afghan youth in Iran.[1] The underlying assumption was that a degree of generalization, or 'lessons learned', would emerge about refugee youth, including Palestinian youth, from a broad regional study where some contextual elements were the same and others were different. The emerging similarities and trends across the seven field sites would then provide an important contribution to comparative studies of youth and their care-givers in forced migration, to the social sciences and to practice in general.

This chapter provides a brief historical background to both the Sahrawi and the Afghani refugee conditions in Algeria and Iran respectively. Both countries are largely off the international humanitarian aid 'radar'. Perhaps this lack of international involvement is because both states are Muslim nations where there is a strong tradition of providing refuge to those seeking asylum at a local and national level without much reliance on international assistance.[2] For this reason, as well as for the largely international political positioning of Iran as a 'socialist' and an Islamic state, refugee assistance in Iran is primarily dependent on state support, with some national non-government organization input, while assistance to Sahrawi refugees is also largely dependent on the Algerian state, with some provision by international and regional NGOs.

This chapter also describes, in some detail, the field research process in each field site which was purposively set up along similar lines to the earlier Palestinian study. The intention was to make it possible to draw out reliable and potentially comparative findings across the seven sites. This introductory chapter looks closely at the contrasting styles and approaches employed by the Sahrawi and Afghan team leaders to gain access to their respective localities, the way in which sites for data collection were identified, the selection, training and support of local researchers, and the interaction, or lack thereof, with humanitarian aid agencies. It also reviews the way in which participatory activities were taken up by the youth among the Sahrawi and the Afghan refugees. The approaches adopted by each of the team leaders were heavily influenced by previous research experience, as well as by the specific political contexts of their field sites.

The chapter closes with a brief discussion of the themes that emerged from the Sahrawi transnational field sites (chapters 1, 2, 3 [Chatty, Crivello and Fiddian, Crivello and Fiddian, and Cozza chapters]) as well as the Afghan field study (chapters 4, 5, 6 [Hoodfar, Kamal and Monsutti chapters]). It reviews the similarities and the differences that have emerged from the data in an attempt to understand how largely Muslim, young people in the Middle East have managed to live with the effects of prolonged forced migration. The ojective is to identify the factors that have contributed to the resilience and agency of these young people as they forge new identities in transnational spaces and create in new places homelands, real and imagined, in which to strive to better their lives and the lives of their parents and caregivers.

Historical Context

The Palestinian, Afghan and Sahrawi refugee communities across the research field sites shared many basic features. They all represented protracted refugee communities of predominantly Muslim peoples.[3] The Sahrawi and Afghan refugee youth shared a background of mobility, one coming largely from a society with a significant pastoral or agro-pastoral base, the other from a society with a long tradition of male (and occasionally family) migration as a 'rite of passage' to full adulthood (Monsutti 2005). All three of these societies were largely illiterate prior to their forced migration; however, other features were significantly distinct. The Palestinians were largely agrarian-based prior to their displacement and had the added difficulty of adjusting to urban life as refugees. Unlike the Afghans in the study who spoke one or more of the languages of Afghanistan, such as Pashto and Dari (Afghan Persian/Farsi), Palestinians and Sahrawis were Arabic speakers, albeit of different dialects. Legal status also varied between and within the groups; all of the Sahrawi camp residents had official refugee status, as determined by the United Nations High Commission for Refugees (UNHCR), and were receiving humanitarian aid and international protection. Palestinians were officially recognized as refugees by the United Nations Relief and Works Agency (UNRWA), but did not enjoy international legal protection. The Afghan refugees were initially welcomed into Iran and encouraged to self-settle. Over time, however, the Iranian government became increasingly reluctant to grant newly arriving Afghans 'official' refugee documentation, or to renew the documentation of those Afghans already resident in Iran.

Sahrawi Refugees

Western Sahara is said to be the last remaining colony of Africa.[4] By 1936, Spain and France had formed an alliance to establish Spanish hegemony in the Western Sahara. In 1966, the United Nations General Assembly called on Spain to organize a referendum in which Sahrawis would vote on self-determination. This was, however, ignored. In 1973, the Polisario (Frente Popular para la Liberación de Saguia El-Hamra y Rio de Oro), the armed forces of the Sahrawi liberation struggle, was formed by a group of Sahrawi students living in Rabat, Morocco.[5] Two years later, in 1975, Spanish General Franco died and the International Court of Justice (ICJ) published its advisory opinion on Western Sahara, rejecting Morocco's and Mauritania's claims to the territory and maintaining the right of the Sahrawi people to self-determination. Soon after the ICJ announced its position, the Moroccan king, Hassan II, assembled the Green March, where an estimated 350,000 Moroccan civilians crossed into the former Spanish Sahara to annex the northern two-thirds of the territory for Morocco. Makeshift camps sprung up inside the Western Sahara to temporarily shelter those who fled their homes but these were bombed soon after in a series of raids by the Moroccan air force. While young men generally stayed behind or eventually returned to fight, many of their family members sought refuge further away across the Algerian border where they remain to this day.

Between 150,000 and 200,000 refugees from the Western Sahara currently live in one of four remotely located camps set up in the harsh desert thirty kilometres from the western-most Algerian town of Tindouf.[6] Some of those who settled in the camps had come from a tradition of nomadic pastoralism; others had fled from the larger urban centres of Western Sahara such as El-Ayoun, Dakhla, La Guera and Smara. They live in tents provided by the UNHCR, while most families have added on sand-brick buildings. Trucks bring water to the camps, as well as food, medicine and other basic supplies.

Despite the remoteness and isolation of the refugee camps, many of the residents maintain transnational networks that link them to families and institutions abroad. Educational networks are particularly necessary in order for students to continue their education, as agreements have been established with ministries of education in such countries as Algeria, Cuba and Libya to enable Sahrawi youth to complete university degree programmes.

The *Vacaciones en Paz* (Vacations in Peace Programme) is also an important channel that links Sahrawi youth to Spain and is organized by the Asociación Amigos de Pueblo Saharaui (registered in 1986 as a national Spanish NGO). *Vacaciones en Paz* is an annual holiday programme that enables between 7,000 and 10,000 Sahrawi children between the ages of eight and thirteen to be hosted by Spanish families in their homes for a two-month period during the summer. During their stay, the children receive medical examinations and treatment, as well as gifts of clothes, toys and money which they take back with them to the camps. The relationships established during the programme often endure beyond the summer months, as proto-familial relationships form between the children and their Spanish host-families, and return trips reinforce these cross-border bonds.

Afghan Refugees in Iran

The presence of Afghan refugees in Iran was seen initially as temporary, and the government, in a gesture of Muslim fraternity, generally welcomed them. The majority of these refugees arrived in Iran during the period of the Soviet military presence in Afghanistan in the 1980s and up till 1992. Many were afforded substantial benefits, including food subsidies, health care, and free primary and secondary-level education for their children (BAAG 1996:8). In 1998, the Ministry of Interior's Bureau of Aliens and Foreign Immigrant Affairs (BAFIA) estimated Afghan refugees in Iran at 1.4 million. Other estimates suggested that the numbers were closer to 2 million (HAMI Association for Refugee Women in Iran). Only 22,000 were believed to live in camps near the Iran-Afghanistan border, or less than 1.6 per cent. Instead most Afghans in Iran were self-settled and scattered throughout the country's villages and cities.

The British Agencies Afghanistan Group (BAAG 1996:5) identified the major flows of Afghans into Iran and grouped them as follows: those who were working in Iran as economic migrants prior to the 1979 Soviet invasion of Aghanistan; those who fled the Soviet invasion during the 1980s;[7] Hazaras who fled in 1991 as a result of massive flooding of their lands; Heratis who fled the Taliban takeover of their land in 1995; Kabulis who went to Iran as a result of economic hardship following the Taliban takeover of the capital; and economic migrants who have entered since 1979.

Those who arrived prior to 1992 were issued 'green cards' which afforded them legal recognition and entitled them to subsidies on health, education, transport and provisions upon repatriation to Afghanistan (BAAG 1996:5). Temporary cardholders and undocumented refugees had little or no legal access to jobs and social services. A number of Afghans who had at one time held proper documentation lost their status after they decided to repatriate. When they again sought refuge in Iran as conditions in Afghanistan worsened, they found themselves undocumented and at risk of being arrested and deported. Currently, those who do not hold proper refugee documentation do not have access to health care nor education for their children.

Education has emerged as an important priority among Afghan families living in Iran. However, the Iranian government has banned Afghan children from Iranian schools in an effort to encourage their families to repatriate to Afghanistan. In response, Afghans have adopted different strategies to overcome the barriers to their children's education; some borrowed the identity cards of Iranians or of Afghans who had legal rights to education. Others mobilized to create informal, self-directed and self-funded schools for their children. During the course of the present study, most of the contact and interaction with the youth took place within these informal schools. Most Afghan refugee male and female children attended schools – either formal Iranian schools or the informal Afghan schools – for some years. Older children and male youth tended to drop out as pressure to earn a wage to support their families increased. Those in the informal Afghan school system were constantly under threat of forced closure by the government.

Setting up the Research: Negotiating the Start of Fieldwork

At the close of our study of Palestinian refugee youth we conducted numerous seminars and round tables in Europe and the United States with policymakers and practitioners to draw conclusions from our work and to extract 'lessons learned' or 'good practice' guides for dealing with refugee youth. We were surprised to hear from some of our audiences that our findings were being labelled as 'exceptional' or 'ungeneralisable' (see Dumper 2003 for a discussion of the perceived exceptionalism of the Palestinian refugee case). That is, as one policymaker in Washington put it, 'the Palestinian case is *sui generis*, you cannot draw any conclusions from it that would have a value in other refugee situations'. Thus, this Sahrawi and Afghan refugee youth study may be regarded as an effort to overcome the narrow policy perceptions which we recognize exist because of limited case studies on refugee youth in the wider Middle East region.[8] Our underlying assumption has been that a degree of generalization, or 'lessons learned' would emerge from this second study where some contextual elements are the same, which would then be applicable to the Middle East region and perhaps more broadly to refugee youth elsewhere.

Here we have refugee youth in, by and large, Muslim countries. We also have situations of prolonged conflict extending back two, if not three, generations. The hope is that the two studies taken together, with their holistic, anthropological approach and action-oriented, participatory methods, would contribute to an alternative understanding of the lives of children and young people that moves beyond the Western model elaborated by developmental psychology. Our aim is to provide deeper insights into the way in which the experiences of refugee youth are mediated through the various social, cultural, political and economic contexts of their lives. The focus of the Sahrawi and Afghan study is then to develop a grasp of the coping mechanism which these young people develop to confront a variety of hardships in their respective host communities – the refugee camps in the Tindouf region of Algeria and the urban refugee quarters of two of Iran's major cities, Tehran and Mashhad.

As with our earlier study of Palestinian youth, the broad aim of the Sahrawi and Afghan refugee youth study was to investigate the direct and indirect effects of forced migration on children. Although we were searching for an understanding of the local social construction of the category of child and youth, we needed to set out a frame of reference for our sampling and interviewing. Our original Palestinian study team had agreed to broadly seek out families with children or youth living at home ranging in age of between about eight to eighteen years. This was an administrative decision for analytical simplicity. We did not seek out legal proof of age from our informants, nor did we use the ages eight or eighteen as a rigid cut-off mark. We all assumed that somewhere in this broad range of chronological age would lie the socially defined 'youth'. We did not intend to be rigid in our child and youth category nor did we accept that this broad sampling guide would be viewed as a tacit reinforcement of Western norms regarding the ages of childhood.

The preliminary findings of the Palestinian study suggested a number of concerns among young refugee people and their caregivers. These included: their multiple, and at times contested, identity as Palestinians, as refugees and as camp residents; their complicated relationship with the occupying state; gender discrimination, particularly expressed by young women; education and the lack of history lessons in the school curriculum regarding their homeland; high levels of unemployment; and the different kinds of violence they witness and experience in their everyday lives (Chatty and Hundt 2001, 2005). Of particular interest to us were the open acknowledgement of multiple identities among refugee youth, the groundedness in the refugee camps in their deterritorialized existence, and the vividness of their 'memory' of the real or imagined homeland of their parents and grandparents. Such contestation of places and spaces was assumed, by many, to be unique to Palestinian refugees. In order to test whether or not this was actually the case, it was important to pursue further comparable studies based on the same fundamental questions and methods in order to facilitate comparison. With these concerns in mind, we set out to examine, among Sahrawi and Afghan youth, the same general set of concerns which had emerged as important for Palestinian youth. Exploring these matters, we hoped, would allow for some analytical comparisons across the seven field sites.

We knew that the past experiences of forced migration amongst the older generations had impacted significantly on Palestinian children and youth.

We wondered whether we would find the same among the Sahrawi and Afghan youth. Knowing how different were the experiences of Palestinian girls from those of boys in terms of exposure, opportunities, constraints and responsibilities within the household and the community, we wondered whether we would find the same to be true in the Sahrawi and Afghan study. Given the Palestinian youth's high profile in political activism, we wondered whether this was also the case among the Afghan and Sahrawi refugee youth. And finally, given the agrarian roots of most of the Palestinian refugees in our study, we wondered whether the tradition of mobility among the Sahrawi in the past would result in findings which suggested a different experience of integrating the reality of forced migration into their current circumstances.

Seville Start-up Workshop

In order to maintain the holistic, anthropological approach to the study of refugee youth, and at the same time develop methods for field research which would permit some comparability between the Sahrawi and Afghan research sites, the project opened with a methodology workshop in Seville, Spain for both teams. The team leaders of each field site, as well as their assistants, were invited to present their research strategies regarding data collection as well as to develop a preliminary timetable for the set of methods to be used in each site. The opportunity was also taken to introduce the school classroom psycho-social 'worry questionnaire' developed by Dr Colin MacMullin, a psychologist at Flinders University, as a potential participatory tool with which to commence fieldwork (MacMullin and Odeh 1999). This 'worry questionnaire', much like the recently revived interest in Q methodology, sought to take into account, clarify and illuminate the perspectives of marginalized and powerless individuals (Brown 1996). MacMullin had applied his 'worry questionnaire' to Palestinian children in Gaza, asking them to identify what they most feared or worried about in their daily lives. The group-centred responses, rather than the usual, Western egocentric ones, were then resubmitted to the children in further 'tests' and games in order to identify priorities and create statistically malleable findings. We found that the first steps of a modified and adapted version of this 'worry questionnaire' in our Palestinian study was particularly useful in identifying youth concerns. But more, it was an ideal tool to draw youth into the study in a participatory fashion. Both the Sahrawi and Afghan teams agreed to try to use aspects of the 'worry questionnaire' in the early stages of their fieldwork when they would be working with local schools to identify potential participants in the study.[9] The later dimensions of the MacMullin study, concerned with creating psycho-social childhood priorities and relevant statistical measures were not taken up by either of the teams. It was also agreed by both teams that basic socio-economic data on each household being interviewed would be coded so that it might be possible to make some associations or comparisons among household variables (for example, youth who were from households with little or no education, who had little or no experience of the homeland, were active in an informal economy).

The team leader for the Sahrawi study was Dr Randa Farah, a Palestinian anthropologist based at the University of Western Ontario in Canada. Dr Farah had previously served as the team leader for the Jordanian field site in the Palestinian study, so she was particularly well placed to implement the same field methods and tools to collect the necessary data from Sahrawi youth. She had also carried out her doctoral research in the same Jordanian field site, and so was very much at home there and was well known and well respected by the Palestinian refugee community. Furthermore, during the late 1970s and 1980s she had been active in the Palestinian cause in Lebanon. Through that experience she had developed personal contacts with some members of the Sahrawi Polisario. The latter were to be very useful to her in facilitating the official permissions she would need in order to set up the Sahrawi field study and in order to appoint her field assistant or manager.

The team leader for the Afghan youth study was Dr Homa Hoodfar, an anthropologist of Iranian origin based at Concordia University in Canada. Dr Hoodfar had already been engaged in extensive research on Afghan refugee women and children in Iran during the previous decades. She was also well connected with the few NGOs working with refugee women and youth in Iran. Official permission was not a requirement for her as an Iranian. Thus her entry into the field had already been established through her previous and ongoing fieldwork and her research teams were well practised in interviewing. However, her field assistant cum local manager, a Chinese Iranian postgraduate student in Comparative Media Studies at the Massachusetts Institute of Technology (MIT), was new to such research.

During the Seville workshop, both team leaders and their field assistants agreed to meet the goal of fifty in-depth interviews and narratives on the impact of forced migration on the lives of the refugee youth and their families. It was also agreed that although youth was to be regarded as a social category, we would need to maintain some consistency with the Palestinian study sample and thus we agreed that each household selected for in-depth interviewing would have children living in it between the age band of approximately eight and eighteen. No effort would be made to confirm these chronologically-stated ages.

The teams agreed that a detailed coding system for socio-economic household data derived from the fifty in-depth interviews in each field site would be developed at Oxford and sent out to each team to be used in the course of their interviewing. It was also agreed that a software package to analyse qualitative information would be utilized to assist in comparisons across the field sites. Several packages were considered, but NVIVO was considered the most sophisticated and flexible and thus the most suitable for this project. We wanted to be able to set our socio-economic variables up against thematic findings in our data. We also wanted to have the opportunity of searching for comparable variables between the two field sites, if our data suggested that such analysis would be of interest.

As with the earlier Palestinian study, it was also agreed that first contact with the communities would be through participatory methods and focused group discussions in order to draw the youth and their families into the study as partners. Thus, although the families to be interviewed were assumed to be representative, the sample was purposive, with youth and their families opting in or out of the study. Such a participatory focus meant that generalizations at the end of the study were going to be harder to come by. Such potential loss, however, we hoped would be compensated by a richness and depth of qualitative material. As well as collecting in-depth interviews, each team was also meant to be conducting participant observation, the notes of which would enrich and help contextualize some of the material to emerge from the narratives of forced migration.

At the end of the workshop it was clear that the two very different contexts of the Sahrawi refugees in Algeria and those of the Afghan refugees in Iran would make it difficult to keep parallel methods and data recording. It might also undermine our efforts to generalize results at the close of the study. Thus it was felt important to make a concerted effort at transparency among all the team members throughout the course of the project. This concern has been translated into a detailed   description of both the administrative features of the field methodology as well as the particular cultural and social context within which each team leader had to work in setting up her team and field site.

Setting up the Research: Getting Started in the Field

For the Iranian team, previous studies undertaken in the same locations with trained research assistants and translators meant that work could start almost immediately. Official permission would not have to be sought as the work could be viewed as a continuation of early research. Dr Hoodfar could maintain the role of supervisor over her new field assistant, backed up by experienced Iranian interviewers who had worked with her in the past on the related topic of women refugees in Iran. This made it possible for Dr Hoodfar to come in and out of the country for short periods regularly throughout the year without having to spend long periods in the field. Sarah Kamal, Dr Hoodfar's field assistant, was also hired as a field researcher and local research team manager to keep an eye on the research teams and to conduct participant observation among the Afghan youth.

For the Sahrawi team, the task at hand was more challenging. Up until the early 2000s very few, if any, long-term studies had been conducted in the Sahrawi camps that were not part of the action plan of the numerous IGOs and NGOs working with the Polisario near Tindouf. Official permission would clearly have to be sought, if only in order to get a visa permitting entry into the field. Gaining permission from the Polisario to undertake independent 'theoretical' rather than 'action-oriented' work was going to be difficult because of its unusual, if not unique, character in the camps. For, although the Polisario relied on an army of NGO/IGO activity in the camps, they had rarely, if ever, agreed to permit an academic study to be conducted among the refugee 'citizens' of the Sahrawi Arab Democratic Republic in exile near the border town of Tindouf in Algeria. In addition, there was the worrying constraint of the limited window of opportunity as far as climate was concerned to conduct such a study once permissions had been gained. Dr Farah, a new staff member at the University of Western Ontario, had a full teaching schedule and so was only available for a few weeks in the winter and spring as well as the long summer break. The latter, however, was the most inhospitable time to be working in south-western Algeria. Dr Farah had to find a way of working with her team during the very high summer temperatures (in the high 40s and 50s C°). Training of the team interviewers and translators was going to have to be conducted during her winter and spring breaks. The summer months, which are so often the main period of data collection for academics not released from general teaching, were largely impractical because of the high temperature. Later we would discover that many camp dwellers also left the camps in the summer. Those who could afford it left for the Canary Islands, Mauritania or simply hired air-conditioned apartments in Tindouf itself.

As both teams began settling into their field sites and initiating participatory activities, a surprising theme began to emerge in both sites from the initial field reports. This theme was not political activism, as had been the case among Palestinian youth, nor was it religious or ethnic identity, as we might have imagined. Rather, it was the theme of food and its relationship to the refugee culture. With two diametrically opposed situations regarding access to and choice of food, it seemed an ideal opportunity to examine the relationship of food to culture and hence, development of identity in exile. Among the Sahrawi youth, there was a total reliance on food-aid – in the form of flour, cooking oil, sugar and other basics donated by the international community – in their bleak and sterile refugee camps in the desert sands several dozen miles away from the border town of Tindouf in Algeria. For the Afghan youth, although there was greater choice with all the markets of Tehran and Mashhad available to them, the desire to replicate the foods of home was striking.

A short complementary study was set up half-way into the project to examine the way in which food mediated the construction of social identities among youth in refugee contexts. The sense of belonging to a group, as well as the need to mark off the group as an entity, was regarded as both an organic and non-essentialist trait as well as an important element of social discourse among refugee youth (Back 1996; Barth 1969; MacClancy 1993). Exploring the way in which food and access and non-access to food associated with parental culture impacted on the development of social identity was felt to be particularly significant in these two extreme cases of food access. In the Sahrawi case, the fieldwork was carried out by Dr Nicola Cozza, while Dr Alessandro Monsutti carried out a parallel study among Afghans in Iran. Professor Jeya Henry of Oxford Brookes University contributed to the design of the food-intake questionnaires and the theoretical framework for studying food among refugee populations. Both researchers benefited from the support system set into place by each of the research teams, but their fieldwork time-frame was relatively short – about six weeks – and their substantive concerns were strongly focused around food-intake, diet and general ideas of identity expressed in what youth ate or sought to eat. Such a specific focus and short period of fieldwork meant that the two 'food' chapters written by these researchers are of a different nature and structure from the rest of the chapters in this book.

Afghan Refugee Youth in Iran (Tehran and Mashhad)

Each team was invited to bring two researchers or other field assistants with them to the opening project workshop at Seville. Dr Hoodar brought with her Sarah Kamal, her field assistant and local team manager as well as Natalie Haghverdian, who would translate the final report of the project document into English. During the workshop they refined their team research strategy, keeping an eye on the way the Sahrawi team was progressing. The emphasis on interactive and participatory methods, particularly at the start of the project work, was a challenge for the Afghan team. Aware of the sensitivity in Iran regarding Afghan refugees – at this point in our research, the Iranian government was actively seeking to shut down Afghan informal schools and deport as many Afghan refugees as they could locate – the team wondered how they could best arrange to have regular access to refugee youth. Why would Afghan youth want to talk to them? The team suggested that the setting up of youth clubs might serve as a central structure for the research effort. It was felt that these clubs could help to develop a relationship with the youth that would be sustainable and long-term, and help the team to establish a presence in the Afghan community that would allow youth and their parents to trust the research team and see them as a support network. It was important, the team felt, that they were not seen as representatives of the Iranian government nor seen as acting in their own interests.

As Iran had no youth organizations or recreational halls that Afghan refugee youth attended regularly, the team felt that the informal Afghan schools would be their best point of contact with youth between the ages of eight and eighteen. They determined to rent rooms in the informal Afghan schools which had sprung up over the last decade, and convert them into youth club offices to give the team a way to develop a relationship with youth and involve them in the study. Because the experiences of Afghan refugees in Iran are quite different in one part of the country from another, the team decided to have two study sites: one in the Afghan suburb of Tehran and the other in an Afghan quarter of the city of Mashhad.

At the close of the Seville workshop, Dr Hoodfar drafted an open-ended questionnaire based on her previous research with Afghan youth. She travelled to Iran the following month to begin organizing the local Afghan research team and to decide definitively on the field sites. While Afghan refugees in Iran did not live in camps, they did tend to cluster in low-income neighbourhoods on the outskirts of the cities. Dr Hoodfar chose one informal school in such an Afghan colony. Choosing a school in Mashhad was more problematic because local government officials were far more rigid about dealing with the informal Afghan schools.

The month of February 2003 was spent selecting research assistants for the team. Dr Hoodfar was determined to find someone who both the Afghan youth and the informal school could trust. Informal schools in Iran were under great pressure from the Iranian government to close down; thus the team research assistants would have to be trustworthy and acceptable to the school administration. Dr Hoodfar also wanted them to be Afghans and female – otherwise she would have lost access to female respondents. During this trip she identified a number of prospective candidates.

Her third major task during this trip was to find a way of managing some kind of governmental protection. Although she did not need official government permission to conduct the research, she felt she needed some kind of semi-official support. She decided to approach HAMI, a semi-governmental Iranian organization which worked with refugee women and children and had branches in both Tehran and Mashhad. Having organized this affiliation, Dr Hoodfar and Sarah Kamal, her research assistant and field manager, finalized their topics for the in-depth interviewing, and decided on a management system for generally tracking her progress, conducting, translating and transcribing interviews, and inputting the household socio-economic data on Excel spreadsheets.

In May 2003 Dr Hoodfar returned to Iran to commence fieldwork. She established her Tehran research centre at Sarollah, an informal and self-funded Afghan-run school. They negotiated a twelve-month lease for a room at the school and planned to do something similar in Mashhad. Fieldwork commenced with an adapted form of the 'worry questionnaire' which had been introduced to both teams by Colin MacMullin at the Seville workshop. This participatory tool/instrument provided an entry into the community and the school and provided the research team with a sense of the anxieties of youth given the pressure on schools to close down.

The results of the community canvassing of the 'worry questionnaire' in Mashhad were good and many youths raised issues that were bothering them. They found the questionnaire a good way of letting others know their feelings and ideas. Consequently, Dr Hoodfar decided to set up the project research centre in the heart of the community and she proceeded to negotiate a seven-month lease in the home of Shocria, an Afghan female writer who had worked with her in the past, instead of at a school as these had been recently closed down by the Iranian government.

During this period Dr Hoodfar also finalized the composition of her research team. In Mashhad she hired Shocria Rezabaksh and her sister Malakeh Batour, as well as Massoumeh Ahmadi, a female Afghan teacher at one of the closed informal Afghan schools. In Tehran she hired Fouzieh Sharifi, a female Afghan teacher at the Sarollah School, as well as Zohreh Hosseini, a female Afghan researcher. She explained the goals of the research and the job requirements and gave training in the use of the computers and digital cameras. Sarah Kamal conducted a series of technical training sessions with the research team over the next few months. Both offices in Mashhad and Tehran were then equipped with desks, computers, chairs, stationery and printers. In Tehran this also meant cleaning out the small dark room she had hired at the informal school and placing a door at the entrance to the room. By the end of the month the basic foundation for the fieldwork was in place. Sarah Kamal remained in Iran to train the team interviewers and also to commence her own participant observation fieldwork.

Dr Hoodfar returned to Iran in September and December for two further field trips. The next phase of the project was to develop youth clubs at both field sites so as to gain trust and also to give something back to the refugee youth. The youth had very little reason to trust either Dr Hoodfar or Sarah Kamal as both were Iranian and hence represented the government and the society that was so unkind to them. In Sarollah School a large youth club and a boys' football team were organized, with 100 participants. In Mashhad a smaller newsletter club and a girls' volleyball team were set up for twenty youths. These 120 refugee youths eventually comprised most of the in-depth interview sample.

The youth club in Sarollah was set up via an open meeting in which the school's youth were invited to sign up for one of seven different committees with up to ten members each. The sign-up sheets for these committees were full within the first few days. A set of introductory meetings were then organized to explain to the youth how these meetings should run and be managed (chairperson, secretary, meeting minutes and agendas). Very quickly the youth learned how to run and manage their own meetings with some light support from the research team, and the club ran successfully for the next six months. Besides the Research Committee, which was deeply involved in the research effort, there was a Committee to Solve Community Problems. When, for example, issues emerged from the 'worry questionnaire', the Research Committee got together with the Committee to Solve Community Problems and set out to improve the condition of the school – a major issue derived from the 'worry questionnaire'. Working together, the youth bought and installed a fan to combat the sweltering conditions in the classroom, they cleaned and made minor renovations to the bathroom, they installed and maintained a large water cooler and they painted the class benches and tables in bright colours. They were clearly very proud of their club. The main youth activity at these clubs was the production of newsletters, the content of which the youth themselves decided. Typically the issues addressed youth concerns such as differences between boys and girls' lives, the life story of an Afghan woman, a seminar on the Afghan constitution, and the reproduction of a great deal of poetry written by the youth and others.

Although the team was not able to create exactly the same kind of structure for the youth club in Mashhad as they had in Tehran, they were still able to develop a strong relationship with the members and to create a participatory research partnership, particularly in the production of the club newsletters. These skills were then also applied to the data collection phase of the research project. They were given training in interviewing and note-taking and were later asked to launch the in-depth interviewing process by conducting introductory interviews with a predetermined list of Afghan youth in Mashhad.

Setting up these clubs was time-consuming and required a great deal of energy on the part of the local research team manager. It is possible that youth club membership may have influenced the kind of data which was gathered from them for this study. However, it does seem that it was the only strategy to take in order to develop and maintain links with the youth at a very unstable time in their lives. Not only were they Afghans under pressure from the Iranian government, but the Iranian state was also under internal pressure with the threat of an attempted overthrow of the Islamic regime very real.

Data collection began with the youth 'worry questionnaire' and then took on a variety of forms. The questionnaire gave the team a quick sense of Afghan youth concerns and helped them to revise their subsequent research tools, such as the Afghan youth essay competition and in-depth interview questionnaire. The main concerns to emerge from this questionnaire revolved around the high cost of school and the dire economic situation at home; not having any documentation, and the subsequent lack of rights; prejudice against Afghans, having no future and the lack of support from the UNHCR. The research team held a number of small, participatory research exercises so that the youth would understand what the research was about. Then after several months of conducting short interviews amongst each other and with their families, the members of the Youth Club Research Committee were sent out to interview each other and their friends, armed with tape-recorders. This process gave them a good sense of the in-depth interview process which the research team was about to embark on.

The team conducted fifty-one in-depth interviews with Afghan youth, seventeen in Mashhad and thirty-eight in Tehran over a period of a few months. These were, shortly thereafter, translated into English and coded according to the topics which had been identified at the Seville workshop. A further fifty-one corresponding in-depth interviews of parents or guardians were also conducted. Every effort was made to sample more or less evenly from the different age groups and by gender. However, the final tally showed a slight skewing towards females and the higher age bracket. The average age of those youth interviewed was 14.8 years.

Table 0.1: Age and Gender of Afghan Interviewees

Age	Tally	%	Gender	Tally	%
8	1	2	Male	21	41
9			Female	30	59
10	2	4	Total	51	100
11	2	4			
12	4	8			
13	5	10			
14	7	14			
15	7	14			
16	8	16			
17	9	18			
18	6	12			
Total	51	100			

As the scheduled end of the research drew near in December 2003, the team began to plan an end ceremony or celebration. However, the youth pressed hard for an extension of the life of the youth clubs beyond the data gathering stage. Dr Hoodfar agreed to continue with modest financial support for a further four months so that they could continue their activities a little longer. The final farewells were made in a large amphitheatre in May 2004 and each youth received an official youth club certificate for their efforts over the past year.

Sahrawi Youth in Algeria and Spain

Dr Randa Farah set about re-establishing her earlier contacts with the Polisario. She was able to locate a former Sahrawi colleague whom she had met when he had worked for the Polisario office in Washington DC in the 1980s. This was Radhi-Saghaiar Bachir, a high-ranking member of the Polisario who was also attached to the office of the President of the Polisario governing body, the Sahrawi Arab Democratic Republic (SADR). After carefully considering the aims of the project, he agreed to work with Dr Farah as her field manager and research associate. The first step was to arrange the obligatory, and as it turned out unusual, permission from the Polisario governing body for this research project to go ahead.

Dr Farah met with representatives of the Polisario in London, in order to acquire an invitation from the SADR (a condition for entering) to visit the refugee camps. While waiting for this permission to come through, she travelled to Spain and started identifying the various NGOs working in the Sahrawi refugee camps. She met with a number of these NGOs and explained the purposes of the research effort in the hope of creating a collaborative environment for herself and her team. These included Solidaridad Internacional; Movimiento por la Paz; Paz y Tercer Mundo; and the Asociación de Amigos del Pueblo Sahraui. While in Spain, she learned that her visa to the Sahrawi refugee camps had been approved and she travelled directly to the camps in Algeria from Spain as an official guest of the SADR.

There she met up with Radhi-Saghaiar Bachir and together they began the process of gaining permission from the Polisario/SADR government-in-exile for this long-term academic study to take place. She met with numerous SADR government officials and informed them of the project. At the same time she canvassed for potential local research assistants and interviewers. As few Sahrawi refugees had travel documents, the pool of possible assistants able to take part in our project workshop in Seville was going to be limited. This exploratory, initial trip confirmed for Dr Farah that there had been no previous academic research on children and adolescents, only policy-driven, short IGO/NGO studies and reports relating to the improvement of service provision. Most of the services provided by NGOs focused on responding to immediate needs, mainly food, shelter and health. The study of the coping strategies of older children and youth, which our project was promoting, was unique among the Sahrawi.

In the past the only 'foreign' activities approved by the Polisario were primarily humanitarian and development projects. Purely 'research' projects tended not to be approved. Academics given access to the camps for a period longer than a week or two were generally already associated with NGOS and were from countries such as Spain and Italy where there was a wide network of support from civil society as well as deep historical links. Whereas the Afghan research team were able to quietly enter the country and commence their work directly with Afghan refugee youth, Dr Farah had no choice but to devote a great deal of time and energy in the early phases of the project to presenting the project to the Polisario leadership, translating the document, and returning to discussions concerning each element of the study in order to secure permission to proceed. This process took a year before the formal commencement of the study. Even with the approval from the highest level which Dr Farah succeeded in obtaining, the research project still faced many unexpected difficulties in being set up; some of these problems were related to the potential for bias commonly found in tight state-control over research processes and team employment.

Dr Farah attended the January 2003 Seville start-up workshop with her project manager, Radhi-Saghaiar Bachir, and a female researcher, Fatima Mohammed Salem. The team presented to the workshop what they saw as the peculiarities and hardships of working in a desert environment, and the problems of being entirely removed from any urban or even suburban context. It was clear from their presentations that this study was going to have to walk a very narrow path between being connected to the government – otherwise it would not be possible to work in the camps – and being sufficiently separate from government so as to enjoy an intellectual independence in the eyes of those being researched. The tight overview by the Polisario over the team's movement, access and facilities threw up important ethical concerns regarding the freedom of voice, participation and agency among the Sahrawi youth and their families. Dr Farah had a very clear sense of these difficulties which in other circumstances it might have been possible to mitigate over the long term, had she been able to remain in residence in the camps over a period of months rather than weeks. Instead, she was only able to spend a few weeks at a time, three or four times a year, working with a largely untested research team unfamiliar with the qualitative and participatory tools which had been agreed upon for this project. Furthermore, here in the Sahrawi camps, she was entering into one of the most inhospitable places on earth, where summer temperatures in the 50s C° – for nearly four to five months of the year – brought activity and movement in the daytime to a near halt.

The immediate issue regarding the Sahrawi study was how to turn the formal permission from the Polisario for this project into a community-wide activity. The team needed to gain widespread support beyond that provided by officialdom. Using mechanisms of SADR state control to the benefit of the project, Dr Farah and her team decided to seek consent from the community by first setting up radio interviews in the camps to discuss the potential benefits of the project to the community. These radio shows, they felt, would be far more effective than any written letters, as oral transmission of information remained important in the formerly partially-nomadic community.

In the Sahrawi team's presentation of their provisional research strategy at the close of the Seville workshop, it was agreed that the fieldwork effort would start in the Sahrawi schools. The team agreed that they would select several classes and ask for permission to conduct a modified form of the Colin McMullin 'worry questionnaire'. This exercise would be conducted by the teams without the support of the class teacher. This modified 'worry questionnaire' exercise would give the team an opportunity to gain an understanding of the concerns of Sahrawi youth and perhaps to modify the topics that would form part of the later in-depth interviewing. It was also hoped that this participatory exercise might help identify youth who would be interested in taking part in this detailed and extensive interviewing.

In the following month, Dr Farah travelled out to the Sahrawi camps where she interviewed potential research assistants. Most of these candidates either had jobs with the various Ministries of the SADR or were heavily committed to volunteer work in the camps. During this same visit, Radhi-Saghaiar Bachir was able to arrange permission from the SADR Ministry of Education to conduct the 'worry questionnaire'. This was administered immediately by Dr Farah to a class of girls and boys between the ages of eleven and fifteen at the 9th of June School. As the 'worry questionnaire' had been originally set up to be administered in school classroom settings, and was so conducted in our Palestinian study, we were not particularly concerned with any particularly methodological issues. Dr Farah did, however, express some concern with the rigid and controlling manner in which the Sahrawi schoolteachers managed their charges. The results of the questionnaire which Dr Farah administered – as with the Palestinian 'worry questionnaires' – focused on community and group issues rather than individual fears. From their responses, the research team was able to derive a general idea of the concerns of youth: worry about the continuing occupation of Western Sahara; fear of failure at school; concern about leaving their families to study abroad; concern about their physical environment; and interest in the community becoming better off. These responses helped Dr Farah and her team to reshape their interview topics. It also gave her some guidance for planning future participatory activity with youth on her next field trip.

In the summer of 2003, Dr Farah returned to the Sahrawi camps in order to complete her selection of researchers and interviewers. She extended her team to include, in addition to Radhi-Saghaiar Bachir and Fatima Mohammed Salem, Abdati Breica Ibrahim, Mohammed Ali, Noueha and Mohammed el Mokhtar Bouh.With these six university graduates, Dr Farah hoped she had found a way around the problems of setting up a research team in this extremely harsh and inhospitable environment. There was the problem of long-distance travel, among a community where travel for extended periods was not unusual. There was the problem of finding those with time to work for her, as all university graduates are obliged to work for the SADR or Polisario upon completion of their education. By spreading out the research load among all six researchers, Dr Farah hoped they would be able to conduct the interviews for her in their spare time. Thus, they could keep their SADR government jobs and at the same time benefit by having this additional employment. Our earlier Palestinian study had relied on a number of researchers who held day-jobs with UNRWA so we did not see this SADR government 'employment' as an insurmountable conflict of interest.

In December 2003, both Dr Farah and I visited the camps for several weeks and met with the extended research team. We spent several days reviewing research methodology and, in particular, the importance of qualitative interviewing. It was clear from these discussions that the team had a strong preference for 'hard' data and were genuinely sceptical of the potential for quantitative research. All of Dr Farah's interviewers had experience with quantitative tools, particularly closed question questionnaires, and would have preferred the study to have had a quantitative focus. Thus, they were all particularly interested in the rather detailed household codes for each extended family group that was to be included in the sample of fifty in-depth interviews. Both Dr Farah and I continued the training of the team members, pressing on with qualitative interviewing training in the hope that they would soon feel comfortable with this, apparently, novel approach to research.

I encouraged Dr Farah to purchase a four-wheel drive vehicle for the project – up to now she had depended entirely on Radhi-Saghaiar Bachir and his vehicle to move around the camps. Generally, she paid for petrol, tyre replacements and any repairs for this vehicle. However, I felt that it was important for the project to have its own means of transportation in a society where mobility was limited but highly prized. A project vehicle would have been seen by many local Sahrawis to represent the a form of independence from the SADR government.

Fearing that the quantitative bent of her research team would overcome her efforts to develop a more qualitative and participatory approach, I also encouraged her to identify her strongest two researchers to give more concerted training in in-depth interviewing, with an eye to shifting the weight of this task on to them alone. During our discussion with her team at this time (December 2003), the following arguments were put forward by her researchers regarding the way in which fieldwork should be conducted and under what conditions:

Movement and transportation were difficult, especially during the hot season. The researchers felt it would be easier for people to work within the neighbourhood, or the camp, in which they lived without having to travel. Many people who worked in a location other than their home camp often slept at the work site. The same was true about visiting (including women) friends in other camps; such visits were often overnight or continued sometimes for days.

When possible (that is when visas/passports and finances are available), Sahrawis go to Algiers, Spain, Mauritania and the Canary Islands, often for months at a time. For this reason it was important to have a large research team to catch people when they were around the camps.

Team members did not feel comfortable interviewing families whom they did not know very well. Thus, there was a general consensus among the team members that it would be easier if they interviewed families that they knew, including relatives. Many began with their neighbours or with their own families. There was a lot of deference in the culture and in-depth interviewing required trust and a certain level of familiarity that was best nurtured by family or neighbours.

Furthermore, some of the male members of the team remarked that it seemed strange for men to interview children. They felt it would be regarded with disbelief by other people and they – the male researchers – might be 'laughed at'. In hindsight, these comments by the research team should have been taken seriously but, at the time, they were regarded as trivial complaints. However, at the end of the research process, it became clear that these remarks should have been grounds to obtain specific undertakings from the male researchers that they would interview children. The research project was, after all, about youth. Furthermore, the field decision to interview family and neighbours raised a number of other ethical issues specifically regarding maintaining the confidentiality of the informants and respecting any wish to remain anonymous. Fortunately for the project, most Sahrawi wanted their story to be told, as they felt, rightly or wrongly, that their story of forced migration and exile has been largely muted by wider international political concerns.

Closing up the Field Sites

In March 2004, I organized a 'dissemination' workshop for the two teams in Damascus to discuss their provisional findings and identify issues, to be included in a 'Lessons Learned Report' for interested IGOs and NGOs working in these fields. Each team invited an important governmental or NGO figure from their field site to take part in the discussions and hear the findings which might influence future policy planning and programming with refugee youth. Dr Farah invited the Sahrawi Minister of Education. At this meeting it emerged that there were, as yet, only a dozen or so interviews completed by either the Afghan or the Sahrawi team. We renegotiated with both teams a new schedule for completing the in-depth interviewing. The deadline of August 2004 was agreed upon at this time and it was decided that all interviews would be completed, translated, transcribed and sent to Oxford by the end of August.

In the summer of 2004, both Dr Hoodfar and Dr Farah returned to their field sites to press forward on collecting the last of the interviews. During this time Dr Farah had the unique opportunity to travel to the Liberated Territories with some of her research team members and visited a number of families, most of whom were herding livestock – mainly camels and goats. This period of time, Dr Farah reported, was extraordinary as it gave her an opportunity to interview a number of respected elders and oral historians of the Sahrawi past. She also had the chance to spend time with youth out of the context of their schools in the refugee camps and to engage in some participant observation as well as some visual photography projects with youth.

By September 2004 the Afghan team had completed their interviews and finalized their field report but the Sahrawi team was struggling to complete the English translation of their interviews. In late August and then again in November Dr Farah travelled to Spain and Italy to enlist the support of the Sahrawi delegation in translating these interviews. Radhi-Saghaiar Bachir, on a tour of Europe for Polisario business at that time, spent a week with her translating these remaining interviews.

Interviewing children proved unexpectedly and particularly difficult for the Sahrawi team. In hindsight, it is hard to separate whether this was due to the rigid Poliario control over so many aspects of the research effort or cultural factors, or a combination of inappropriate training and a powerful cultural discourse. Dr Farah had reported from very early contacts that it was much easier to hold informal conversations with children than with adults. Such encounters formed a body of participant observation notes from which she was able to get a general sense of children's place in society, their concerns and worries as well as sense of their social identity, or belonging to the group. The themes raised by the children she came across in this informal fashion focused on issues such as the extreme and harsh climate they lived in, their general poverty, and the lack of school materials or even toys. However, collecting data on children in more formal settings through household interviewing and narrative collection proved very difficult. Male team members, in particular, expressed discomfort at having conversations with the younger generation. The best information came from informal and spontaneous conversations with young people in the camps and in the Liberated Areas.

In the spring of 2005, when all of the fifty Sahrawi household interviews had been completed, translated, transcribed and sent to Oxford, I realized that only thirteen of the fifty household interviews actually included a young informant between the ages of eight and eighteen. The household coding had been completed to perfection, but in most cases the voices of Sahrawi youth were muted, the text reflecting an adherence to official Polisario narrative not often found in informants so young. Where the voices of the youth were heard, they appeared in the interviews which had been conducted by Dr Farah's female researchers.

What the fifty interviews did reveal was a strong focus on movement in and out of the camps, mainly of children going to summer camp in Spain, but also of adults travelling to Mauritania, the Liberated Areas and Spain. Young and old alike spoke of the summer experience in Spain. I asked Dr Farah whether she would be able to send her team back to the camps to try to tap into the voices of youth. Dr Farah unfortunately felt that cultural constraints were such that she could not ask her team to do any more than they had done.[10] In order to bring out the voices of Sahrawi youth, I commissioned a further study in the summer camps of Spain where the words of young people could be recorded. The project research assistant, Gina Crivello, and my doctoral student, Elena Fiddian-Qasmiyeh, agreed to spend a month in Spain in the summer of 2005 interviewing Sahrawi children and their Spanish hosts in order to bring to life the voice of Sahrawi refugee youth. The findings from this month-long study have contributed to the development of chapter 1 on identity and territory as well as chapter 2 focusing on transnational networks and Sahrawi children.

The Sahrawi and Afghan teams faced very different field sites and extremes in welcome and accommodation. The Afghan study was smoothly integrated informally – without official government involvement – into a community already familiar with the research team and which was seeking expression and agency. The Sahrawi study, on the other hand, had to negotiate a strong-armed government effort to control and manage the research effort. No step could be made without official sanction among a people – much like the Palestinians in the 1960s – who largely voiced a formalistic, government-approved discourse. The details of this section regarding the processes of setting up, administrating and closing down this research effort among largely Muslim refugee youth in very different social and political contexts are valuable in assessing and comprehending the findings of the chapters which follow.

Chapters in this Volume

This volume is divided into two parts: Part I includes chapters related to Sahrawi refugee youth; Part II is drawn from data on the Afghan refugee youth. Part I is made up of three chapters: chapter 1, Identity with/out Territory: Sahrawi Refugee Youth in Transnational Space; chapter 2, The Ties that Bind: Sahrawi Children and the Mediation of Aid in Exile; and chapter 3, Food and Identity among Sahrawi Refugee Children and Young People. Chapter 1, by Chatty, Crivello and Fiddian-Qasmiyeh, sets out the contested history of the Sahrawi people and explores the social and political conditions which have lead to the pre-eminence of formal education and learning-based activities within Sahrawi society as well as the emergence of significant transnational education networks. Based upon both the in-depth family interviews in the Sahrawi camps as well as the individual interviews with children and youth participating in a summer host programme in Spain, the chapter examines how Sahrawi youth identities have emerged in such a transnational context and how the Sahrawi government 'in exile' has promoted and encouraged this development. The chapter also looks at how Sahrawi youth come to terms with their reintegration into the refugee camps after months, if not years, abroad. It suggests that the original tribal ideology of pastoral-based mobility, while not representative of all Sahrawi people, may help to explain the relative ease with which many adults, if not the youth themselves, have accepted and tolerated long physical and temporal absence of close kin as part of the duty of a good Sahrawi citizen.

Chapter 2 by Crivello and Fiddian-Qasmiyeh then explores the way in which Sahrawi refugee children taking part in the annual *Vacaciones en Paz* (Vacations for Peace) in Spain came to mediate the flow of humanitarian aid and other expressions of solidarity for their families and the broader Sahrawi community-in-exile. This chapter is based on nearly fifty interviews with Sahrawi refugee children in the summer of 2005 in Madrid. It documents the views of Sahrawi children in relation to their daily lives in refugee camps, their 'guest' experience in Spain, and their aspirations for the future. The chapter also looks at the views of the Spanish host-parents and integrates information about the kind of support which they offer their guest child(ren) over the years. Crivello and Fiddian-Qasmiyeh see the *Vacaciones en Paz* programme as a vital transnational network that facilitates the shared care of Sahrawi children. The hosting scheme also illustrates the way in which mobility has become a necessary feature of Sahrawi childhoods in exile.

Chapter 3 by Cozza examines the relationship between food and social identity among young Sahrawi camp refugees and complements the later chapter by Monsutti on issues related to food and social identity among Afghan youth. Although the social importance of food is widely acknowledged, little work has appeared in refugee studies on this subject. In this context, this chapter and that by Monsutti in Part II have sought to explore how the condition of forced migration and prolonged displacement might affect food practice, and to what extent changes in food practices and possible resistance to such changes might play a role in the reproduction of social ties and the construction of group identities. Cozza intends the chapter to provoke further debate on the relationship between food, displacement and identity. He finds that there are three categories of food among Sahrawi camp refugees: traditional food, food-aid and new food. For youth, there was an assumption among adults that a preference for new food was widespread and derived from their experiences in the Spanish summer camps as well as their general lack of ability in knowing what is best for them. Such explanations of youth's preferences for new foods, Cozza argues, reveal how food practices have taken part not only in the social construction of adulthood and childhood but also in intergenerational relationships. The relationship between food, gender and ideas of beauty are also examined in this chapter, together with a discussion of how youth's distinctive food preferences have acquired political significance.

Part II consists of three chapters: chapter 4, Refusing the Margins: Afghan Refugee Youth in Iran; chapter 5, Afghan Refugee Youth in Iran and the Morality of Repatriation; and chapter 6, Food and Identity among Young Afghan Refugees and Migrants in Iran. In chapter 4, Hoodfar sets the focus clearly on education while at the same time providing a general overview of the research effort in Iran. Drawing on her long research association with refugee women and children in Iran, Hoodfar prioritizes the remarkable development and manipulation of education, particularly for girls, among Afghan refugees. What is a defining element in the lives of these refugees is the way in which what was once cited as a major reason for fleeing Afghanistan – the imposition of compulsory education by the Soviets – had become a major priority – the acquiring of education, particularly for their daughters, as a requirement of good Muslims. Despite restrictions on access to education imposed on Afghan refugees by an Iranian government tired of looking after millions of refugees, the Afghan community developed informal, self-directed and self-funded schools. The Iranian government policy of banning Afghan children from Iranian schools, Hoodfar argues, has had far-reaching and unintended social, economic and political consequences. The chapter analyses the political and social conditions that led to the emergence of education as a priority for Afghan refugees over the last decade and explores how the attendance of Afghan students in Iranian schools led to their developing a sense of 'Muslimness' as their primary identity, legitimizing their entitlement to education, security and equity.

Chapter 5 by Kamal examines the repatriation concerns of Afghan youth. It looks at the way in which they expressed and acted out their concerns in 2003 and then follows up four youth who moved to Afghanistan in 2006 and another four who remained in Iran. Kamal offers a comparative account of 'return' from the perspective of these Afghan youth as embedded within their family and peer group. In particular, the chapter explores the Afghan youth's experiences of return as related to their construction of self and their future during the three-year time span she observed following a coercive Afghan repatriation programme. Contrary to her expectations, Kamal found that the returnee youth were happier and expressed greater satisfaction with their living conditions. She suggests that perhaps for these Afghan refugees born in exile, enduring the suffering of return was a rite of passage which initiated them into Afghan society.

Chapter 6 by Monsutti is the companion piece to chapter 3 by Cozza. It examines food practices among young Afghan refugees and migrants in Iran and finds this to be an arena where identities are negotiated in their complexity. Monsutti examines three areas of tension related to food and food habits. At the impersonal level, there is the ideal of equality which is implied by commensality; this conflicts with the reality of hierarchy which is inherent to hospitality. At the personal level, migration to Iran has led to a process of urbanization and detribalization and with it an abstract sense of 'Afghan-ness' which is embedded in emblematic dishes. These coexist with the narrower concept of self and everyday foods related to the specific regions of origin in Afghanistan. Finally Monsutti finds that food also expresses the ambivalent perception among Afghans of their Iranian host society. Among Afghan refugee youth and migrants there is an oscillation between a fascination with the modernity of Iran and bitterness towards the Iranian authorities who make them feel used and despised.

Conclusion

The chapters which follow offer a fascinating insight into the lives of refugee youth on the edges of the Middle East and North Africa. Their experiences call for some generalizations – both in the similarities of responses to prolonged forced migration, and in the differences which the specific contexts of lives caught in limbo take on – and may lead to further research questions being tested in the future on refugee youth in the region Four key areas which have emerged as particularly significant in this study of refugee youth on the margins of the Middle East include: multiple or contested identification with places and spaces; opportunism and agency related to gender discrimination and education; resilience and optimism expressed through further migration, and transnational networking in the face of poverty and limited political expression.

Multiple or Contested Identification with Places and Spaces

Ethnic or national identity is cultivated among all peoples through a variety of social processes and institutions. The family and oral history narration are particularly important to refugee youth as well as 'hegemonic social narratives that are not of their own making' (Somers 1994). For the Sahrawi in their camp schools and the Afghan students of the informal schools in Iran, schooling instils a deep sense of identity. Most of the young people in our research programme could describe the villages, towns and urban centres from which their families originated even though many had never been there, providing another layer of identity and connection to the imagined homeland and place of belonging. Afghan youth sought out ways to learn more about their homelands through the internet and by setting up peer-group circulated newsletters and poetry readings as well as historical prose competitions about their places of origin.

Much like the heteroglossia identified among the elderly former settlers of Algeria (*pieds-noirs*) of non-French European origins, contradictory narratives or the juxtaposition of competing voices (Bakhtin 1981, 1986) is a multivocality which is increasingly becoming recognized not only in research into popular memory but also in the narratives of the past by people of any subject position (Smith 2004:252). In the case of the material presented by Smith, former settlers of Algeria narrated their past integration in Algeria with both positive and negative memories. Sometimes the same informant spoke both of successful integration and in a later narration of its failure.

We did not expect to find contestation in terms of belonging and identity among refugee youth in the Sahrawi and the Afghan case material. However, we were surprised to find that multiplicity of identity and some contestation over social memory did exist among these youth. This finding suggested to us that there may, in fact, be a commonality, a multivocality and a heteroglossia among refugee youth in situations of prolonged forced migration across the Middle East and North Africa. The importance of identity and the sense of being 'different' and 'the same', of belonging and of being excluded, is shared by all the refugee youth who participated in the study. This may be explained by the reality of prolonged migration, of being different and marginal in a largely otherwise homogenous society or as an integral part of the social category of youth.

Gendered Opportunism and Agency of Youth

A commitment to helping the family, by taking any opportunity to work, generally in the informal economy, while also attempting to maintain a presence in schooling, was common across our data sets. However, a closer examination of this material revealed widespread gender discrimination which affected access to opportunities for employment as well as support for remaining in education. Throughout, girls faced restrictions on their movement and expression, and had heavier workloads in the household. Furthermore, early or arranged marriage often impacted on the girl's education; in most cases marriage marked the end of their educational opportunities. Clearly gendered similarities in findings become less obvious, however, in terms of the ideology of education. Across the field education was described as the most significant element in terms of future betterment.

Among Afghan refugees, the education of females was often the reason the family went to Iran (due to a fear that the Taliban in Afghanistan, who had banned education for girls, might still be restored to power). One of the greatest fears among Afghan families in Iran was that upon returning to Afghanistan, their girls and young women would lose many perceived freedoms, in particular, their right to employment and public mobility as well as education.[11] Many refugees argued that it was a religious duty to educate women, supported by the example of women in the Quran who had been educated. Among the Sahrawi refugee communities, the access to education was almost equal for girls and boys, up to university scholarships for male and female youth in Cuba, Algeria, Spain and Syria. On their return to the camps from abroad, Sahrawi male youths often leave for extended periods of time to tend to their family's herds, engage in trade, or participate in political activities. The presence of females in the camps is very noticeable. Women are particularly active in the daily administration of camp life and civil society. The progressive socialist agenda of SADR promotes an official image of gender equality and democratic organization in the Sahrawi camps. The role that women play in various aspects of camp life is important, as they comprise an estimated eighty per cent of the adult population.

Resilience and Optimism

Although economic and political activities are particularly gendered in the Palestinian and Afghan communities and not so formally in the Sahrawi, the refugee youth all exhibited remarkable resilience in the face of adversity, poverty and political morasses. Refugee youth looked to the future with optimism whether it involved leaving school and working, or emigrating and supporting their families through remittances. It was not unusual for school-age children to drop out of school or take on informal work outside of school to supplement their families' incomes. The financial hardships faced by Afghan children and their families in Iran did not undermine the youth's determination to get as much schooling as possible. Afghan children were often expected to contribute to the family income, and made to juggle the demands of school and work on a daily basis. When school interfered with their ability to generate an income, however minimal, youth often had to abandon their education in order to work full-time. The jobs for which they were hired were often dangerous (e.g. assembly line work lacking safety nets, garbage collection and sorting without protective clothing or gloves). At the same time, we observed that young Afghans undertaking manual labour regarded it as a source of pride and a trait that distinguishes them from the Iranian population. However, political activism among Afghan refugee youth in Iran was, out of necessity, muted. Here it was important to blend in with the surrounding Iranian population and not be easily identified as an Afghan refugee. Instead the youth demanded an outlet for their self-expression in the form of newsletters, and poetry and prose competitions.

However, among Sahrawi youth political participation was largely shaped by the governance structures in the refugee camps. The school curriculum, planned by SADR, included a political education. Reliance on humanitarian food packages and a general lack of employment opportunities encouraged young people to continue their education to secondary and tertiary level.

Emigration, or the desire to emigrate, to find work and send remittances back to their families, is a form of hope among all these refugee youth. Among Sahrawis, permanent emigration is limited as SADR encourages the formation of transnational links in Spain, Cuba and other places in the Middle East over settlement abroad. Afghans, on the other hand, have a long history of migration to Iran. Many of the families who participated in the study had members who had first migrated there over fifteen or twenty years ago.

Many of the conclusions drawn in the earlier Palestinian refugee youth study resonate in the following chapters. Yet their expression has varied, highlighting the importance of local context and historical specificity. Seeking an education, while also committing to helping the family, was, among each of these sets of refugee youth, significant. So, too, was their resilience and optimism expressed through the constant searches for identity, work or self employment in the informal economy and their awareness and response to gender discrimination. By drawing together in this volume these two related but distinct examples of young refugee lives at the margins of the Middle East and North Africa, it has become possible to identify features that are shared across the region. At the same time it allows us to better understand the specificities of each refugee case and so improve our understanding of both the commonalities and the differences that exist in refugee youth's response to prolonged forced migration.

Notes

1. The perception of exceptionalism can be overcome by setting up further studies, using a similar methodology, allowing for the comparisons between the data sets on other refugee youth. However, critics of comparative studies frequently assert that anthropological and especially participatory studies are not framed in such a way as to be empirically comparable. I take the position that generalization is at the core of the anthropological knowledge project of cross-cultural or cross-societal comparison and that social science is the study of meaningful human behaviour.
2. The United Nations High Commission for Refugees (UNHCR) does have a presence in Iran and in the Sahrawi refugee camps, but both operations have limited budgets.
3. The Palestinian group, however, had a particularly significant Christian minority.
4. According to United Nations' figures for 1998, there were 275,000 inhabitants in Western Sahara, excluding Moroccan settlers in the territory, as well as refugees in neighbouring countries.
5. On 27 February 1976, the day after the Spanish officially withdrew from the territory, the Polisario proclaimed an independent Western Sahara (Sahrawi Arab Democratic Republic, or SADR).
6. The Smara, Auserd and Aaiun camps are located in close proximity to one another and each claims around 40,000–45,000 residents. The fourth camp, Dakhla, is located at some distance from the others and claims a higher population of between 45,000 and 50,000 residents. Each camp is intended to function as a self-contained wilaya or province of SADR. Each wilaya is divided into six daira or districts, with Dakhla having seven due to its slightly higher population. Each daira is subdivided into four hay or sub-districts (UNHCR (2003/4/5) Statistical Overview 2002/3/4). Available at www.unhcr.org.
7. By 1998, their official numbers reached some 2.35 million and by 1992, nearly 3 million.
8. The Middle East is here defined as stretching from Mauretania to the West and Afghanistan to the East. This broad geographical definition has been widely used in recent years by a number of scholars working in the region (see for example Eickelman 2001).
9. The very high regard in which the Palestinian, Sahrawi and Afghan communities held education meant that the school classroom was an ideal initial point to commence fieldwork for this project. Permission was sought, and gained from – in the case of the Sahrawi – the Polisario government in exile and – in the case of the Afghan refugee community in Iran – the individual informal school headteachers. Any bias or compromise which such authority figures may have had on the research were compensated for by the ease of access and gradual transition to a less structured field situation.
10. Dr Farah was invited to write chapter 2 for this volume. However, she declined the invitation and passed a message through the Chair of her department at the University of Western Ontario that she might engage with this material at some time in the future.

11. Kamal remarks that although some of the refugees who returned to Afghanistan recognised that the quality of education was higher in Iran, the prospect of not being able to attend university or having schools shut down in Iran was a big factor in promoting their return to Afghanistan (personal communications, August 2007).

References

Ager, A. 2002. 'Psychosocial Needs in Complex Emergencies', *The Lancet Supplement* 360: 43–44.

Ahern, F. and J. Athey. 1991. *Refugee Children, Theory, Research and Services.* Baltimore: The Johns Hopkins University Press.

Back, L. 1996. *New Ethnicities and Urban Culture. Racism and Multiculture in Young Lives.* London: Routledge.

Bakhtin, M. 1981. *The Dialogic Imagination: Four Essays*, translated by Caryl Emerson and Michael Holquist. Austin: University of Texas Press.

———. 1986. *Speech Genres and Other Late Essays*, translated by Caryl Emerson and Michael Holquist. Austin: University of Texas Press.

Barber, B. 2001. 'Political Violence, Social Integration, and Youth Functioning: Palestinian Youth from the Intifada', *Journal of Community Psychology* 29: 259–80.

——— (ed.). 2008. *Adolescents and War: How Youth deal with Political Violence.* New York: Oxford University Press.

Barth, F. 1969. *Ethnic Groups and Boundaries: the Social Organisation of Cultural Difference.* London: George Allen and Unwin.

Boyden, J. 1994. 'Children's Experience of Conflict Related Emergencies: Some Implications for Relief Policy and Practice', *Disasters* 18(3): 254–67.

Bracken, P., J. Giller and D. Summerfield. 1995. 'Psychological Responses to War and Atrocity: The Limitations of Current Concepts', *Social Science and Medicine* 40(8): 1073–1082.

——— and P. Thomas. 2005. *Postpsychiatry.* Oxford: Oxford University Press.

British Agencies Afghanistan Group (BAAG). 1996. *Exile and Return: Report on a Study on Coping Strategies among Afghan Refugees in Iran and Returnees to Afghanistan.* BAAG.

Brown, S 1996. 'Q Methodology and Qualitative Research', *Qualitative Health Research* 6 (4): 561–567.

Chatty, D. and G. Hundt. 2001. *Lessons Learned Report: Children and Adolescents in Palestinian Households: Living with the Effects of Prolonged Conflict and Forced Migration.* Oxford: Refugee Studies Centre.

——— and G.L. Hundt (eds). 2005. *Children of Palestine: Experiencing Forced Migration in the Middle East.* Oxford: Berghahn Books.

———, G. Crivello and G.L. Hundt. 2005. 'Theoretical and Methodological Challenges to Studying Refugee Children in the Middle East and North Africa: Young Palestinian, Afghan and Sahrawi Refugees', *Journal of Refugee Studies* 18(4): 387–409.

Dawes, A. and C. Tredoux. 1989. 'The Impact of Violence on Children: A Study from South Africa', Paper presented at the Fourth Ethnography of Childhood Workshop. Victoria Falls, Zimbabwe.

Dumper, M. 2003. 'Comparative Perspectives on Repatriation and Resettlement of Palestinian Refugees: the Cases of Guatemala, Bosnia and Afghanistan', Paper prepared for the International Conference on Israel and the Palestinian Refugees, Max Planck Institute for Comparative Public Law and International Law, Heidelberg, 11–13 July 2003.

Eickelman, D. 2001. *The Middle East and Central Asia: an Anthropological Approach.* 4th ed. Englewoods Cliffs, NJ: Prentice Hall.

El Bedour, S., R. Bensel and D. Bastien. 1993. 'Ecological Integrated Model of Children of War: Individual and Social Psychology', *Child Abuse and Neglect* 17: 805–19.

Ennis-McMillan, M. 2001. 'Suffering from Water: Social Origins of Bodily Distress in a Mexican Community', *Medical Anthropology Quarterly* 15(3): 368–90.

Hart, J. 2007. 'Empowerment or Frustration? Participatory Programming with Young Palestinians', *Children, Youth and Environments* 17(3): 1–23.

——— (ed.). 2008. *Years of Conflict: Adolescence, Political Violence and Displacement.* Oxford and New York: Berghahn Books.

MacClancy, J. 1993. 'Biological Basques, Sociologically Speaking', in M. Chapman (ed.), *Social and Biological Aspects of Ethnicity.* Oxford: Oxford University Press, pp. 92–129.

MacMullin, C. and J. Odeh. 1999. 'What is Worrying Children in the Gaza Strip?', *Child Psychiatry and Human Development* 30(1): 55–72.

Monsutti, A. 2005. 'La migration comme rite de passage: la construction de la masculinité parmi les jeunes Afghans en Iran', in C. Verschuur and F. Reysoo (eds), *Genre, nouvelle division internationale du travail et migrations.* Paris: L'Harmattan (*Cahiers genre et développement*, no. 5), pp. 179–186.

Rogoff, B. 2003. *The Cultural Nature of Human Development.* Oxford : University of Oxford Press.

Rousseau, C., M.S. Taher, M.-J. Gagne and G. Bibeau. 1998. 'Resilience in Unaccompanied Minors from the North of Somalia', *Psychoanalytic Review* 85(4): 615–37.

Scheper-Hughes, N. and C. Sargent (eds). 1999. *Small Wars: The Cultural Politics of Childhood.* Berkeley: University of California Press.

Smith, A. 2004. 'Heteroglossia, "Common Sense", and Social Memory', *American Ethnologist* 1(2): 251–69.

Somers, M. 1994. 'The Narrative Constitution of Identity: a Relational and Network Approach', *Theory and Society* 23: 605–649.

Wessells, M.G. 1998. 'Children, Armed Conflict, and Peace', *Journal of Peace Research* 35(5): 635–46.

Young, A. 1982. 'The Anthropologies of Illness and Sickness', *Annual Review of Anthropology* 11: 257–85.

SAHRAWI SECTION

1
Identity With/out Territory: Sahrawi Refugee Youth in Transnational Space

Dawn Chatty, Elena Fiddian-Qasmiyeh and Gina Crivello

Introduction

Thirty years after the first wave of refugees from Western Sahara fled their territory and took refuge along the border areas of south-western Algeria, a second generation has grown up without territory, patently committed to supporting its government-in-exile's goal of return.[2] Sahrawi refugee youth are highly politicized and imbued with a sense of the importance of education, which they perceive as a major weapon in their nation's fight for economic and political survival. Educational opportunity also instils Sahrawi youth with a sense of hope for a better future. They accept the transnational reality of their education and recognize that the limited resources within their refugee camps mean that they must leave their families and kin from an early age in the pursuit of education. This mobility and networking across vast distances and often several nation states is a common feature of life for these youth. Although the four (or five, if we count the smaller 27th February Camp) Sahrawi refugee camps near the Algerian border town of Tindouf are the physical locus of their lives, most Sahrawi youth recognize that they must travel for education as well as for the support networks their movements create. Whether it is summer camps in Spain or Italy, or high school and university training in Algeria, Spain, Libya, Cuba, Syria and, more recently Mexico, Venezuela or even Qatar, these placements are regarded as a 'national' duty to support their government-in-exile and eventually also their families. Their homes are cast widely, wherever their extended families are found, be they in Mauritania, Algeria, Spain, in the Western Sahara itself, or elsewhere. But the message remains the same: they are refugees from a territory currently occupied by Morocco. The transnational spaces which make up the core of Sahrawi young people's lives remain organized around the theme of education for the betterment of the nation as well as the more immediate needs of their family and kin.

This chapter examines the social and political conditions which have led to the emergence of significant transnational education and networking phenomena primarily among Sahrawi children and youth. Based upon family group interviews in the Sahrawi camps and individual interviews with youth in a summer host programme in Spain, the chapter examines how Sahrawi youth identities in a transnational context have emerged and how the policy of the government-in-exile has promoted and encouraged this development. The chapter then examines how Sahrawi youth come to terms with their reintegration into the refugee camps after months, and often years, abroad. We suggest that the original tribal ideology of pastoral-based mobility (Chatty 1996: 129–35; Zutt 1994: 7–9, 33–35), whilst not representative of all Sahrawi people, may help us to understand the relative ease with which many Sahrawi adults, if not the youth themselves, accept and tolerate long physical and temporal absences of close kin as part of the duty of a good Sahrawi citizen.[3] The tradition of movement and dispersal among and outside the kin group – particularly by male youth – in the nomadic pastoral camps, the urban centres of the past, and in the settled refugee camps today is a cultural continuity which needs to be taken into account (Claudot-Hawad 2005). Furthermore, the almost complete material dependence of the Sahrawi state based in the refugee camps near Tindouf, Algeria – although not always fully understood by Sahrawi youth – has meant that creating transnational educational opportunities for the young is a major state, as well as individual, survival strategy. Upon their return, these transnationalized youths face numerous difficulties, including those of a broadly cultural nature: how to acclimatize to the physical and intellectual emptiness of their desert refugee base after years spent abroad, sometimes in situations of relative deprivation and at other times in a richness of social experience and knowledge. The adjustment is hard, sometimes traumatic, and only just hinted upon in the data.

This chapter will open with a brief overview of the regional and global politics which superseded the flight of the Sahrawi from their home towns and desert camps to the Algerian border area of Tindouf. It will then describe the Sahrawi refugee camps themselves on the desert edge of the town of Tindouf, followed by a review of the main characteristics of the Sahrawi refugee community as they emerge from the project household interviews. Finally, we turn our attention to Sahrawi youth themselves and discuss the significance which transnational education has had on the formation of both their social and political identities, and how their reintegration has shaped that process.

Contested History

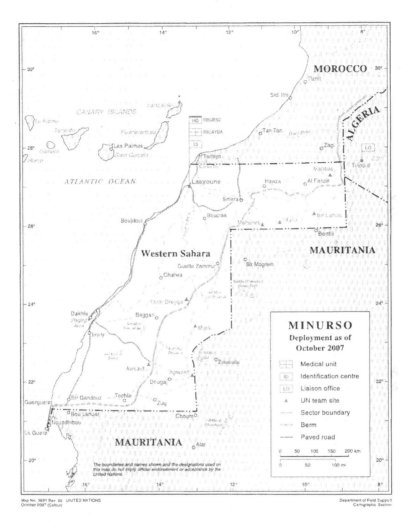

Figure 1.1: Map of Western Sahara.
Reproduced with the permission of the UN Cartographic Section.

The Western Sahara, Africa's last non-self-governing territory according to the United Nations (UN),[4] became a Spanish colony in 1884. While the Spanish presence in the territory remained minimal until the mid-twentieth century, by 1936 Spain and France had formed an alliance to establish Spanish hegemony in the Western Sahara. In 1920, 253 Spaniards were present in Villa Cisneros, the main 'urban' centre in the territory (Yara 2003), but the discovery of phosphates in 1947 led to a massive shift in Spanish interest in the territory, which was paralleled by a mass influx of Spanish civilians and soldiers. The total Spanish civilian population reached 1,220 by 1950, more than quadrupling by 1960 to 5,304 (Damis 1983), and multiplying again almost fourfold to reach 20,126 in 1974 (Barbier 1982). Spain's desire to exploit the territory's natural resources, in addition to the need to keep emerging Sahrawi anti-colonial movements under control, led to the military presence soaring from only 700 Spanish troops in 1925 to some 15,000 Spanish soldiers by 1970 (Damis 1983).

This ever-expanding number of Spanish civilians and soldiers in the territory was accompanied by the settlement of large numbers of nomadic pastoral Sahrawi people, who increasingly moved to live around the territory's growing urban centres: Aaiun, Villa Cisneros (now known as Dakhla) and Smara. This process of sedentarization of the region's nomadic peoples occurred both as a result of the several severe periods of drought in the territory between 1949 and 1974, and also following the Spanish administration's pressure to 'civilise' the population.[5] By 1974, between 55 per cent and 72 per cent of the Sahrawi people still based in the territory, estimated to number around 73,500 according to that year's Spanish census,[6] were living in or around the main urban centres, although not all of these had given up nomadic pastoralism entirely.

Throughout the colonial period, animosity and tension towards the Spanish administration cumulatively intensified, with the first major urban-based anti-colonial movement emerging in 1968. Four years before this major organized resistance started, the UN first asked Spain to decolonize the Spanish Sahara, a request which was reiterated in December 1965, and on a systematic basis from then onwards. The UN and the Organisation of African Unity (now the African Union) stressed, as they continue to do today, that a referendum for self-determination should be held, in order for the inhabitants to decide their future. In 1973, a group of Sahrawi students, many of whom had studied in Morocco and Spain, formed the Polisario (Frente Popular para la Liberación de Saguia El-Hamra y Rio de Oro), the armed forces of the Sahrawi liberation struggle. The Polisario demanded independence from Spain, and rejected any claims made by Morocco and Mauritania to the territory. In 1975, the International Court of Justice (ICJ) published its advisory opinion maintaining the right of the Sahrawi people to self-determination. On the same day, the Moroccan king, Hassan II, announced his intention to 'reclaim' the Sahara through a civilian 'Green March' (Damis 1983; Chopra 1999). Six days after the Moroccan armed forces crossed into the former Spanish Sahara, an estimated 350,000 Moroccan civilians followed (Saxena 1995; Pazzanita and Hodges 1994). Mauritanian forces invaded from the south. Makeshift camps sprung up to temporarily shelter those who fled their homes, but these were bombed soon after in a series of raids by the Moroccan air force. Young men generally stayed behind or eventually returned to fight, while their families sought refuge in Algeria where they remain to this day.

Sahrawi Society in 'Exile'

Contemporary Sahrawi society is widely dispersed throughout north-western Africa. The numbers of people in 'exile', that is, not living in the Western Sahara, are not precisely known, but are distributed primarily in Algeria, Mauritania and Spain.

According to the United Nations High Commission for Refugees (UNHCR) statistical yearbooks of 2002, 2003 and 2004, the Sahrawi refugee population of concern to UNHCR in Algeria was distributed as shown in Table 1.1.

Table 1.1: Sahrawi Population of Concern to UNHCR by Camp.

Location	Population of concern to UNHCR at location
Smara Camp	41,850
Dakhla Camp	40,440
Aaiun Camp	38,740
Auserd Camp	34,410
Tindouf (City)	9,570
Total	165,010

This is a total of 165,010 Sahrawi refugees in the camps around Tindouf, although the estimate is limited in several respects. Firstly, the UNHCR has not been able to complete a reliable census, so these figures must, indeed, be seen as merely an estimate. Secondly, the total figure is limited by an absence of information regarding the number of refugees living in the 27th February Camp. Furthermore, as the figure remains the same from 2002 to 2004, it clearly does not account for population growth.

Mauritania also hosts some 26,400 Western Saharan refugees whose situations are monitored by the UNHCR but who do not directly receive assistance from the UN body.[7] This would suggest that the total population of Sahrawi refugees spread out over a number of nation states is between 190,000 and 200,000 refugees.[8]

The Sahrawi Refugee Camps

The emergence of the Sahrawi refugee camps took place at a time when young and adult men were at the military front, meaning that female-centred extended families played a central role in social life from the mid-1970s until the mid-1990s.[9] While fathers and husbands would return to the camps on short visits during these first two decades, most men were absent from the camps on a daily basis, leading to women being in charge not only of their families, but also of camp structures as a whole. Given women's centrality in daily social and political life in the camps, Sahrawi children have been cared for by a broad selection of individuals in social and institutional settings. In addition to being looked after by older sisters, aunts and grandmothers in their respective *khaimas* (tents/households), the creation of crèches for young children whose mothers work outside of their *khaimas* has been an integral part of the social structures developed in the refugee camps.

Sahrawi women's contemporary centrality, both within the *khaima* and at all levels of camp life, reflects a syncretic response to the demands and opportunities of exile.[10] Similarly, the diffuse familiar and institutional forms of childcare currently offered in the refugee camps represent the adaptation of some elements of social structures which characterized Sahrawi life before the occupation of the Western Sahara.

An estimated 150,000 and 200,000 refugees from the Western Sahara currently live in one of the five remotely located refugee camps set up in the desert thirty kilometres from the south-western-most Algerian town of Tindouf. Some had been nomadic pastoralists; others had fled from larger urban centres such as Aaiun, Dakhla, La Guera and Smara. UNHCR provided them tents to which some families have added on sand-brick buildings. Trucks bring water to the camps, as well as food, medicine and other basic supplies. Camp residents are almost entirely dependent on externally-provided humanitarian supplies, although food-aid is supplemented by a small amount of vegetables (mainly potatoes, onions and carrots) grown in gardens in the camps, some eggs produced in one of three (air-conditioned) hen-houses (E.U. 2004), and the milk and meat from goats and camels kept by individual families.[11]

Sahrawi refugees live in camps set up, with Algerian permission, in 1975 by the Polisario Front and the Sahrawi Arab Democratic Republic (SADR), an entity whose existence was proclaimed by the Secretary General of the Polisario Front (El Ouali) on 27 February 1976, the day that Spain officially withdrew from the territory. Initial assistance was offered by the International Committee for the Red Cross (ICRC), who, forty-eight hours after receiving a call from the Sahrawi Red Cross, sent a plane from Sweden carrying tents and medical items (Wirth and Balaguer 1976). Other NGOs and IGOs, including the International Federation for Human Rights and

UNHCR,[12] sent missions to the camps to evaluate the requirements of medical and humanitarian assistance, and documented the abuses which had taken place during the invasion. Between 1975 and the mid-1990s, humanitarian aid and projects in the camps were managed by the refugee community itself, with only a minimal presence of international NGO/IGO workers in the camps.[13]

There are four major camps, one small camp (27th February Camp, also known as 'The Women's Camp'), and one administrative centre (Rabouni). The camps are named after the four major urban centres in Western Sahara: Aaiun, Smara, Dakhla and Auserd. These camps, called *wilaya* (pl. *wilayat*, provinces), are located approximately twenty-five to a hundred kilometres from the Algerian military border town of Tindouf. Most of the camps can be reached in half an hour to an hour's driving time from Tindouf, although Dakhla is considerably further away to the south, located closer to the Mauritanian border. Each camp is intended to function as a self-contained *wilaya* of the SADR. Each *wilaya* is divided into six *dawa'ir* (sing. *daira*) or districts, with Dakhla claiming seven due its slightly higher population. Each *daira* is subdivided into four *ahya'a* (sing. *hay*) or sub-districts.

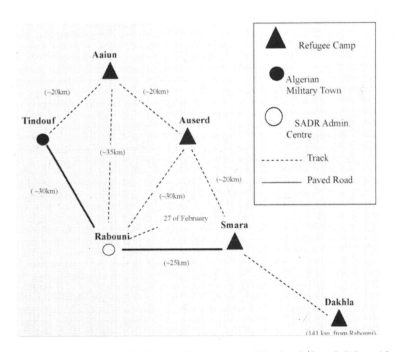

Figure 1.2: Map of Sahrawi Camps near Tindouf (South-West Algeria). Adapted from Train in Caratini (2003).

Thirty years following the war which prompted the Sahrawis to flee to Algeria, the refugees have become a highly organized community and participate in institutions ranging from local committees that run and manage small neighbourhoods, to larger organizations that include the National Union for Sahrawi Women (NUSW) and the Union for Sahrawi Youth (UJSARIO). Consequently, the individual refugee's daily life and activities intersect to a large degree with programmes and projects funded and run by international humanitarian organizations, the camp-based state, with its various governmental departments and community organizations, and the family. Moreover, the government, especially through the Ministry of Cooperation, ensures that external interventions, regardless of their nature and objectives, are screened and examined, a process that is bureaucratic in structure and character. All visits related to research or journalistic reporting are also first screened by this and/or other ministries. The purposes of such visits, their duration as well as their interface with camp residents are examined in detail. Our own research effort was closely scrutinized by the Ministry of Cooperation before permission was given to travel to the camps, and our Sahrawi local research manager was carefully vetted before we could proceed with hiring and training local assistants and getting the research process underway. (See introduction.)

Sahrawi Research Participants

This chapter draws on interviews carried out in 2002, 2003 and 2005 with Sahrawi refugee youth and their families in two research contexts – in the refugee camps of Algeria (2002 and 2003), and in Madrid, Spain in 2005, where many of the Sahrawi youth spend their summers staying with Spanish host-families.[14] The researchers in the Sahrawi camps were all young adults who had completed university training in Spain, Algeria and Syria. Existing research skills were augmented by further training in semi-informal interviewing techniques by the team leader, a naturalized Canadian anthropologist of Palestinian origin who conducted the training and interviewing in Arabic. The researchers in Madrid were European and American Spanish-speaking academics.

There were a total of ninety-two youth in the study's core age group (eight to eighteen years old), representing both groups of youth participants. Of these, thirty-three were male and fifty-nine female and their median age was 11.9 years old. The average number of siblings in their families was 5.4; sixteen reported that they were the eldest sibling, seventeen the youngest, and the remainder somewhere in between. They were all born in the refugee camps and reported that their families lived in the following camp locations: Aaiun (33), Auserd (29), Smara (12), Dakhla (9), and 27th February (9).

Table 1.2: Project's Core Youth 8–18 years old.

Gender		Age	# Siblings	Family's Camp Location	
Male	33	Avg. = 11.9	Avg. = 5.4	Aaiun	33
Female	59			Auserd	29
Aaiun				Smara	12
				Dakhla	9
				27 February	9

In addition to the data collected from youth aged eight to eighteen, several hundred of their family members were also interviewed, the youngest aged five and the eldest aged eighty-nine. In the refugee camps, interviews were carried out in an extended family setting with several generations of household members present and participating in the recorded conversations. Given this wide range of speakers, we have classified interviewees according to their generation, as outlined in Table 1.3.

Table 1.3: Interviewees by Generation.

Generation	Description
G1	Born in Western Sahara (WS)
G1.5	Born in WS but left at 9 years old or younger
G2	Born in the refugee camps (to parents born in WS)
G3	Born in the refugee camps (to parents born in the refugee camps)

In Madrid, interviews were generally conducted on a one-on-one basis with youths, although in several cases one or more members of their Spanish host-families were present.[15] Collectively, the youth and family interviews gathered in both research contexts provided important, sometimes contrasting, perspectives on Sahrawi childhoods, their past experiences, current challenges, and implications for their future.

The Camp Interviews

The interviews were carried out with fifty families living in the Sahrawi refugee camps in Algeria and information was collected at the level of the household. Personal data were therefore recorded for individuals who were present and spoke during the interviews, as well as for individuals who were considered members of the household but who were absent, for whatever reason. The field researchers collected information on a total of 380 individuals, composed of 164 men and 216 women. Of these, 214 were born in the refugee camps. Of the 166 born in Western Sahara, nearly half of them fled their birth country for Algeria when they were nine years old or younger.

The education levels reported for all members of the refugee households who participated in the camp-based research are indicated in Table 1.4.

Table 1.4: Refugee Generation and Education: Refugee Camp Households.

		Elem	Prep	Second	Univ	Tech	Lit	none	other	Quran	
Refugee generation	G1	13	2	7	3	8	43	15	4	17	112
	G1.5	5	8	16	12	12	1	0	0	0	54
	G2	73	57	36	11	10	2	11	5	0	205
	G3	6	1	0	0	0	0	1	1	0	9
	Total	97	68	59	26	30	46	27	10	17	380

[Elem = elementary, Prep = preparatory, Second = secondary, Univ = university, Tech = training school, Lit = Literacy Programme, Quran = Quranic school]

The leap in educational levels between the generations is made clear in Table 1.4. Their educational attainment can also be presented according to gender (see Table 1.5). Because there were more women in the sample, it is important to represent this information as a percentage of the gender group.

Table 1.5: Gender and Education: Refugee Camp Households.

		Education									Total
		Elem	Prep	Second	Univ	Tech	Lit	none	other	Quran	
Gender	M	29%	12%	21%	10%	5%	5%	6%	5%	7%	164
	F	23%	22.5%	11%	5%	10%	17%	8%	5%	3%	216
	Total	97	68	59	26	30	46	27	10	17	N=380

[Elem = elementary, Prep = preparatory, Second = secondary, Univ = university, Tech = training school, Lit = Literacy Programme, Quran = Quranic school]

This chapter highlights the international education networks that both require and contribute to the mobility of Sahrawi refugee youth. Table 1.6 indicates where household members received their preparatory/secondary schooling, according to generation. Table 1.7 presents the same information according to gender.

Table 1.6: Refugee Generation, and Location of Preparatory/Secondary Education: Refugee Camp Households*.

Refugee Generation						Total
		G1	G1.5	G2	G3	
Second ed loc	Algeria	3	31	103	1	138
	Libya	3	2	3	0	8
	Cuba	3	11	5	0	19
	Spain	0	1	1	0	2
	other	6	0	2	0	8
	Total	15	45	114	1	175

* The n/a and 'unknown' reponses have been removed. N=175

Table 1.7: Gender and Location of Preparatory/Secondary Education: Refugee Camp Households*.

		male		female		Total
		#	% of male	#	% of female	#
Second ed loc	Algeria	52	67	86	88	138
	Libya	2	3	6	6	8
	Cuba	17	22	2	2	19
	Spain	0	0	2	2	2
	other	6	8	2	2	8
	Total	77	100	98	100	175

* The n/a and 'unknown' responses have been removed. N=175

Tables 1.6 and 1.7 indicate that, amongst our interviewees in the camps, Algeria was by far the most frequent location for preparatory and secondary education of Sahrawi students and that Cuba, as a location for further education, is dominated by male students.

Tables 1.1–1.7 provide a sense of the characteristics of all reported household members (N=380), but further patterns can be identified for the sub-sample who spoke during the interviews (N=171). Based on data collected on 162 of these 'speakers', we know that they represent the generations as shown in Table 1.8.

Table 1.8: Refugee Generation: Speakers in Camp Interviews.

Generation	# Speakers
G1	64
G1.5	28
G2	67
G3	03

The average age of the speakers was thirty-four, and more than 70 per cent of them were female. Forty-three per cent were born in the refugee camps, with the remainder born in Western Sahara (and one in the Liberated Territories). Nearly 40 per cent reported being married, with the remainder single (45 per cent), divorced or widowed. Their households have an average of nine members, and the speakers reported an average of six siblings.

NVIVO

All of the interviews collected for this study were transcribed in their original languages and then translated into English. These interviews and a separate spreadsheet containing the personal attributes of each individual speaker formed the basis of the project database. NVIVO, a computer software package for the analysis of qualitative data, was used to store, code and analyse the project data. Each of the interviews was coded thematically using an emergent approach: a basic set of core themes was initially applied, with subsequent themes emerging from the interviews during the coding process. Some of these themes were non-hierarchical, or 'free nodes', while a second category of codes represents hierarchies of themes. Some of the key themes which emerged were: adult reflections on being refugees; adult reflections on childhood; child reflections on being refugees; and nomadism and mobility.

Conceptualizing the Mobility of Sahrawi Youth

Many of the surviving members of the older generation of Sahrawis living in the refugee camps recalled in detail aspects of their own childhoods, long past. Many had lived out their childhoods in mobile contexts, their *friq* (pl. *firqan*, group of nomadic tents) moving periodically. A forty-one year-old woman recalled her earliest childhood memories:

> we were organised into *firqan*. We had camels and goats … men used to go to towns or cities and return carrying goods that lasted for a month. Women made the tents and took care of everything related to the running of domestic life.

Another woman, aged forty-five, described the way these *firqan* were made up of several extended families who moved together as a group:

> My father, my mother, and brothers and sisters, as well as the tent of my grandfather and my uncles, along with other children. We always had neighbours living close by, many people living together … We lived like this and moved seeking better pasture for our livestock. When we moved from one place to another, all the *friq* moved together … we were like one family.

As reflected above, mobility has historically been an integral feature of the fabric of Sahrawi society[16] and lives on in the collective memory of the older generations, despite the temporal and spatial distance from their childhoods. We argue, therefore, that one consistent feature of Sahrawi society that has survived among the refugees, despite their forced sedentarization as a community, is their continued mobility. Indeed, in addition to some families travelling to the Liberated Territories during the summer months, or visiting relatives in Mauritania throughout the year, it is estimated that approximately 10,000 Sahrawis continue to practise a nomadic pastoral life in the Liberated Territories despite the constant danger presented by landmines in the area (Smith 2004).[17]

There are, however, some differences between the forms that mobility currently takes among children and youth in the refugee camps, and mobility as accepted and previously practised by the older generation. In the past, movement and mobility of the kin group were commonly a response to ecological and seasonal weather factors to access grazing for their herds of, mainly, camel. Additionally, for male youth, there was a tradition of movement either in support of satellite herding groups, or to 'seek their fortune' before returning to the core kin group to marry and take on the responsibilities of adulthood. The latter type of activity was generally conducted within a common age-group so that the peers or age-cohort built intra-group support networks (on similarities with the Algerian Tuareg see Keenan 2005; and on the Bidan in Mauritania, see Villasante Cervello 2005). We hold that the contemporary movement of youth is framed primarily by the requirements of gaining an education, which has become one of the Polisario's core political aspirations. Its manifestation, however, remains embedded in, and must be interpreted in light of, traditional nomadic practices.

Mobility in relation to education also has a strong historical basis amongst the Sahrawi. Both prior to and during the Spanish colonial period, some children received a Quranic education in what may be described as mobile religious school groups. A forty-five year-old woman remembers that around the time she turned seven, she began attending a Quranic school and studied with a *lemrabet* (Quranic teacher) with other children in her *friq*. In addition to these mobile schools, there was also at least one established seat of religious learning within the territory of the Western Sahara, namely that created by Sheikh Mael-Ainin in the sacred town of Smara. A small number of male adolescent students reportedly attended the sedentary *mahadra* there, leaving their nomadic groups behind for long periods to do so (Perregaux 1987). In the current refugee context, children's early education is far more universalized and institutionalized within fixed schools established in the refugee camps. For older children, however, formal links with middle schools, high schools and universities abroad lead them to travel great distances to attend school.

The mobility of Sahrawi youth in the refugee camps may be conceptualized as a form of 'serial circular migration' for education. On the one hand, there is a commonality with the kinds of mobility practised by the older generation who recalled childhoods marked by comparatively frequent, ecologically-determined seasonal movement with their family groups. The contemporary mobility of youth who grow up in the refugee camps, however, is driven more by academic and holiday calendars and the availability of funds to support their travel. When they do travel it is usually with their peers and not with their family groups.

Interviews carried out in 2005 with young Sahrawi children (under the age of twelve) who were participating in the Spanish hosting programme revealed that for many of them, prior to their trips to Spain, their lives in the camps were quite insular and immobile. Many of them reported never having left the refugee camps, some even claiming to have never travelled beyond their particular camp. A twenty-five year-old female teacher living in Aaiun camp described the importance of children being able to leave the camps, saying:

In the camps, we live in difficult conditions. In the schools, the desks and chairs are old and dilapidated and used by generations ... [Outside] the desks and chairs are good and the environment helps us psychologically and encourages us to study ... We watch cartoons and programs for children which help us develop our minds. As for the camps, there is nothing. They try as much as possible to provide entertainment, such as sports, but these are not enough and are always deficient.

During an interview in Madrid, a ten year-old Sahrawi girl described what she liked about Spain, saying:

I like the houses. I like the streets ... And I like the beach and the pool. And playing here ... over there [in Sahara] there aren't places to play, like the park ... I like the places that are really big ... these really big buildings.

Young children's immobility is eventually interrupted by the need or opportunity to travel abroad, either as part of a summer hosting scheme or for longer-term schooling. In their new residences, they usually live 'settled' lives, as school boarders or in the homes of their host-families. It appears that those students living in Algeria or Spain had opportunities to return annually to spend their summer breaks with their families in the camps, in Tindouf or Mauritania. Students placed at greater distances, such as Cuba, Libya or Syria, have described being unable to return to the camps for periods of up to ten years. In these contexts, peer groups and proto-familial relationships become important for providing children with a sense of place and belonging.

Cycles of migration over the period of childhood and adolescence ensure that children have the opportunity to access valuable resources and services unavailable in the camps. This is not to suggest that all experiences abroad are characterized by relative abundance, the kind observed, for example, in the cases of children placed with well-off Spanish host-families. In fact, one of the challenges repeatedly mentioned during the family interviews in the camps had to do with the lack of material support available for students studying abroad. An extreme example of this was offered by a thirty-eight year-old woman living in Aaiun camp who talked about the early years, when the first groups of children were being sent to study abroad:

I remember my young brother was only seven and he was sent away so he could get an education. He only had one pair of shoes and when he returned his shoes were stuck on his feet and we had to cut the shoes to take them off and put some ointment on his toes.

This strong imagery of extreme deprivation counters the assumption that children leave the camps primarily to access valuable material resources. A twenty-nine year-old man who had studied in Cuba for several years described the hardship endured by Sahrawi students studying there in the late 1980s:

> At one point, especially in 1989 and 1990, the embargo got worse and there was no food except vegetables ... we also had rice, most often spoiled and old and one glass of milk with sugar in the morning ...We did not have clothes. A person had just one set of clothes to wear and two people often shared one pair of shoes. One would wear them during the day and the other in the evening ... A towel was used by three or four people.

Within the current system of transnational education, experiences are wide-ranging, depending on where and with whom the children and youth are placed. In addition to their age and legal status, all of these factors will determine the material and nutritional resources they can access.

With the exception of longer periods of separation, such as those endured by students based in Cuba in the 1980s and 1990s, the circularity of migration, whether a child returns after a three-month period away, annually, or only once every few years, means that family ties can be reinforced periodically. In the context of an ideology of mobility, such absences tend to be quickly absorbed, and returning students rapidly adjust to home life in the camps until the next migration cycle begins. The transnational space throughout which thousands of children and youth circulate is both an extension of, and a formative factor in the ideology of movement which characterizes Sahrawi refugee society. As new cohorts of Sahrawi children set out each year to be educated abroad, scores of other students are returning to their families in the camps.

On the whole, when the children interviewed in Spain were asked where they wanted to live as adults, they insisted they would eventually return to live with or near their families in the refugee camps. Some of them even articulated the possible return, with their families, to an independent Western Sahara, in what may be conceived as the final leg in the migration circle. Their main concern was to return to their families, wherever they may be located, once again reinforcing the link to people rather than place which is so common among mobile peoples (Chatty 1996, 2005; Keenan 2005).[18]

Youth and Education

We have suggested that mobility is an essential part of Sahrawi refugee youth's experiences, and that it is through the practice of accessing an education outside of the camps that the historical connection between Sahrawi identity and mobility is reproduced. Youth experience of obtaining an education is a formative factor which enables a new generation of Sahrawis who have not lived in nomadic encampments, like the generations before them, to recognize the significance of mobility to their individual, family, community and national identities.

In this section, we focus on the education system which is present in the camps, and indicate how the camp-based system is connected to, and reliant upon, international educational networks provided through both study-abroad and summer-hosting programmes. By means of contextualizing the contemporary education system in the refugee camps, we will start by outlining the form of access which Sahrawi youth had to a formal education during the Spanish colonial era.

Education prior to 1975

During the late Spanish colonial era, education opportunities for Sahrawis only slowly gained ground. Between 1948 and 1974, the Spanish Sahara's educational system jumped from two primary schools with 91 students, to 6,059 students in primary school (including 909 girls) and 111 in secondary schools (including 3 girls). By 1972, 260 Sahrawi students were enrolled in the Spanish Sahara's two vocational schools, and 169 attended the two domestic science schools which had opened in the colony. The literacy rate of the native population in the Spanish Sahara was equal to, or just under, 5 per cent when the mass exodus to Algeria took place (Damis 1985).

By 1975, with a population of 73,497 Sahrawis in the territory, there were only 75 Sahrawi students in Spain, 52 of whom were in Spanish universities or other further education establishments (Barbier 1982). By the end of the Spanish colonial era itself, only two Sahrawi had higher university degrees and twelve had advanced technical diplomas (Damis 1983). The miniscule number of Sahrawi tertiary degree holders in 1975 is explained by the fact that it was not until 1968 that Spain allowed Sahrawi students to access Spanish universities; this was only seven years before Spain abandoned the territory (Gaudio 1978). Those Sahrawi students who were allowed to study in Spanish universities[19] encountered an additional limitation: only specified subjects were permitted to them. While they could study law, technical engineering, economics, philosophy, medicine, advanced engineering, pharmaceutical studies and nursing, they were not allowed to follow political sciences, sociology or journalism (Wirth and Balaguer 1976).

Education post-1975: in the refugee camps and beyond

In common with other liberation movements, education emerged as a central feature of the Sahrawi anti-colonial movement in the 1960s and 1970s. It is worth noting that many of the Polisario's earliest (male) leaders were amongst the most educated of the colonized population, and the movement and Sahrawi struggle was influenced by the anti-colonial, socialist and non-aligned theories, frameworks and models which permeated the region at the time.

Rather than adopting these ideas directly, however, the Polisario promoted a particular fusion of the old with the new, aiming to maintain key features of Sahrawi pre-colonial and colonial society and identity whilst developing specific ideas about their aims for social and political organization. This fusion affected the way in which the Polisario engaged with the Sahrawi population more broadly, including the creation of a certain degree of tension between the younger and older generations both during the anti-colonial struggle and later on in the refugee camps. Hence, while elders had traditionally been the community leaders and main authority figures, during and after the anti-colonial struggle Polisario youth replaced their fathers and grandfathers. This younger generation led the colonized Sahrawi firstly against the Spanish, then against the Moroccan and Mauritanian invasion; eventually they also founded the refugee camps and a new Sahrawi refugee society.

The centrality given to education is an embodiment of the Polisario's aim for its nation-in-exile to be wholly self-sufficient in the camps, and also in an independent Western Sahara when/if the long-awaited referendum takes place. In the early days, however, education was also a means of 'socializing' the formerly nomadic population, which had to become accustomed to their enforced sedentarization in the newly created refugee camps. This 'socialization' ranged from campaigns regarding public health and hygiene, in order to avoid epidemics, to the Polisario's determined attempt to eradicate the hierarchical tribal system in order to create a nation formed by equals.[20] One of the main campaigns aimed to encourage parents to send their children to school, a practice which most parents were at first reluctant to do.

Schools were amongst the first structures to be built in the camps, and both children and adults benefited from the literacy campaigns run by the small number of individuals who had received an education during the colonial era. In addition to building primary schools, the need for secondary schools emerged, leading to the construction of two boarding schools which offered an education to children from all of the camps, and maximized the students' access to the small number of teachers.

Reflecting the centrality given to women's rights and participation by the

Polisario, a National Women's School (27th February School) was created in 1978, followed by the construction of a second one (Olaf Palme School) in 1989. The 27th February School has accepted approximately 800 women each year, enabling the female students to temporarily set up their *khaimas* around the school, move their families with them, and have their collective educational and medical needs catered for during their studies. Courses offered in the women's schools include literacy, crafts, teacher training, nursing and kindergarten training.[21] More specialized training centres were gradually established in the camps, currently including a Nursing School and a Vocational Training School. There are also specialized schools for disabled children.

At this point, it is important to note the structure which exists in the camps, and beyond, to provide for Sahrawi children's and youth's welfare. Hence, while the Polisario and/or SADR are responsible for coordinating and helping to manage most projects in the camps, they depend entirely on funds and materials brought to the camps from outside. Figure 1.3 offers a preliminary overview of the organizational structures which are in place in the camps to provide, primarily, for children's educational and health needs.

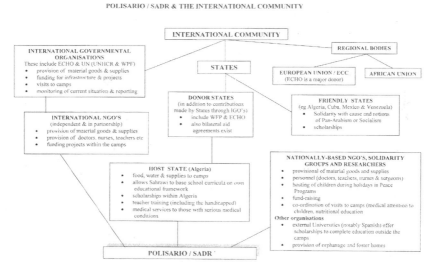

Figure 1.3: Organigram of Structures directed at Children's Needs. Designed by Elena Fiddian-Qasmiyeh from UNHCR and other sources.

The refugee camp population is young, with a large proportion of the Sahrawi inhabitants having been born in the camps between 1975 and today. According to UNHCR statistics for 2004, 19 per cent of the population was aged between 0 and 4 years of age, 37 per cent between 5 and 17, with a total of 59 per cent of the refugee camp population being under the age of 18; 31 per cent were aged between 18 and 59, and only 13 per cent of the population was aged over 60. It is worth reiterating that there is no recent reliable UN census of the camp population, and we suggest that the figures quoted in this chapter should therefore be considered to be estimates which reflect general trends in the camps.[22]

Table 1.9 indicates the percentage and number of children who were enrolled in schools in the camps according to UNHCR statistics for 2003 (note the different total populations given by the organization for 2003 and 2004):

Table 1.9: Percentage and Number of Children in Camp Schools, 2003.

Camp	Total Population	% population aged 5–17 enrolled in school	Number of children aged 5–17 not enrolled in camp school	% of qualified / trained teacher in each camp
Smara Camp	39,466 (2003)	57.6	6,210	67.2
Dakhla Camp	38,180 (2003) 40,440 (2004)	43.3	8,030	56.6
Aaiun Camp	36,675 (2003) 34,410 (2004)	60.1	5,440	39.7
Auserd Camp	32,624 (2003)	61.2	4,690	44.2
Totals	146,925 (2003) 155,440 (2004)	Average: 55.5	24,370	Average: 51.9

While the information available does not account for residents in the 27th February Camp, and unfortunately does not indicate the male-female ratio of the population enrolled in school, the percentage, and overall number, of children and youth who are not enrolled is higher than expected, especially given the extent to which the Polisario and/or SADR prioritize education in the camps. It is not clear whether it may be younger children who are not attending primary school, or older children who are unable to enrol in the camp-based boarding schools due perhaps to insufficient school places, infrastructural limitations and poor conditions (as suggested in an ECHO report, 2005).

A seventeen year-old woman from Dakhla camp remembered her experience as a student in the 12th October boarding school:

I studied ... far from my family. Three months of boarding school and then ten days vacation. I spent the summer holidays with my family. The boarding school was difficult and required discipline... Toys were non-existent, no TV, no puppets, no dolls. We used old sandals to make a doll or an oilcan to make a truck and we played with these. [HHD35]

The infrastructural limitations of the boarding schools have been addressed by the Polisario since the camps were created by sending some Sahrawi youth away to study, as we shall now discuss.

Education abroad: Algeria, Cuba, Libya, Spain and Syria

Upon the creation of the refugee camps, the Polisario almost immediately recognized that to educate its youth inside the camps would be a complicated task. This was due to the limited camp infrastructure, the small number of primary and secondary school places, the lack of an adequate teaching body, and, of course, the absence of any university. Hence, when the Sahrawi Ministry of Education, Health and Social Affairs was created in 1976, its main aims included not only creating and organizing schools in the camps but also requesting that friendly countries welcome as many Sahrawi children and youth as possible to educate them abroad (Velloso de Santiseban 1993).

It is for this reason that every year varying numbers of children leave their families in the refugee camps to study abroad. These students usually depend on scholarships offered by friendly states, such as Algeria, Spain, Libya, Syria and Cuba,[23] although there are great differences in the kind of financial and social support available from one programme to another.

Cuba. The first group of Sahrawi children arrived in Cuba in 1977, initially enrolling in the SADR-Cuba Friendship School in the Isla de la Juventud (Petrich 2005 a and b), and eventually entering tertiary Cuban institutions on the completion of their secondary level studies. Cuban media reports calculate that approximately 300 Sahrawi students have trained specifically as doctors in Cuba (RHC 2002a, 2002b; SPS 2002) while the total number of beneficiaries of the Cuban scholarship programme is estimated as being well over 4,000 (Salazar 2002). It has been assumed from the programme's inception that all children participating in the scheme will return to the refugee camps to work for their community upon graduation.[24]

The Cuban study-abroad programme is a long-term experience, with the children's stay on the island ranging from a few years to over a decade, depending on their course of study. Those students who studied in the Isla de la Juventud and then completed graduate studies in Cuba have often spent over fifteen years there, returning only infrequently to the camps during that time. Given the distances and period of separation involved, Sahrawi children's Cuban school directors and staff have played a particularly important role in ensuring their well-being. A small number of Sahrawi teachers also accompany the students, living with them and sharing responsibility for their care with the aim of 'helping the adolescents to preserve their linguistic and cultural identity' (UNHCR 2003a). Since 1994 the UNHCR has also monitored these adolescents' protection situation in Cuba.[25] The UNHCR covers most international transportation costs for students who arrived in Cuba in or before 1996, and offers them a small stipend (to pay for clothing, shoes, hygienic items and school supplies) during their stay (UNHCR 2005a).[26]

Table 1.10 offers a brief overview of the available statistics indicating the total number of Sahrawi students in Cuba per year, and, where information is available, the number of Sahrawi children arriving from, and flying back to, the refugee camps.

Table 1.10: Sahrawi Students in Cuba from 1977 to 2006.

Year	Sahrawi students in Cuba	Returnees to the camps
1977	20	
1978–93	No data available	
1994	1,493	
1995	Over 1,400 (± 200 females)	
1996	1,328 (1,247 by end of year) (± 200 females)	
1997	1,099 (1,000 assisted by UNHCR)	238
1998	963 (880 assisted by UNHCR) (140 females)	142
1999	862	
2000	802	
2001	901 (60 females)	185 (29 female)
2002	878 (27 females at start of year; 9 at end)	167 (21 female)
2003	721	
2004	719	
2005	597	143
2006	600	

Table compiled by Elena Fiddian-Qasmiyeh from UNHCR reports, Cuban media reports and other sources.

One young man in the camps described travelling to Cuba for what would be a five-year stay:

After I completed elementary school, I went to Cuba in September 1985 with 800 other Sahrawi students in a big boat. We left from Oran harbour to Havana and from there to the Island that has been allocated to foreign students. A new and more difficult stage in my life began then when I was far away from my family. Previously, I used to see them every three months. Now I became separated from them for years and years.

Spain. In Spain, Sahrawi refugee children are usually individually fostered or adopted by families who support them during their studies. Spanish families sometimes take in children who they had previously hosted in the *Vacaciones en Paz* programme. When this occurs, the education programme usually builds upon existing connections between the child and the Spanish hosts who would most probably have already travelled to the camps to meet the child's parents there (see chapter 2). It is worth noting that many Sahrawi children who leave the camps to study in Spain also have medical conditions which influence their parents' decision to send them to live and study outside. In some cases, the children do not live with Spanish families, but are rather housed in a *casa cuna* (a children's home), where their medical needs can be addressed.

Sahrawi children who study in Spain are able to return to the camps with greater frequency than those who travel to Cuba, and these children's direct contact with their families appears to be much more frequent. It is possible for them to travel on one of the many charter flights which take thousands of Spaniards to the camps each year.[27] The students can therefore either visit the camps (accompanied by their Spanish host-parents) for about a week a year, or return during the summer holidays when many other Sahrawi children are spending two months in Spain. Such students often then play a key role in the camps, teaching in the summer adult literacy programmes.

When living with a Spanish family, specific agreements are usually made between the Sahrawi family and the Spanish hosts before a Sahrawi judge in the refugee camps. The conditions specified in these agreements (RASD 2000) include the following:

- the host-family is granted temporary custody and guardianship of the child and is responsible for all expenses related to the child's stay in Spain,
- the child is to return to its birth-family at the family's request, and
- the host-family is responsible for maintaining the child's family and cultural ties and facilitating regular communication with the child's parents and family.

Students travelling to Spain are usually funded and supported by their Spanish host-families, although local solidarity associations and various local municipal governments may offer financial support in different ways (on

Valencia, see Guía Activ 2001; Asturias see ARSO 2001; and Universidad de Vigo 2003). The main role played by the Spanish government appears to be in processing the young refugees' residency documents, which allow them temporary but legal residency. UNHCR plays no role in this Spanish programme, and, accordingly, no UNHCR statistics have been identified indicating the number of refugee children who have participated in this Spanish-Sahrawi initiative. We have also been unable to locate statistics confirming the number of Sahrawi girls and women who have studied in Spain, or regarding the proportion of students who return to the refugee camps upon completion of their studies.

In terms of Sahrawi children's contact with other Sahrawi youth in Spain, this varies considerably depending on their place of residence, and the programme under whose auspices they may have travelled to Spain. Some children are unable to maintain frequent contact with other Sahrawi youth, while other projects ensure that a community of Sahrawi children are regularly brought together. Children participating in the *Escola en Pau* (School in Peace) programme in Mallorca (Balearic Islands) stay with local families, attend Spanish schools on weekdays, and take intensive Arabic classes together on Saturdays.[28]

Algeria, Libya and Syria. There is a distinct absence of news items, and apparently no UNHCR statistics, regarding Sahrawi refugee youth who have studied in Algeria, Libya or Syria.[29] Despite this absence of statistics, however, it is possible to briefly reflect on the broad nature of these programmes, which will permit some comparison with the Spanish and Cuban projects.

Algeria appears to offer the largest number of Sahrawi students access to both secondary and tertiary education. The government grants full scholarships, and children are housed in group accommodation in Algiers and other cities and towns. Given the proximity to the refugee camps, youth are able to return there with relative frequency, and a large proportion of girls are reported to study in Algerian schools and universities. According to the children interviewed, the main difficulties encountered whilst in Algeria include a limited knowledge of French (which is used in the Algerian educational context), and problems adapting to the higher educational standards in Algeria.

One teenage girl living in Auserd camp described how, after living two years in the camp boarding school, she went to Algeria to receive her secondary school education, saying:

In Algeria, the society is different and one had to adapt and get used to the environment there... one had to spend nine months [at a time] in Algeria... In Algeria, the subjects were different. We had foreign and

Algerian teachers. We had to study French which we did not study here in the camps... there, the Algerian students study it from grade three. [HHA12]

Libya has also systematically offered support to Sahrawi youth since the creation of the Polisario Front, despite changing diplomatic relations between Colonel Gaddafi and the Polisario/SADR. As is the case in Syria, one of the principal motivating factors behind the Libyan scholarship programme appears to be the government's commitment to Pan-Arabism.[30] The only information offered regarding the number of students in Libya is from news items. For example, a Sahara Press Service report claims that in 2001, 700 Sahrawi students were studying in Libya at different levels, with 350 female students amongst them (SPS 2001). According to a female Polisario representative who studied in Cuba, in 2003 there were '2,000 students in Libya, 3,000 in Algeria, and 1,400 in Cuba' (Coggan 2003). While these numbers may be somewhat inflated, they most likely reflect the general ratio of students based in Algeria, followed by Libya, and then Cuba.

For the **Syrian** study-abroad programme, no information was found either in the media or from the UNHCR regarding the nature of the project or numbers involved.[31] However, during a visit to Damascus during the summer of 2006, one of the authors [Elena Fiddian-Qasmiyeh] met informally with six Sahrawi male students completing university studies in Syria, and spoke with the Polisario Representative based in Damascus. She was informed that in the past, up to about forty students (all male) had taken up Syrian government university scholarships, but that less than a dozen students were based there in 2006. While the government scholarship covered university fees, the students depended on a small maintenance grant from the Polisario Front to cover all other expenses. The youth lived together in small groups in shared student accommodation, and tended to meet regularly. Due to the high expenses involved, returning to the camps to visit family before the end of their studies was very difficult, and some of the students had been unable to return for between five and eight years.

Summer Hosting Programmes in Perspective.

While not all children travel to Spain, Algeria, Syria, Libya or Cuba to study, a very large number of Sahrawi children leave the camps on a yearly basis during the summer months (when temperatures in the camps often reach 50°C). Some 9,000 Sahrawi children were hosted by Spanish families in 2005 alone, indicating the extent of the programme. These summer hosting programmes have been operating since the mid-1980s, and originated through a partnership between Spanish solidarity organizations, the Polisario Front and the Polisario-affiliated Union for Sahrawi Youth

(UJSARIO). Other countries soon developed similar programmes, and children were invited to spend their holidays at 'summer camps' in, for instance, Spain, Belgium, Italy or France. These children spent the summer together in groups, in the company of Sahrawi monitors, and often slept in schools or halls that were not being used over the summer.

Group-based camps have continued to take place in the past few years: 600 Sahrawi children stayed in a number of Italian youth centres in 2002 (Farah 2005) while in 2000, ten children participated in a summer camp in the United Kingdom and twenty-eight young Sahrawis spent almost a month in Swiss holiday camps (ARSO 2000a; 2000b). Outside of Europe, 250 Sahrawi children spent their 2006 summer holidays in the Algerian regions of Annaba and El Tarf, following an initiative organized by the Algerian National Committee of Solidarity with the Sahrawi People (CNASPS) (SPS 2006).

Gradually, however, the nature of the summer holiday programme has changed and it is currently more common for children to be hosted by individual families. In addition to the Spanish initiative, many other such opportunities for individual hosting exist, mostly within Europe, but also further afield: between 1999 and 2004, 170 Sahrawi children were hosted by American families in six states (Lenz 2004). Such a change ideally offers the children closer, more personalized attention during the months that they are away from their own families. While the nature of the Spanish programme is discussed in detail in chapter 2, it is worth noting that the major benefits of this individual hosting programme include the possibility of children obtaining medical treatment and material support from their host-families. The hosting programme also enables the host-families to become more aware of and involved in the Sahrawis' political situation, with many host-family members becoming active supporters of their quest for self-determination.

Moving away from home, for months or years, is part of growing up for Sahrawi children. Once past primary education levels, children and youth have no choice but to leave their families if they are going to continue to receive an education. For some, the move is to one of the secondary-level boarding schools in the refugee camps, where instruction is in Arabic and Spanish. But most leave to the secondary schools of Algiers which require mastery of French, or further afield to Libya, Spain, Cuba and other Spanish- or Arabic-speaking countries. This movement, and return, fitting into the scholarly annual cycle, is tolerated and even promoted by adult Sahrawi and many youth. On some levels it prompts comparisons between the present situation of the sedentarized adults, whose current possibilities for mobility are severely restricted, to the peripatetic character of their own childhoods (Villasante Cervello 2005; Keenan 2005). For Sahrawi youth today, however, this mobility for education brings with it challenges for themselves and their kin back at 'home' in the refugee camps.

The Challenges of Return and Reintegration

Sahrawi youth face several challenges when they return to the refugee camps after having spent periods away from home, with the nature of these challenges depending on where, for how long, and from what age they have studied abroad. We start with a brief overview of children's comments following their 'short', two-month stay in Spain, then turn to the experiences of students who return after living outside the camps for longer periods of time. Understanding the experiences and challenges faced by children and youth who spend only two months away from the camps provides information not only about these brief experiences themselves, but also helps to draw out the possible implications for the older children and youth of longer periods of time spent away.

Summer Programme: the challenges

The majority of young children interviewed during their summer holidays in Spain were eager to return to their families. Most said they had missed them and did not express any concerns about having to 'readjust' to the conditions of life in the camps. It was mainly the Spanish hosts and the children's natural parents in the camps who voiced their worries about what might happen when the children return home after spending two or three months living in Spain. The vast differences in material wealth between Spain and the refugee camps underpin these parental concerns on both sides but did not seem to be a concern among the children themselves.

At the close of summer, when the host period ends, Spanish host-parents regularly proclaimed how much weight the Sahrawi children had gained while in their care. Many of them lamented the fact that when the children returned to the camps they would be subject to the limited rations of food-aid, a diet they equated with poor nutrition, hunger and weight loss. While children did mention 'less food' as one of the characteristics that distinguishes Sahrawi from Spanish society, they never raised it as something that prevented them from wanting to return. Some of the parents interviewed in the camps, however, suggested that children returned from abroad with new expectations that are often difficult to fulfil. One mother in her mid-forties, whose children had spent several summers living with Spanish families, described the adjustments which were necessary when they returned home:

[There they] have refrigerators, fresh vegetables, and fruits and take what they want ... so when they return ... they start to see things differently. They look at our tents as dirty, because they were exposed to clean and tidy houses and in good condition. They begin demanding things we cannot afford. Sometimes we are forced to sell our rations to fulfil their demands. [SL01FFG1MO44]

Another mother in the camps described the difficulties in meeting children's expectations when they returned home after being abroad:

They are used to having butter and jam for breakfast. So when we offer them olive oil they do not like it. This forces us to do things beyond our means, sometimes we have to sell our *melhafa* (women's clothes) in order to please them.

Of particular interest here is that the adults' anticipated concerns were not expressed among the young children at the end of their two- or three-month stay in Spain. However, when we consider the interviews completed with youth who spent a longer period of time away from the camps, these concerns begin to coalesce. The following section focuses on some of the particularities faced by youth when they experience a long separation from their families and from the refugee camps.

Study-abroad: the immediate challenges of return

In order to better understand the challenges faced by youth upon their return to the camps, it is first useful to outline some of the characteristics of the countries where they have lived. Clear socio-economic and political differences exist between the Cuban, Spanish and SADR contexts. Life in Cuba is heavily influenced by a strict embargo and a strong socialist ideology; in Spain by wealth and capitalism; and in the SADR by a dependence on humanitarian aid and its own form of social democracy in a protracted refugee camp setting. Furthermore, students who have lived in Cuba or Spain for several years will have been based in societies that are not primarily Muslim. They will have mingled with non-Sahrawi students, and generally been exposed to a social world which is very different from the peculiar context that is the Sahrawi refugee camps. Youth who have studied in Algeria, Libya or Syria, on the other hand, will have been exposed to different versions of Pan-Arabism, as well as a range of socio-economic living conditions. Although all three of these states are officially secular, they permit individual adherence to any of the four schools of Islamic jurisprudence (Hanafi, Shafi'i, Hanbali and Maliki), meaning that yet again, Sahrawi students would be exposed to more than just the Maliki School of Islam which is adhered to by the Sahrawi community in general.

In addition to differences related to the location of study, the period of time which students may have spent abroad (ranging from a few months to over a decade), together with the age at which they left their families (as young children or more mature adolescents), are key issues which influence youth experiences of returning home and their expectations for the future. Given the wide range of programmes outlined in this chapter, we will reflect on only a selection of challenges faced by each group of students, highlighting the heterogeneity of Sahrawi refugee youth's experiences during their time away from the camps, and suggesting some of the major difficulties they may face upon their return. Indeed, bearing this heterogeneity in mind, when they return 'home' students must not only readapt to the camps, but also to the other youth who have studied elsewhere. Imagining the encounter between a student who has lived for ten years in Cuba, and one who has lived in Libya for seven, suggests that, besides the language barrier, there would be serious social and cultural differences to recognize and to work through. At the same time, the camps' more permanent residents (including the students' families and those youth who have 'stayed behind') need to find some commonality with the returning students, some of whom no longer speak fluent Hassaniya, but prefer to communicate in French or Spanish.

Older youth who spend long periods of time away may confront multiple challenges upon reintegration into home and camp life, challenges that relate primarily to 'who they are' (identities) and 'what they do' (social roles). Hence, identity markers such as gender may influence experiences of studying abroad, and of returning to the refugee camps.

In general, Sahrawi girls and young women in the camps are expected to be educated, and actively participate in transnational education networks, often travelling long distances for schooling or to participate in one of the summer holiday programmes. Female participation at this level represents a real departure from the gender expectations experienced by older female generations of Sahrawis. Describing these changes, one forty year-old woman in Aaiun camp observed that:

> now things have developed… In the past, we could not send a young girl alone even to a neighbour's without someone. Now, girls travel all over the world alone to study. [T]hey enjoy freedom under the auspices of the SADR. Transportation is available and there are guides that go with the girls and boys.

Indeed, since the refugee camps were established in the late-1970s, female students have travelled 'alone' in the sense that they are without their families, but they are usually accompanied by a Sahrawi *monitor* (guide). Some students are fostered individually by Spanish families who take on most aspects of their care. However, despite the widespread participation of girls in the programmes, there are also families who prefer their girls not to leave home to study. A fourteen year-old girl in the camps insisted,

Girls also have problems pursuing their education. This depends on the family. Some of the families do not like to see their girls go abroad. Some prefer that the boys study more than girls. [SF50YFG2Y14]

In other cases, even when arrangements have been made between Spanish and Sahrawi parents for children to temporarily live in Spain, problems, some of which are gender-based, sometimes emerge between the families involved. Sometimes the child's birth-family may request or demand their son or daughter's permanent return to the camps, embodying conflicts between the Sahrawi and the Spanish families' understandings of what is best for the child involved. General issues considered by the families include the educational, nutritional and medical benefits which they feel can only be offered to the child by living in Spain, and the emotional difficulties of medium- to long-term separation from the child. Gender-specific reasons may include a desire to be closer to daughters upon adolescence (when sexual maturity and the potential for sexual activity might become a concern for Sahrawi families), and, in the case of eldest daughters, the assumption that these girls will take on major household responsibilities and support their parents in old age. There have been several high-profile cases in Spain of Sahrawi and Spanish families fighting for the custody of adolescent girls after they have lived in Spain for several years, indicating the complex realities faced by these refugee children and their families (Fiddian 2006).

There have also been cases where girls have decided themselves, following visits to Spain during the summer months, that they do not wish to return to Spain, either in the short or longer term, rejecting many 'Spanish ways' such as women's dress sense and the predominance of pork-based foods and alcohol. A seventeen year-old girl in 27th February camp described her reactions to Spanish life in this way:

I was in Spain many times, but I do not like Spain. The people have very different customs, they do not respect the elders, and they go out without clothes, naked. (she laughs)… That is very difficult for the Sahrawis to do. I was shocked when I was in Spain, and since then I refused to go back. (HHF42)

Regarding this ambivalence of sending, or not sending, girls to certain countries, it is also interesting to note changes that have taken place in relation to the Cuban study- abroad programme. While it is difficult to determine the total number of Sahrawi girls and young women who have studied in Cuba due to the absence of statistical information covering the first twenty years of the programme, Table 1.10 suggests that only a relatively small number of girls and young women have more recently participated in it. Hence, although 200 girls were studying in Cuba in 1995 and 1996, the number reported by UNHCR has decreased considerably, reaching nine at the end of 2002. Indeed, no girls apparently accompanied the 252 boys who arrived in Cuba in 2001. The current gender ratio is particularly interesting given that in the refugee camps observers are frequently told that large numbers of girls have studied in Cuba and the authors have met many Sahrawi refugee women who did indeed study there. It appears that although many girls were sent to study there in the late 1970s and early 1980s, this is no longer the norm.

In order to understand the reasons for this shift, it is, on the one hand, important to note that the total number of children, both male and female, travelling to Cuba has decreased dramatically since the 1980s. Another major change is that while young children (aged eleven or twelve) were initially sent to Cuba, there is a tendency nowadays to send only older adolescents aged sixteen or seventeen, to prepare for starting university. One motivation behind this may be that while parents were initially willing to send their children to study abroad, they had not expected that this would involve such a long-term separation: the first groups of children were in general unable to return to the camps at all for up to ten years. Recognition of the implications for the youth and families involved has led to many changes in the programme, and alternative locations for study have more recently been prioritized to try to minimize such long-term and long-distance separations, even leading to suggestions of increasing the institutional capacity within the camps themselves.

However, beyond these general shifts in the number and the age of youth being sent to study in Cuba, we must ask why the number of girls in particular has decreased so dramatically. Reports in the camps suggest that the reduction in female participation has taken place since the early 1990s. This change may have come about simultaneously due to some young women's difficulties in readapting to life in the refugee camps, and to their community's difficulty in accepting them upon their return.

Having spent so many of their formative years exposed to, and experiencing, Cuban culture and lifestyles, readjusting to Sahrawi traditions, social expectations and practices invariably takes months, if not years, for many Sahrawi young women (Farah 2005: 43). While Fatma Hmada of the Sahrawi Women's Union, the NUSW, has stressed that Sahrawi girls who study abroad have 'no problems when they return because they are Sahrawi inside', some women who studied in Cuba have stressed otherwise (Fiddian 2002). While highlighting the importance of their Sahrawi identity and their adamant support for the Sahrawi right for self-determination, some women stated that they still often felt like 'outsiders within' and several of them described their return to the camps as a 'radical culture-shock' (Fiddian 2002, also see Fiddian-Qasmiyeh, forthcoming 2009b).

For young women in particular, it appears that becoming accustomed to the differences between Cuban and Sahrawi traditions, surrounding everything from clothing to interactions with members of the opposite sex, may be especially difficult. Indeed, Cuban gender roles and relations are starkly different from those considered appropriate in the Sahrawi context, and young women returning from Cuba (unlike women who have studied in Algeria or Libya) have sometimes faced a degree of stigmatization from kin and community who were certain that the women had been 'bad girls' in Cuba – a Spanish film, *Las Cubarauis* (Márquez 2005), documents the experiences of Sahrawi women who studied in Cuba (ibid). While much of this information is anecdotal, some of these women have indicated that their morality and sexual integrity were questioned, both explicitly and implicitly, no matter how they behaved upon their return to the camps (Fiddian 2002). The families who experienced the return of the first groups of female students from Cuba may have decided that alternative study locations, such as Algeria or Libya, might be preferable, due to geographical proximity, as well as greater cultural and religious similarities.

This brief discussion suggests some of the ways in which gender and education programmes interact, both in terms of who is currently encouraged to study where and for how long (boys in Cuba but not girls), how girls may experience their return to the camps, and how the community may react to their return after prolonged periods of absence. It also indicates that students may react differently to the more liberal social realities of Spain and Cuba, some of them enjoying their times there, while others may reject these differences, preferring the security and social frameworks offered by their families and neighbours in the camps who make up the moral community underpinning their social lives.

Other challenges relate to distinctions conventionally associated with ethnic markers, such as language. The potential for the personal transformation of youth is highlighted below in the words of a twenty-four year-old Sahrawi man in Auserd camp who spent several years studying in Cuba. He points to the identity shifts he and other Sahrawi students experienced there, in terms of the initial emphasis on differences between them and local Cubans, and later, upon return to the camps, differences between the students and the camp residents.

As to our situation in Cuba, we left for a different country and we lived with them. They are not like us. The language and culture are different, so is their political life... Many spent their entire youth among the Cubans and forgot their Sahrawi customs. This different experience in Cuba affected us when we returned ... people here made fun of us and the way we spoke. (HHA13)

The difficulties of reintegration were not limited to those who had studied in Cuba.

Many Sahrawi children and youth based in Spain also had no access to Arabic lessons, and encountered linguistic difficulties upon their return to the refugee camps. This indicates that participants of programmes both based around peer-groups living together (Cuba) and individually-based opportunities (Spain) encounter linguistic difficulties upon return, due to their having lost fluency in their mother tongue (Hassaniya Arabic). However, even those who had studied in nearby Libya report experiencing feelings of marginalization upon return, unlike those youth who had returned from Algeria, the latter country perceived by camp residents as having a greater Sahrawi presence and perhaps as being culturally less distant. The passage below, from a thirty-four year-old woman in Auserd camp, highlights her memory of what it was like to return to the camps from Libya:

> I returned to the camps and lived with my family who I had left when I was seven years old. [When I returned,] I began living in a society that was different from the societies I had lived in previously, and therefore our lives were very difficult in the beginning. We were ridiculed a hundred times a day. They did not let us speak the Libyan dialect. If we behaved differently they used to laugh at us and make jokes. However, while studying in Algeria, it was easier to get accustomed again to the Sahrawi ways, because we returned to the camps every summer and we met many Sahrawi students which helped us to adapt to our traditions. Then the routine of daily life began ... whatever you do one day, you repeat the next.

This sense of having had one kind of life abroad and having to adapt to a new way of life back in the camps was also expressed by a thirty-three year-old woman from Aaiun camp who described how after studying in Libya and Algeria she returned to the camps and got married: 'Life changed, and another kind of life began. I had finished education and was among students. Now I have four children and have a different social life.'

One of the ways in which students cope with the initial ridicule and marginalization on their return is by maintaining the peer networks that they had established while studying abroad and tapping into them for emotional support. A former Sahrawi student from Cuba describes it as follows:

> I have many friends, especially from Cuba. We have the same mentality and stick together. We gather for coffee from time to time and try to help and understand each other. We have something like a club and we meet girls and boys and give them advice.

In addition to developing support mechanisms to deal with the temporary marginalization, Spanish speakers often have some advantages over mono-lingual Arabic speakers in the camps. Through their knowledge of Spanish, for instance, these young men and women are often invited to become guides for Spanish NGO workers, journalists and solidarity groups visiting the camps. This not only allows them to keep busy in an arena which has limited possibilities for employment, but also provides them with a way of gaining access to gifts and money (Fiddian-Qasmiyeh 2009a). In addition, they are able to act as intermediaries between the refugee camps and the outside world. The reality of their marginalization, paralleled by the potential benefits experienced by some of the youth returning to the camps, suggests the often ambivalent nature of the overseas education programme and of return to the camps.

Indeed, given the many challenges that youth face upon their return, a few of which have been hinted at above, it is important to ask why parents continue to allow and even encourage their children to leave the camps and travel abroad. Although major shifts have taken place in this respect over the last three decades, such as increasing the age at which students travel to Cuba, and changing the locations where youth are sent to study in order to facilitate frequent return visits to the camps, some reasons for this continued acceptance of youth studying abroad may include the following: the protracted nature of the refugee situation and the continued limited educational infrastructure in the camps; a strong desire to maximize local self-sufficiency by educating youth; and the fact that studying abroad often allows youth to access medical care and accrue nutritional and economic benefits, as well as developing important social and professional networks which may assist them in the future (Crivello, Fiddian and Chatty 2005). As we have already suggested, it is also important to reiterate the historical importance of mobility amongst the Sahrawi, both as a rite of passage and a connection to the culture of the older generation. Indeed, the factor of mobility and movement is one trait which links the old and the new generations despite the growing cultural differences between them, largely due to the specific educational experiences of the younger generation. In this respect, one further reason for the continued existence of these study-abroad programmes is the recognition by both the state (SADR/Polisario) and many Sahrawis that education is a key impetus for societal change.

Education is one of the characteristics which differentiate pre-colonial (largely pre-literate) society from Sahrawi refugee society, and also the older from the younger generation of refugees. A seventy-two year-old grandmother in Aaiun camp described these differences, saying:

The new generation is developing with the world ... it has new ways, it has learned a great deal ... the new generation is aware of new and modern things of which they learn through education and studying.

One forty-two year-old mother believed that as a result of their education and experiences abroad, the younger generation has developed higher expectations for life, indicating that

> The new generation wants more modern things, for example, we used to ride the camels, they want to drive a car and have better things... In fact, they want to learn how to fly and sail boats and travel on land and in the sky and across the sea. They want to talk to the world far away.

However, the act of leaving the deprivation and hardship of the refugee camps to study abroad in relative comfort (real, or imagined) was identified by members of the older generations as one of the main forces responsible for widening differences between the young and old. The way in which one sixty-four year-old man in Smara camp described these differences suggested that they were embodied, in the sense that the younger generation 'cannot tolerate heat or hunger'. He went on to say,

> We the people of old could stay without food for a whole month or more. We can walk from here to Zouerat on foot ... such stamina you will not find in the younger people ... they live in a different and developed age and are exposed to more luxuries.

So, while youth are more educated than their parents and grandparents, the latter believe that they are themselves more robust. It is a point of distinction for them, which they probably explain in relation to the extreme physical, social and emotional conditions they had to endure in their previous nomadic lives, as well as in their exodus, often on foot, towards the safety zone in Algeria thirty years ago.

Hence, on the one hand, the older generations are proud of their educated youth and support their long-distance travel for short to medium lengths of time. However, elders also voice worries about what has been sacrificed as a result, once again stressing the ambivalent nature of the study-abroad programmes. Unlike the challenges which are faced upon return, one major element of loss relates to the fact that the children spent extended periods away from their families while they participated in these study-abroad programmes. A forty-three year-old mother claims that the distance created between her children and herself because of their need to study abroad (in Libya, Algeria and Cuba) compromised her ability to parent them, saying 'they grew up alone ... and I have been unable therefore to bring them up as I wish'.

Further expanding upon the experience of separation, one thirty-three year-old woman described her experiences as an eight year-old child when she left her family to study in 1978:

The children who went to Libya were very young, some six or seven years old... The Libyans provided us with everything that we needed and tried to compensate for the separation from our families. Can you imagine the effect of this separation on the children? They were forced to leave their families due to the conditions at a very early age and under very difficult conditions ... they suffered a great deal...

Clearly noting the difficulties faced by these children, she continued:

The efforts made by schools and other organisations do not make up for the time lost with family where one feels love and warmth... Can you imagine what a child of six or seven feels when he gets sick ... lying there sick among the other children? When a sick child is with his family ... they provide him with love, something a school or other children cannot provide.

A thirty-four year-old woman in Auserd camp had similar memories of loneliness and yearning. She recalled how, only two years after arriving in the refugee camps, she left as a young girl to study in Libya:

I used to cry all day long, looking for my mother. There, they gave me toys to distract me... with time I became accustomed to my mother's absence. At that time we visited the camps and our families every two years during the summer holidays. Each time we left the camps back to Libya we cried and remembered the camps and our families. However, as the years passed, we got used to this also and now I do not see anyone crying when they leave the camps.

Nonetheless, despite all of the emotional difficulties encountered, even those who spent many years of their childhoods living away from their families consider that their parents played a crucial role in their upbringing. A thirty year-old woman who studied in Cuba from her preparatory years through to her bachelor's degree – at a great distance from her family – said, 'We went through a lot of hardship. But thanks to God, my mother took care of us and we were raised under guidance and care.'

Sahrawi children and youth are viewed as having a positive influence on their refugee society when they return to the camps. In particular, the purposeful formal education of the younger generations born in the camps over the past thirty years has placed them at the centre of societal changes. Although these children and youth may not be actively involved in making decisions about their education (i.e., where they go and when), they are nonetheless seen as critical elements in shaping a highly educated refugee society. Indeed, the main rationale of both the Polisario and the older generation for sending their children and youth to study abroad is to ensure that Sahrawi society becomes and remains self-sufficient, both in the refugee camps (with Sahrawi youth working as doctors, teachers, engineers, lawyers, ministerial aides and so on) and someday also in an independent Western Sahara. The mobility and educational outcomes of young people's lives may also therefore be framed in terms of the relationship between individual and several forms of collective strategies. When children leave the camps, it is to fulfil their immediate needs for education and to access other vital resources. They also leave in peer groups which may or may not reflect family and old tribal linkages. It is essentially their commitment and eventual return to live in the camps, however, that reflects a collective strategy among peer groups of youth as well as the broader 'new' socialist society being promoted by the Polisario/SADR. Refugee youth are seen as an investment in the future, with great hope placed on the roles that they might play in a future independent Western Sahara.

Conclusion: Transnational Lives

We should not forget that we are here as visitors, and a visitor eats a little and leaves.
Seventy-nine year-old woman, Smara camp

Sahrawi youth, the second generation to live in the refugee camps, have come to see their lives as one of movement interspersed with stretches of settlement. Their lives, like those of their parents and other relatives, have come to be defined by the links and networks which have been set up for them by the Polisario/SADR. In the case of Sahrawi youth these links are shaped by the drive for education, perhaps one of the state's foremost political goals. In accepting this fundamental political goal on a personal level, Sahrawi youth are driven into migrating for education and, as an aspect of that migration, they become key links in networks between their educational hosts and their families in the refugee camps. Whereas their parents' networks were often based on an ideology of nomadic pastoralism and associated seasonal movements, contemporary networks revolve around the movement of youth and the transnational support units which shore up such mobility. It is grounded in a cycle of movement for education and also, peripherally, for medical care.

The older generation often fears that their transnational youth are losing their culture and traditions, and so go to significant lengths to maintain a focus on their original culture through various support, mentoring and supervisory activities. The youth, meanwhile, search out and hold on to their histories as a way of remaining linked to their Sahrawi families in the refugee camps of Algeria. Those youth who are sent to Arabic-speaking states such as Algeria for education recognize the special solidarity which their hosts have for the SADR and their political ambitions. The networks they create in these locations are based on political solidarity. They are reminded that they are guests of the Algerian state, awaiting the chance to return to their own homeland. Those youth who are sent to non-Arabic speaking states, such as Spain or Cuba, must make greater efforts with regards to their cultural and political identity. The networks they create are closely tied to their social and economic needs. On their return to the camps, they often have to work at regaining their mother tongue, but they also form a large cohort of youth with similar cultural experiences. They create a social solidarity amongst themselves grounded in the impermanence of the refugee camps in the desert sands near Tindouf, Algeria.

In its early years, the Polisario/SADR push to educate youth was accessed almost equally by male and female Sahrawi children in keeping with the modern socialist promise of the new state. This push embodied a major shift from traditional Sahrawi society, in which it might have been common for male youth to leave the kin group (sometimes for years at a time), but female children were expected to be closer to home, with puberty generally marking the end of non-kin-based movements. As the study-abroad programmes have developed, many shifts have taken place, including a sharp decline in the number of females going to study in Cuba. The distances and time-periods involved, together with an increase in knowledge about the social and religious environment of the host country, and gender expectations and responsibilities in the camps, appear to have affected the ease with which Sahrawi adults allow their daughters to study abroad following adolescence. While large numbers of girls continue to participate in Spanish, Algerian and Libyan study-abroad programmes, several key characteristics are worth noting: a large number of pre-adolescent girls still study for their secondary, and often tertiary, education outside of the camps, but many girls are encouraged to return to the camps in their mid- to late-teens, either to complete further studies there (in the camp-based nursing or teaching colleges, for instance), to take on household responsibilities (especially in the case of eldest daughters), to marry and create a family of their own, or a combination of these.

Not all Sahrawi students spend their childhood and adolescence separated from their family and kin group. Some only participate in the *Vacaciones en Paz* programme for a few summers in Spain, elsewhere in Europe, and now also in the US, and decide not to carry on with their education. As education beyond primary school generally means leaving home to attend boarding school (only one of which currently exists within the camps), some youth and their families decide not to continue the cycle of migration for education. Our data does not give us any idea of how these decisions are made; whether it is the youth themselves who take the decision or whether it is the parents or the extended family who decide that the benefits of participation do not outweigh the losses to the child, family and community. The emotional costs may be accompanied by those of a more practical nature, especially in the case of youth who perform key household tasks (especially eldest daughters), tend to animals, or assist in small family businesses in the camps. It is unclear whether the decision to drop out of a formal education, and the separation and mobility that this education entails, is an active choice indicating some agency among the youth and family. It might even be the case that dropping out of the education network is a decision taken by families wishing to disengage from the Polisario/SADR structure which has so diligently created international opportunities to educate its youth.

Sahrawi youth are members of a nation living in a temporary and symbolic territory – the refugee camps near Tindouf. Their lives are highly politicized and their future is built upon an education which is dependent on transnational networks. One of the major issues confronting youth who have studied abroad for prolonged periods and then returned to the refugee camps with university degrees and specialized training is 'what to do'. As there is no formal economy in the camps, paid jobs are rare and formal appointments highly competitive. Instead, returning graduates are expected to volunteer to work in committees and institutions that underpin the organization and maintenance of Sahrawi camp society (for example, working in a pre-school, teaching in a primary school or distributing food-aid). It is not always the case that youth will have no paid employment on their return, but they will often be expected to participate in activities for which they were not trained or in which they lack interest, for instance, as guides for tourists, journalists and academics visiting the camps.

For many returning youth, the lack of appropriate work to suit their newly gained educational qualifications is a fundamental problem. A twenty-five year-old female teacher described the situation of returning students, saying:

> When they return they do not find jobs or a position ... the graduate remains without anything to do, and occupies himself or herself with other responsibilities; for example, he becomes an administrator or joins the military. Thus, the graduates lose their knowledge and the specialty which they had eagerly pursued and exerted a great deal effort.

She asserts that the youth 'suffer a great deal due to the emptiness they feel' because 'the state cannot employ them' and 'there are no jobs where they can develop their talents and the special skills they acquired'.

Although personal histories of serial cyclical migration throughout childhood and youth may prepare individuals for future emigration as adults, their desire to emigrate should not be considered a given. Long absences away from family may in fact strengthen the desire to return and remain in the camps, as this testimony from a twenty-six year-old male medical volunteer suggests:

> I do not want to go to Spain, although I had many offers from my Spanish friends who need people like me to work in Spain. They can pay a lot of money but I do not want to go because of my mother and father who have suffered a lot in the camps for me to be educated. I also want to support my sisters who still need guidance.

Although this young man has the opportunity to migrate, he chooses to stay near those family members from whom he was separated for so long as a child and to whom he feels responsible. Other able-bodied youth, however, are looking outward for possibilities to provide for their families' basic needs, as this fifteen year-old boy suggests:

> Sometimes I think it is better to go to Mauritania and work there, or to Spain. But you need a passport and a visa to go to Spain, and I cannot afford to leave my family now. My father does give us some money from time to time but it is not enough. My neighbours also help us when they can.

The gap between students' expectations and the reality they confront upon return to the camps is exacerbated by the general uncertainty of the future of the Sahrawi refugee camps in relation to self-determination and the international arena. As the quotation above suggests, Sahrawi youth are searching for options, often outside the confines of the camps. A thirty-four year-old man in Aaiun camp claimed that,

> There isn't the same enthusiasm regarding education as there was in the past. Students do not study as much as they did in the past. They are being distracted by other things such as working in market activities and in general they are more materialistic.

The desire to work in a market economy is also reflected in a recent survey reportedly conducted amongst 540 Sahrawi refugees aged between seventeen and thirty-five in the camps by a locally-produced Sahrawi magazine called *Futuro Saharawi* ('Sahrawi Future'). While no information is available regarding the methodology used in this survey, and therefore the reliability of the data is somewhat uncertain, the result reported by the magazine is that eighty-seven per cent of those 540 interviewed wished to obtain a visa to work outside of the camps (Futuro Saharawi 2006). Nonetheless, even if this data is not wholly reliable, the fact that such a survey was carried out, and that the magazine has included a special report on the matter, suggests the importance that is given to this issue by much of the refugee camp community. Indeed, it suggests that one type of difficulty which may accompany having such a highly-educated population, in a place where opportunities for paid employment are so limited, is that many of the members of that population may want to leave the camps, and, in a sense, continue the serial circular migration which they first experienced as children.

The Polisario/SADR'S highly successful campaign to educate its people has resulted in a new generation of Sahrawi youth who are comfortable with cyclical patterns of movement away from the extended family and kin group. It is a movement reminiscent of traditional migration patterns: seasonal movement punctuated by brief periods of return to the core group. Many members of this new generation, a transnational one, at home in the desert camps as well as the cities and towns of their educational host-countries, are now looking to continue their migrations in order to contribute to the well-being of their kin back at home. The rationale may appear different, but there are many parallels with the traditional migrations of nomadic youth to seek their fortune and return to their families having made good.

Whereas the Sahrawi youth migrations for secondary and, for many, tertiary education may not have been personal choices, the decision to leave the desert camps after receiving a complete formal education is certainly a matter of personal agency with individual, family and collective implications. Given the harsh reality of the refugee camps, and with the opportunity for education being a fundamental principle of the Sahrawi state which is generally supported by the older generations, youth have had little choice but to accept the opportunities which were handed to them by Spanish families, and friendly states such as Algeria, Cuba or Libya. There was also little opportunity for youth to express a preference as to where they would travel, and when; they have often simply cooperated with the state's agenda. However, on their return to the camps after protracted periods abroad and with established social networks transcending national borders, many are now flexing their ability to take charge of their lives and to contribute actively to their families, kin groups and the state. For many highly educated youth, this means considering emigrating in another cycle of movement in order to set up a chain of remittances to support their society, from afar.

Notes

1. Dawn Chatty was the principal investigator for the Andrew Mellon Foundation funded project on Sahrawi Refugee Youth; Gina Crivello was the project research assistant; Elena Fiddian-Qasmiyeh was a doctoral student as well as co-researcher – along with Gina Crivello – on the Andrew Mellon sub-project commissioned by Dawn Chatty to study the summer placement of Sahrawi youth in Spain. Elena Fiddian-Qasmiyeh has drawn significantly on her Master's thesis (Fiddian 2002), a presentation given at Cambridge University (Fiddian 2006), as well as her doctoral research (Fiddian-Qasmiyeh 2009a), for sections of this chapter.

2. The term 'government-in-exile' is frequently used in the literature to refer to the Sahrawi Arab Democratic Republic. However, as an entity it came into being after the flight of much of the population of the Western Sahara along with the Polisario, the political party and guerrilla organization representing the Sahrawi people. The state, as such, is physically in-waiting and temporarily housed in the four refugee camps near the Algerian border town of Tindouf.

3. In other refugee situations with youth from recent nomadic backgrounds, such as the Dinka and Nuer 'lost boys' of the Sudan, humanitarian aid workers have been surprised by the resilience and ease with which some of these young people tolerated and thrived despite oceans separating them from their families. The cultural continuity of 'nomadic ideology', whereby youth are expected to leave their homes and camps for long periods of time, returning only when they are ready to formally become adults, is thought to have played an important part in the adjustment of these youth in their resettlement countries (Zutt 1994).

4. The Western Sahara is the last territory in the African continent still on the agenda of the UN Special Committee on Decolonisation. It is defined by the UN as a non-self-governing territory [resolution 1514 (XV)], and the organization considers that the question of the Western Sahara is still that of decolonization. The territory was never formally and legally decolonized by Spain (its original colonizer) and has been occupied by Morocco since the territory was invaded in 1975.

5. It was not until 1963 that Madrid set up a formal administration in the territory (Damis 1983).

6. Pazzanita and Hodges (1994) suggest that 'at least as many Sahrawi were in the neighbouring territories' either as a result of population movements fleeing from military unrest which engulfed the territory in 1958, or the process of sedentarization prompted by drought.

7. On 27 February 1976, the day after the Spanish officially withdrew from the territory, the Polisario proclaimed an independent Western Sahara (Sahrawi Arab Democratic Republic, or SADR).

8. Only the situation of those Sahrawis who live in Mauritania close to the border with the Western Sahara is monitored by UNHCR (2003c). The precise number of Sahrawi refugees in Mauritania, however, is not known.

9. According to United Nations' figures for 1998, there were 275,000 Sahrawi inhabitants in Western Sahara, excluding Moroccan settlers in the territory.

10. The United Nations and the African Union sponsored a cease-fire between the Sahrawi and Moroccan armed forces in 1991, with groups of soldiers demobilizing and returning to the camps from that date onwards. Many soldiers continue to complete military training, in case renewed military action is deemed necessary in the future.

11. The historical centrality of Sahrawi women in family and communal life has more recently been reinforced, largely due to men's absence from the camps. While it is misleading to speak of 'Sahrawi women' in this homogenizing fashion, especially if we consider the existence of slavery during the precolonial and colonial eras, the contemporary Sahrawi national project is founded upon an idea(l) of Sahrawi women's freedom and agency. Sahrawi women's participation in all areas of social and political life is heralded by Sahrawis and non-Sahrawi observers alike as a positive feature of Sahrawi society.

12. Pensions from the Spanish government, as well as some remittances from summer holiday schemes, also provide further input into the growing informal economy, as we have previously argued in Crivello, Fiddian and Chatty (2005).

13. According to Miske, the first UNHCR aid programme was planned after a UNHCR visit to the Sahrawi refugee camps in January 1977, when assistance was estimated for 50,000 refugees (Miske 1978). The UNHCR gave the Sahrawi refugees only limited assistance from a special emergency fund under the personal direction of the High Commissioner, independent of the UNHCR's normal eligibility process. It was not until the 1980s that the High Commissioner reportedly felt able to allocate funds from the UNHCR General Fund.

14. Sven Lampell, a League of Red Cross Societies' representative who liaised with the Sahrawi Red Crescent in 1975-77, noted that even in the earliest days of the exodus, these were 'the most unusual refugees' he had known in that they were organized, cooperative and determined to be self-sufficient even when they were entirely reliant on externally provided aid (Lippert 1987).

15. The team leader for the Sahrawi field site was Dr Randa Farah. The local research coordinator was Radhi-Saghaiar Bachir. The research assistants were Fatematou Salem, Abdati Breica Ibrahim, Mohamed el Mokhtar Bouh, Mohammed Ali, Noueha and Fatima Mohammed Salem. The research undertaken in Madrid in 2005 was conducted by Gina Crivello and Elena Fiddian-Qasmiyeh.

16. See chapter 2 for a fuller description of the research carried out in Madrid.

17. For an historical overview of the origin of the inhabitants of the Western Sahara, see Pazzanita and Hodges (1994), Smith (2004) and Norris (1962).

18. The 'liberated territories' are located to the east of the 2,000 km-long structure built by Morocco to keep the Polisario out of the area under its control, and to the west of the political border between Western Sahara and Algeria (see map 1).

19. This, it could be argued, may be related primarily to the age of the interviewees, since, as young children, they wish to be close to their families. Older youth, however, express more interest in finding ways of supporting their camp-based families by working abroad, as we argue in our conclusion.

20. Most students (approximately forty) went to study in Madrid (in the Colegio Mayor Africa), while others went to various cities in the Canary Islands, Malaga, Cordoba, Barcelona and Asturias (Wirth and Balaguer 1976).

21. Regarding the continued significance of tribal identities in the refugee camps and Sahrawi society, see Cozza (2004).
22. More recently, the area surrounding the 27th February Women's School has become a more permanent settlement, with women and their families staying on after completing their studies. This school has now, in essence, become a small fifth refugee camp.
23. In 1999 a preliminary registration of refugees wishing to return to the Western Sahara after a referendum has been conducted did take place in the camps, and confirmed that at least 107,000 camp-based refugees wanted to return under the auspices of a UNHCR programme. We suggest that all other UNHCR statistics should be viewed as estimates.
24. Other countries, such as Mexico and Venezuela, also invite Sahrawi youth to study in their universities. There are, for instance, nine Sahrawi students in Mexico's UNAM University (Petrich 2005).
25. It is clear from interviews and the available statistics that large numbers of Sahrawi students do indeed return to the camps following the completion of their studies, although it is not possible to confirm how many (or how few) may have decided to stay in Cuba since the programme began in 1977.
26. The UN refugee agency has confirmed that the Sahrawi children are well cared for and supervised throughout their stay, that they participate voluntarily (and with their parents' consent) in the project, and also return voluntarily to the refugee camps. Two of their monitoring and evaluation visits are documented in UNHCR (2003a) and UNHCR (2005b).
27. It is worth stressing that UNHCR's role has been relatively minimal, covering only four per cent of all Cuban governmental expenses for the entire scholarship programme in 2001, and only attending to Sahrawi children who arrived in Cuba before 1996 (UNHCR 2003c).
28. Indeed, it is interesting to note that Tindouf, the Algerian city closest to the camps, is the city which receives the largest number of tourists in Algeria.
29. For more information on the programme, see the Escola en Pau website, www.escolaenpau.org.
30. Unlike the Spanish and Cuban programmes outlined above, which are referred to quite extensively in the English-, Spanish- and French-language solidarity pages on the internet (such as www.arso.org), only three references to the Libyan and Syrian scholarship programmes were found on these solidarity pages.
31. Indeed, Libya played an essential role in the 1970s, supporting the Polisario Front's application for the youth organization to be admitted to the Congress of Euro-Arab Youth and the PanAfrican Movement of Youth.
32. The only news item identified on the Syrian study-abroad programme read, in its entirety, 'Syria recognized the SADR in 1980; for the last twenty years, a Sahrawi representative has been based in Damascus. Thanks to Syria, the university formation of Sahrawi students is guaranteed' (ARSO 2000c: our translation).

References

Abjean, A. 2003. 'Histoire d'exils: Les jeunes Sahraouis', *Collection L'Ouest Saharien,* Hors Serie 3: 19–129.

ARSO. 2000a. *Weekly News*: 27 August–2 September 2000. Accessed at http://www.arso.org/01-e00-35.htm on 18 October 2006.

ARSO. 2000b. *Weekly News*: 13–18 August 2000. Accessed at http://www.arso.org/01-e00-33.htm on 18 October 2006.

ARSO. 2000c. 'Siria', 11 June 2000. *Weekly News*: 11–17 June 2000. Accessed at http://www.arso.org/01-s00-24.htm on 26 September 2006.

ARSO. 2001. 'Asturias: the government has granted 5 university scholarships to Sahrawi students', 10/02/01. *ARSO Weekly News*: 11–17 February 2001.Accessed at http://www.arso.org/01-e01-07.htm on 27 September 2006.

ARSO. 2006. *Western Sahara - News.* Weeks 07–08: 12–25 February 2006. Accessed at http://www.arso.org/01-e06-0708.htm on 26 September 2006.

Barbier, M. 1982. *Le Conflit du Sahara Occidental.* Paris: L'Harmattan.

Caratini, S. 2003. *La République des Sables: Anthropologie d'une Révolution.* Paris: L'Harmattan.

Chassey, F. de. 1977. *L'Etrier, la houe et le livre 'sociétés traditionnelles' au Sahara et au Sahel Occidental.* Paris: Editions Anthropos.

Chatty, D. 1996. *Mobile Peoples: Development Planning and Social Change in the Sultanate of Oman.* New York: Columbia University Press.

——— (ed.). 2005. *Nomadic Societies of the Middle East and North Africa: Entering the 21st Century.* Leiden: Brill.

Chopra, J. 1999. *Peace-maintenance: the Evolution of International Political Authority.* London: Routledge.

Claudot-Hawad, H. 2005. 'A Nomadic Fight against Immobility: theTuareg in the Modern State', in D. Chatty (ed.), *Nomadic Societies of the Middle East and North Africa: Entering the 21st Century.* Leiden: Brill, pp. 682–710.

Coggan, F. 2003. 'Sahrawi leader tours New Zealand', *The Militant* 67(21), 23 June 2003. Available at http://www.themilitant.com/2003/6721/672110.html.

Cozza, N. 2004. *Singing like Wood-birds: Refugee Camps and Exile in the Construction of the Saharawi Nation.* Thesis submitted for the degree of Doctor of Philosophy in Development Studies. Oxford: University of Oxford.

Crivello, G., E. Fiddian and D. Chatty. 2005. *The Transnationalisation of Care: Sahrawi Refugee Children in a Spanish Host Program.* Refugee Studies Centre, QEH, University of Oxford. Available at http://www.forcedmigration.org/guides/llreport3/llreport3.pdf.

Damis, J. 1983. *Conflict in northwest Africa.* Publication 278. Stanford: Hoover Institution Press.

——— 1985. 'The Western Sahara Dispute as a Source of Regional Conflict in North Africa', in H. Barakat (ed.), *Contemporary North Africa: Issues of Development and Integration.* Washington: Center for Contemporary Arab Studies, pp. 138–53.

ECHO. 2001. *Evaluation des plans globaux humanitaires de echo en faveur des réfugiés sahraouis. Rapport final. Secteurs: réhabilitation/produits non-alimentaires.* Report accessed at http://ec.europa.eu/echo/evaluation/country_en.htm#sah and annexes at http://ec.europa.eu/echo/pdf_files/evaluation/2001/sahara3_annex.pdf on 19 October 2006.

——— 2005. *Decision to grant humanitarian aid*. ECHO/DZA/BUD/2005/01000.

EU. 2004. *EU humanitarian aid to Sahrawi refugees in Algeria*. 22 July 2004.

Farah, R. 2005. Final Report 'Vacaciones en Paz Programme', in *Sahrawi and Afghan Refugee Youth (SARC*, Final Project Report, unpublished). Oxford: Refugee Studies Centre.

Fiddian, E. 2002. *Promoting Sustainable Transformations in Gender Relations During Exile: A Critical Analysis With Reference to the Sahrawi Refugee Camps*. Dissertation submitted in partial fulfilment of the requirements of the degree, MSc in Gender and Development 2002, London School of Economics, University of London.

——— 2006. 'Education, Gender and Solidarity: the Cases of Three Sahrawi Girls', seminar paper presented at the *Gender Theory and Methodology Seminar Series*, University of Cambridge, 9 February 2006.

Fiddian-Qasmiyeh, E. 2009a. 'Representing Sahrawi Refugee's "Educational Displacement" to Cuba: self-sufficient agents and/or manipulated victims in conflict?' Journal of Refugee Studies, Vol. 22: 3.

——— 2009b. Gender, Islam and Sahrawi Politics of Survival, DPHIL in International Development Submitted to the University of Oxford in April 2009.

Firebrace, J. 1987. 'The Saharawi Refugees: Lessons and prospects', in R. Lawless and L. Monahan (eds), *War and Refugees: The Western Sahara Conflict*. Refugee Studies Programme. London: Pinter, pp. 167–185.

Futuro Saharawi. 2006. '87% de los jovenes saharauis desea emigrar al extranjero'. Accessed at http://www.futurosahara.jeeran.com/es10.htm on 18 October 2006.

Gaudio, A. 1978. *Le Dossier du Sahara Occidental*. Paris: Nouvelles Editions Latines.

Guia Activ. 2001. *Gandia colabora en el proyecto de ayuda a jóvenes estudiantes saharauis,*17 January 2001. Accessed at http://www.guia-activ.com/comunidad/noticias/vernoticia.html?ref=4150 on 27 September 2006.

International Court of Justice. 1975. *Case Summaries: Western Sahara*. Advisory Opinion of 16 October 1975. Accessed at http://www.icj-cij.org/icjwww/idecisions/isummaries/isasummary751016.htm on 18 April 2003.

Keenan, J. 2005. 'Sustainable Nomadism: The Case of the Algerian Tuareg', in D. Chatty (ed.), *Nomadic Societies of the Middle East and North Africa: Entering the 21st Century*. Leiden: Brill, pp. 916–40.

Lenz, J. 2004. 'The Question of Western Sahara'. Statement from Janet Lenz: U.N. Address. 6–7 October 2004. Accessed at http://arso.orc.site.voila.fr/4commLenz.htm on 23 September 2006.

Lippert, A. 1987. 'The Sahrawi Refugees: Origins and Organization, 1975–1985', in R. Lawless and L. Monahan (eds), *War and Refugees: The Western Sahara Conflict*. Refugee Studies Programme, London: Pinter, pp. 150–166.

Márquez, A. 2005. *Las Cubarauis*. Azul Media.

Martínez, G. 2003. 'Las mujeres saharauis gobiernan el dia a dia mientras los hombres van a la Guerra', *Ahige,* 14 October 2003. Accessed at http://www.aige.org/texto_noti.php?wcodigo=12023 on 28 September 2006.

Mercer, J. 1979. *The Sahrawis of Western Sahara*. London: The Minority Rights Group.

Miske, A.B. 1978. *Front Polisario: l'âme d'un peuple*. Paris: Editions Rupture.

Norris, H.T. 1962. 'Yemenis in the Western Sahara', *Journal of African History* III, 1:317–22.

Pazzanita, A.G. and T. Hodges. 1994. *Historical Dictionary of Western Sahara. African Historical Dictionaries,* No. 55. 2nd edn. Metuchen, NJ and London: The Scarecrow Press.

Perez, E.C. 2004. 'Cuba es el más grande ejemplo de cooperación con otros pueblos.' *Granma,* No. 64, 4 March 2004. Accessed at http://www.granma.cubaweb.cu/2004/03/04/nacional/articulo07.html on 29 October 2005.

Perregaux, C. 1987. *L'Ecole sahraouie. De la caravane à la guerre de libération.* Paris: L'Harmattan.

Petrich, B. 2005a. 'El impulso a salud y educación, clave para remontar la adversidad: De Cuba, educación y salud.' *La Jornada* (n.d) Accessed at http://www.jornada.unam.mx/reportajes/2005/sahara/41/?seccion=3 on 26 September 2006.

––– 2005b. 'El impulso a salud y educación, clave para remontar la adversidad', *La Jornada* 13 May 2005. Accessed at http://www.jornada.unam.mx/2005/05/13/022n1pol.php on 29 October 2005.

R.A.S.D. 2000. *Acogimiento Provisional.* Accessed at http://www.elparchedigital.com/pags/huria/ on 1 November 2005.

RHC/Radio Habana Cuba. 2002a. 'Una Visita Muy Provechosa, Dice Presidente Saharaui.' *RHC,* 31 January 2002. Accessed at http://www.blythe.org/nytransfer-subs/2002-Caribbean-Vol-I/Radio_Habana_Cuba-31_de_enero_2002 on 29 October 2005.

––– 2002b. 'Presidente Saharaui Visita la Isla de la Juventud.' *RHC,* 24 January 2002. Accessed at http://www.blythe.org/nytransfer-subs/2002-Caribbean-Vol-I/Radio_Habana_Cuba-24_de_enero,_2002 on 19 October 2005.

Rodríguez Molina, D. 2004. 'Agradece dirigente saharaui apoyo solidario de Cuba.' *Granma,* 22 January 2004. No.22. Accessed at http://www.granma.cubaweb.cu/2004/01/22/nacional/articulo06.html on 10 January 2006.

––– 2005. 'Destacan aprovechamiento de estudiantes saharauíes.' *Granma,* 23 June 2005. No.174. Accessed at http://www.granma.cubaweb.cu/2005/06/23/nacional/articulo03.html on 29 October 2005.

Salazar, E. 2002. 'Mandatario Saharauí Continúa Viaje Por Cuba.' *Radio Reloj,* 25 January 2002. Accessed at http://www.radioreloj.cu/noticiasdia2/notidia25-1-02.htm#2 on 29 October 2005.

San Martín, P. 2005. 'Nationalism, Identity and Citizenship in the Western Sahara', *Journal of North African Studies,* Vol. 10: 3, 565–592.

Saxena, S.C. 1995. *Western Sahara: No Alternative to Armed Struggle.* Delhi: Kalinga Publications.

Smith, D. 2004. 'FMO Research Guide: Western Sahara', August 2004. Accessed at http://www.forcedmigration.org/guides/fmo035/title.htm on 18 October 2006.

S.P.S. 2001. 'Libya.' *Sahara Press Service,* 17 October 2001. Accessed at http://arso.org/01-e01-4245.htm on 23 September 2006.

––– 2002. 'Le Président de la république affirme que son séjour à Cuba aura une influence positive.' *Sahara Press Service,* 1 February 2002. Accessed at http://www.spsrasd.info/sps-240102.html on 29 October 2005.

––– 2006. 'End of the summer holidays of the Sahrawi children in the Algerian cities of Annaba and El Tarf.' *Sahara Press Service*, 31 August 2006.

Um Draiga. 2001. 'Cena de Solidaridad Apoyo Estudiantes Saharauis'. Accessed at http://www.umdraiga.com/actividades/cena01.htm on 29 October 2005.

UN General Assembly. 1960. Declaration on the granting of independence to colonial countries and peoples. Resolution 1514 (XV), 14 December 1960.

UNHCR. 1996. *Statistical Overview 1995*. Available at www.unhcr.org.

––– 1997. *Statistical Overview 1996*. Available at www.unhcr.org.

––– 1998. *Statistical Overview 1997*. Available at www.unhcr.org.

––– 1999. *Statistical Overview 1998*. Available at www.unhcr.org.

––– 2000. *Statistical Overview 1999*. Available at www.unhcr.org.

––– 2003a. 'Summary Update of Machel Study. Follow-up activities in 2001–2002' Refugee Children Coordination Unit, United Nations High Commissioner for Refugees, pp.48ff.

––– 2003b. *UNHCR Global Report, 2002: North Africa*. Available at www.unhcr.org.

––– 2003c. *UNHCR Cuba-Country Report (1 January to 31 December 2002)*. Available at www.unhcr.org.

––– 2003d. *Statistical Overview 2002*. Available at www.unhcr.org.

––– 2004a. *Statistical Overview 2003*. Available at www.unhcr.org.

––– 2004b. *Refugee Education Indicators, 2003*. Available at www.unhcr.org.

––– 2005a. *Statistical Overview 2004*. Available at www.unhcr.org.

––– 2005b. 'Information note in relation to the Moroccan delegation's questions to the EXCOM session 2004', addressed to the 2005 session of the Executive Committee.

Universidad de Vigo. 2003. *La Universidad se compromete para la formación de estudiantes saharauis*, 4 December 2003. Accessed at http://www.universia.es/portada/actualidad/noticia_actualidad.jsp?noticia=38264 on 27 September 2006.

US Committee for Refugees and Immigrants. 1999. *Cuba Report 1998*.

Velloso de Santiseban, A. 1993. *La Educación en el Sahara Occidental*. Madrid: UNED.

Villasante Cervello, M. 2005. 'From the Disappearance of "Tribes" to Reawakening of the Tribal Feeling: Strategies of State among the Formerly Nomadic Bid n (Arabophone) of Mauretania', in D. Chatty (ed.), *Nomadic Societies of the Middle East and North Africa: Entering the 21st Century*. Leiden: Brill, pp. 144–76.

Wirth, R. and S. Balaguer. 1976. *Frente Polisario: la última guerrilla*. Barcelona: Editorial Laia.

Yara, A.O. 2003. *L'Insurrection sahraouie, de la guerre à l'Etat, 1973–2003*. Paris: L'Harmattan.

Zutt, J. 1994. *Children of War: Wandering alone in southern Sudan*. New York: UNICEF.

2
The Ties that Bind: Sahrawi Children and the Mediation of Aid in Exile

Gina Crivello and Elena Fiddian-Qasmiyeh

Sahrawi children are like young ambassadors of their people and through them people get to know about the Sahrawi people.
Sahrawi refugee camp resident, Algeria.

Fawzia's Story

In June 2005, eleven year-old Fawzia, with little more than the clothes she was wearing, boarded a chartered flight to Madrid, Spain. She travelled without her family, yet surrounded by hundreds of other children who, like herself, live in the Sahrawi refugee camps in the harsh Algerian desert. For many of the children it was their first time leaving the refugee camps and, more importantly, their mothers, for an extended period of time. But for Fawzia, the journey has become a relatively familiar one, this being her fourth trip to Spain to spend the summer with the Romero family in their high-rise apartment on the outskirts of Madrid. Nearly 9,000 children from the Sahrawi refugee camps were hosted by Spanish families through the Vacaciones en Paz *(Holidays in Peace) programme in 2005.*

Kin relations tend to be closely-knit among Sahrawi families living in the camps, but the need to leave one's family, however temporarily, has become a feature of Sahrawi childhood and youth in exile. Both of Fawzia's parents were born in the refugee camps and as teenagers left their respective households to attend secondary schools in Algeria and Libya. She expects that when she turns twelve (and local schools are unable to support her education) she will do the same. Her elder sister, Sultana, has already taken up her studies in the Algerian capital, spending most of the year living in a dormitory with other Sahrawi students. Unfortunately, Sultana's visits home largely coincide with Fawzia's trips to Spain. Their nine year-old brother Mohammed has also started spending his summers in Spain, and in 2005 was with a family in Andalucía. When Fawzia and Mohammed returned to the camps at the end of the summer they each took back a suitcase packed with food, clothing, medicine, school supplies, toiletries and toys provided by their respective host-families.

During the summer of 2005, the Romeros hosted three Sahrawi girls. Lina had returned for the second summer and made a nice companion for Fawzia, as they are close in age and come from the same refugee camp. Lina's older sister, Mariam, was ill as a child and was taken in by the Romeros so that she could receive appropriate medical care. Mariam was eventually adopted by the Romeros with her parents' consent and, now aged eighteen, is pursuing a nursing degree in Madrid.

Fawzia had only one more summer in Spain ahead of her before reaching the host-programme's upper age limit. Aged eleven, her thoughts on the future were ambivalent. Like many children her age around the world, she wished she could live in the same tent with her mother and father forever and never have to marry. She nonetheless liked the idea of being a teacher in Spain where she could live in a house 'with walls' and enjoy parks and swimming pools. After some reflection, she said what she really wanted was for the camps to be more like Spain.

Introduction

This chapter focuses on the way in which Sahrawi refugee children participating in the *Vacaciones en Paz* host-programme mediate the flow of humanitarian aid and other expressions of solidarity for their families and the broader Sahrawi community-in-exile. Thousands upon thousands of Sahrawi families live in the refugee camps that were established in the mid-1970s in the harsh Algerian desert, some thirty kilometres from the westernmost town of Tindouf. This study draws on interviews conducted with nearly fifty children from the refugee camps, including Fawzia and Lina above, who took part in *Vacaciones en Paz* during the summer of 2005 in Madrid, Spain.[1] It captures inter-generational perspectives on the programme, including the experiences of participating children, their caregivers in the refugee camps and their adult Spanish hosts. The study aimed to document the views of Sahrawi refugee children in relation to their daily lives in the camps, their experiences of being hosted in Spain, and their aspirations for the future. The research integrated the views of host-families who shared information on the kind of support, material and otherwise, they offered their host-children throughout the year(s). The findings were enhanced by data generated in the main study with caregivers who brought into focus the complex and often ambivalent relationships that make up this apparently necessary transnational network of care.

In *Children of Global Migration*, Rhacel Salazar Parrenas (2005: 12) argues that 'a growing crisis of care troubles the developing world'. She offers as an example the case study of the Philippines where parents, particularly mothers, rely on migration to secure work in order to provide their children with quality nutrition, education and healthcare. The long-term absence of mothers results from the vast disparities in care-resources that characterize contemporary relations between developed and developing countries. We borrow Parreñas' conceptualization of care as 'the labor and resources needed to ensure the mental, emotional, and physical well-being of individuals' (2005: 12). The Philippine example is typical in the sense that it is the mothers and fathers who are compelled to migrate. In contrast, among Sahrawi families in the refugee camps, it is usually children and youth who must leave for varying lengths of time in order to secure necessary resources for themselves and their families.

At least three conditions have driven the trend towards transnationalizing childcare among Sahrawi refugees. Firstly, they are wholly dependent on humanitarian aid for survival. The most basic resources, from water to wheat, are brought in on trucks, with primary donors including the European Commission's Humanitarian Aid Office (ECHO),[2] the Algerian government, and the World Food Programme/United Nations High Commissioner for Refugees. Secondly, such transfers require that the borders of the refugee camps be relatively porous to allow for the passage of goods (food, medicine and so on) and services (provided by doctors, aid workers and others) into the camps. Thirdly, the limited camp infrastructure (e.g., secondary education, healthcare and other services) requires a parallel movement of people outwards. Children and youth in particular must be able to access food, medical care, and secondary and tertiary schooling abroad. The mobility of youth, their willingness to leave home for varying lengths of time, and the vitality and accessibility of international solidarity networks are therefore integral to the raising of Sahrawi youth in exile.

The young people who seasonally migrate to Spain as part of the *Vacaciones en Paz* programme are part of a broader network of transnational migration. Goldring (1998: 179) has argued that in the case of Mexican migration to the US migration networks encourage further migration, and the same can be said in the case of Sahrawi children youth crossing the border to Spain. In the Sahrawi context, the viability and legitimacy of the network is as much about the Spanish families who host the children as it is about other Sahrawis in Spain or who have been in Spain who can report on their experiences.

We argue that this entrenched pattern of mobility across various borders (and back again) has deepened the transnationality of Sahrawi refugee families. In *The Transnational Family*, Bryceson and Vuorela (2002: 3) describe this phenomenon as 'families that live some or most of the time separated from each other, yet hold together and create something that can be seen as a feeling of collective welfare and unity, namely "familyhood", even across national borders'. They also point to the losses and gains of this kind of migration, with the physical absence of certain members of the family altering the kinds of 'at home' emotional and material need fulfilment that can happen. At the same time, with family members 'moving out', however temporarily, they are often able to send remittances home which affords greater scope for fulfilling the needs of the family (p. 14). This underscores the way in which Sahrawi family relationships are characteristically interdependent; decisions to 'send' children abroad for school or for *Vacaciones en Paz* reflect a broader family strategy and decision.

This chapter provides a case study of the *Vacaciones en Paz* host-programme as a vital transnational network that facilitates the shared care of Sahrawi children. The hosting scheme also illustrates the way in which mobility has become a necessary feature of Sahrawi childhoods in exile. We highlight the different forms of care that are expressed through the host/hosted relationship, from the strictly financial to the deeply emotional, and show how children are simultaneously beneficiaries and conduits of valuable aid. This study demonstrates how Sahrawi children are more than the victims of adult wars; they actively mediate the flow of material goods and political solidarity for their families and the broader Sahrawi community-in-exile. Their participation in the host-programme may affect their own individual trajectories in life (through decisions made in relation to education and work), as well as shape the way in which outsiders respond to the broader economic, social and political needs within the refugee camps.

Vacaciones en Paz

Since 1975, Spanish civil society has emerged as a significant source of material support and political solidarity for Sahrawi refugees. Through *Vacaciones en Paz*, between 8,000 and 10,000 children between the ages of seven and twelve are hosted each summer by Spanish families throughout the country, with many children returning year after year to the same host homes until they reach the programme's upper age limit. The programme was formally established in the late 1980s, organized by some 300 Spanish solidarity associations (*Amigos del Pueblo Saharaui*) in partnership with the Union of Polisario Youth (UJSARIO) in the refugee camps.

With its child-centred focus, *Vacaciones en Paz* is one element of a broader solidarity network which Sahrawi refugees depend upon. The host-programme is also one of many projects coordinated by Spanish solidarity associations who campaign throughout the year in support of Sahrawi interests. Some of their activities in Spain are aimed at raising local consciousness of and support for the Sahrawi people, through visits to Spanish children's classrooms, hunger strikes and political marches. Their other contribution is in the form of humanitarian aid and development projects benefiting the refugee camps' residents. The solidarity associations regularly carry out food-drives and solicit funds from local councils in order to send large 'caravans' of food and supplies to the camps, with some projects aimed at specific schools, clinics or neighbourhoods. Several of the groups in Spain have 'twinned' themselves with specific neighbourhoods in the refugee camps where they subsequently focus their humanitarian efforts. These twinning schemes have also impacted the way in which children participating in *Vacaciones en Paz* are matched with host-families. Children from specific neighbourhoods may be assigned to families living in their Spanish partner-town, as was the case in 2005 with Tres Cantos (Madrid) and Aguanid (a neighbourhood in Auserd refugee camp).

Sahrawi children living in the refugee camps are selected to participate in the host-programme on the combined basis of need (for example medical or material), family history (parent/s killed in conflict) and academic achievement. Once in Spain, their host-parents are responsible for all aspects of their care, including an obligatory medical examination and any medicine or treatment reasonably prescribed. Host-families usually give the children they host a variety of gifts, including clothes, toys, food and money to take back with them to the camps. Many host-parents stressed how difficult it was to not exceed the twenty-five kilogram luggage allowance which the children have for their return trip. Local associations (and some local governments) may also donate items for the children in their areas to take back with them, such as solar panels or backpacks of school supplies.

The host-programme is intended to be a positive experience for the Spanish participants as well. Their encounters with Sahrawi children and their families encourage self-reflection, with many host-parents commenting on what they had learned about themselves, their own family and Spanish society. In an effort to facilitate communication between Spanish host-families and the Sahrawi children they host, local programme organizers provide host-families with information packs to prepare them for the experience. These typically include information on the basic tenets of Islam, the history of the territorial conflict over Western Sahara, the organization of the refugee camps and Sahrawi family relations. A vocabulary list of common words and phrases in Hassaniya, the Sahrawi dialect of Arabic, is usually appended to facilitate communication. Such topics emphasize the non-material aspects of the hosting experience and represent Sahrawi children as social and cultural beings.

The Research

During the summer of 2005, 8,600 Sahrawi children were hosted by Spanish families, 424 of whom were assigned to families in the Autonomous Region of Madrid where the current study was based (see Table 2.1). Two researchers from the University of Oxford carried out semi-structured interviews with a total of forty-six Sahrawi children, eighteen of whom were male and twenty-eight female. Of these, three children (two girls and one boy) were hosted by Spanish families in the locality of Arona in Tenerife (Canary Islands), and were interviewed by Fiddian-Qasmiyeh in August 2006. Because the host-programme is geared towards seven to twelve year-olds, our sample mirrored this age-range, with the exception of a few older children who were in Spain for outstanding medical treatment (see Table 2.2). The average age of children in the research sample was ten years. Children were represented from each of the refugee camps, with most of them coming from Auserd (19) and Aaiun (15). That fewer children were from Smara (8), 27th February camp (3) and Dakhla (1) may represent the way in which children were assigned regionally to families throughout the country. The number of times the children had been to Spain through *Vacaciones en Paz* ranged from one (first time in Spain) to five. For most of the children (19) it was their third trip to Spain through the host-programme. Of the children interviewed 82 per cent had been to Spain more than once and 60 per cent of them were staying with a family who had hosted them in the past.

Table 2.1: Distribution of Sahrawi Children in Spanish Households, *Vacanciones en Paz* 2005.

Andalucia	2500
Castilla-La Mancha	1008
Catalunya	804
Galicia	601
Castilla y Leon	547
Valencia	546
Extremadura	540
Pais Vasco	473
Madrid	424
Canary Islands	259
Asturias	198
Beleares	157
Aragon	155
Murcia	155
Cantabria	97
Navarra	79
La Rioja	56
	Total = 8599

Table 2.2: Children's Attributes.

N=46		CAMP	
		Auserd:	19
GENDER		Aaiun:	15
Male: 18	Female: 28	Dakhla:	1
		Smara:	8
AGE		27th of Feb:	3
7 years old:	3		
8 years old:	5	SPANISH EXPERIENCE	
9 years old:	10	Number of Times in Spain	
10 years old:	12		
11 years old:	6	# Visits	# Children
12 years old:	7	1:	8
14 years old:	1	2:	8
16 years old:	2	3:	19
		4:	5
Average age: 10 years old		5:	3
		Avg. # of Visits per Child: 2.5	

Several levels of consent were obtained before the interviews took place, including approval by the Polisario delegation in Madrid, the local solidarity groups, the host-families and the children.[3] It was necessary to go through this long chain of gatekeepers and to explain, at each step, the purpose of the research and the reasons why we wanted to interview the children in their collective care. After receiving approval from the Polisario delegation in Madrid and the central NGO, we were given the telephone numbers of the various Spanish coordinators who were often hosts themselves and who were in charge of the hosting scheme in their locality. The coordinators would then contact host-families in their area to gain permission to pass on their contact details. The researchers would then contact the host-families directly to arrange a home visit for the interview.

Most of the interviews took place in the children's host-homes and various members of the host-families were often present in the home for some or all of the interview period.[4] We were mindful that the presence of host-parents was potentially intrusive and when given the opportunity expressed our preference to speak with the children alone. Host-parents tended to 'float' in and out of the room, and therefore in and out of the conversation. Contrary to being disruptive, on the whole, their interventions were very useful. They were often effective in encouraging the children to speak more and were useful in that they were able to put what the children said in the context of their families. For example, when one child said that he had visited his sister in Barcelona, the host-mother was able to explain in detail the history of each of his siblings' participation in the programme, how the sister had been adopted by a Spanish family, and how the boy had not seen her for years. Especially with the younger children, we sensed that some of host-mothers in particular were protective of them, and wanted to make sure our intentions as researchers were honest. In addition to the youth interviews, a questionnaire for the Spanish host-parents was designed to obtain information on their hosting patterns, the degree to which they maintain contact with their host-children throughout the year, and the quality and quantity of economic and other forms of support they provide. The twenty-six host-families who decided to collaborate returned their completed, anonymous questionnaires through the mail, using pre-addressed and stamped envelopes.

The Refugee Camps in Context: Education and Mobility

We shall now discuss the ways in which two key features of Sahrawi social life have developed in exile: education and traditions of mobility. As was the case in most liberation and anti-colonial movements, education was one of the Polisario Front's primary aims from its inception. The importance placed on education in the camps is linked to the Polisario's desire to cultivate a self-sufficient nation-in-exile. Schools were amongst the first structures erected in the camps and literacy campaigns were launched by the small number of individuals who had received an education during the colonial era (Velloso de Santisteban 1993). Two boarding schools were eventually constructed to provide secondary education; these served children from all of the camps, including some from nomadic families. A national women's school was also created in 1978, followed by the construction of a second one (Olaf Palme school) in 1989. The approximately 800 women who were accepted to study there each year moved their families near the schools. Among the courses they were offered were literacy, crafts, teacher training, nursing and kindergarten training. A Nursing School and a Vocational Training School serving men and women were eventually established (Lippert 1987). There are also specialized schools for handicapped children in the camps.

In addition to its main aim of constructing schools in the camps, however, the Polisario recognized that the limited camp infrastructure, the small number of secondary school places and teachers, and the total absence of universities in the refugee camps, necessitated the development of alternative modes of formally educating its youth. Hence, when the Sahrawi Ministry of Education, Health and Social Affairs was created in 1976, its main aims included not only creating and organizing schools in the camps but also requesting that friendly countries welcome as many Sahrawi children and youth as possible to educate them abroad.[5] One seventeen year-old student in the refugee camps described how from first to fourth grade she studied near her home and was able to return each afternoon to eat lunch in her tent:

> Then grades five and six we study in (*jihawiyyah*) ... the 9th of June and 12th of October schools (national schools) ... we leave our families and stay away from them for nine months ... we study two or three months then we have fifteen days holiday with our families. Then we go to Algeria ... we make an effort to adapt with other people.

Small numbers of children have been leaving their families to study abroad since the Sahrawis' mass arrival in the camps thirty years ago. These students have been wholly dependent on scholarships offered by friendly states, such as Algeria, Spain, Libya, Syria, Russia and Cuba. Although the scholarship system and agreements with specific countries have changed over time, Algeria, Cuba and Spanish solidarity groups have continually offered support since the 'early days'.[6]

In this brief overview of the development of the camp-based educational system, a key issue emerges: that the provision of education, be it in boarding schools, in the National Women's school, or through the international scholarship programmes, is essentially connected to mobility.

Traditions of Mobility

The Sahrawi have traditionally been a nomadic people, and their identity has continued to be based on movement even after the events which forced large sections of the population to sedentarize to greater or lesser degrees throughout the twentieth century.[7] Despite the droughts experienced last century, and explicit colonial efforts to sedentarize the Sahrawi population, mobility still plays an essential part in Sahrawi identity to this day. The camp population continues to be mobile, and many of the children we interviewed described travelling between camps to visit family and friends, taking a taxi to Tindouf, or going to Mauritania to visit relatives.

However, the key feature, and the central focus of this chapter, is the connection between mobility on the one hand, and the provision of different forms of care on the other. It is therefore worth noting that while few Sahrawi children received a colonial education during the twentieth century, a longer-standing tradition existed amongst some Sahrawi tribes which allowed selected boys to receive a Quranic education away from their families. Different models of Quranic education existed, given the population's nomadic lifestyle. In many cases, teachers travelled with the mobile encampments to ensure that children received a formal education, but there was also at least one established seat of religious learning within the territory of the Western Sahara *per se*, namely that created by Sheikh Ma el-Ainin in the early 1900s in what is still the sacred town of Smara. Small numbers of male adolescent students reportedly attended the sedentary *mahadra*, leaving their family and nomadic groups to do so.[8]

The connection which currently exists between education, care and mobility in this sense accentuates and broadens a selection of pre-existing social structures. Sahrawi youth's reliance on mobility to access institutionalized learning and other forms of care[9] is to a certain extent historically rooted, although it had previously been limited to only a small number of boys from certain Sahrawi tribes. Since the creation of the refugee camps, the connection between care and mobility expanded and intensified, with greater numbers of both male and female children and youth leaving their families to receive educational, medical and other forms of care. The cultural memory of mobility that persists may help families accept that their children must leave the camps for varying lengths of time, rather than produce a traumatic response to their absence.

Vacaciones en Paz and the Participation of Youth in Transnational Networks

In July 2005 ten year-old Hamid made his third trip to Spain where he was hosted by Aurora, an elementary schoolteacher, and her fiancé, Juan, a pilot, who live in the centre of Madrid. The experiences of Hamid's nine siblings illustrate the transnationalization of care and the parallel need for children in the camps to be mobile. His sister Khadija studied in Cuba as a teenager, and when she returned to the camps, she married and relocated with her husband to the Western Sahara. His brothers Salam, who studied in Libya, and Karim and Mohammed, who studied in Algeria, returned to the camps after their studies. Like most of the camp inhabitants, and despite being well-educated, they do not have paid work there. His other brother, Ali, left the camps to join Khadija in the Western Sahara and to look for work. Hamid's sister Jamila, born with Downs' Syndrome, was adopted five years ago by a Spanish family in Barcelona. She is now sixteen. The three youngest siblings, including Hamid, were all being hosted by families during the summer of 2005. Hamid and his sister Aisha were in Spain, while Muleika was in Italy.

A variety of networks exist to support the Sahrawi refugee population in different ways, and in this section we provide an overview of how some of these support refugee youth on the one hand, and the broader refugee community on the other. These programmes and networks, including *Vacaciones en Paz,* often rely heavily on the element of mobility to provide

Sahrawi refugee youth with access to formal and informal education, as well as to medical, emotional and economic forms of support.

Informal Learning

As mentioned above, the institutionalized and formal education of Sahrawi refugee youth is provided primarily in the camps, although some children also receive an official education via study-abroad projects, including in Algeria, Cuba, Syria and Spain. Although formal education does not figure in the scope of *Vacaciones en Paz,* the host-programme is certainly an avenue through which the provision of informal learning takes place. The children learn about a new society, develop new ways of looking at and engaging with their environment, and obtain practical skills relating to the usage of modern technologies and appliances to which they have only limited access in the camps.

Many of the youth interviewed in the camps commented on their experiences in Spain, with one eighteen year-old woman, saying:

> I saw the ocean and trees for the first time … I began to discover nature and the colour green which is non-existent in this desert land where we live. I also experienced rain and noticed the difference in life between there and here.

Through the programme, the children learn or improve their knowledge of spoken Spanish, while some of the older children are pushed by their host-families to practise their reading and writing in that language. This not only facilitates their communication with others whilst in Spain, but also enables children to play a central role upon their return to the camps, acting as interpreters and translators for family members and neighbours when Spanish visitors arrive, often staying with them in their *khaimas.* These language skills are gaining importance in the current camp context, given the small, emerging camp economy, where basic shops sell goods to the ever-increasing number of 'tourists' visiting for a few days, or to humanitarian workers who spend a few weeks or months in the camps. Improving children's Spanish is therefore of both social and economic significance.

Some Spanish host-parents also set the Sahrawi child homework, for example in mathematics, in order to bring them up to Spanish standards while their foster siblings concentrated on the tasks set by their own teachers. While the majority of hosted-children are not fostered long-term by Spanish families, many of them do go on to participate in one of the study-abroad programmes outlined above, and therefore benefit from the home-based efforts to assist them academically, especially those who later study in

Spanish-speaking Cuba. More broadly, *Vacaciones en Paz* may be considered a 'trial-run' for children who are going to leave their families in the longer term to study abroad by establishing how well they deal with family separation and adapt to new social environments and forms of interaction.

Physical Well-being

Aged eleven, Zaynab arrived in Tenerife for the third year, looking forward to spending the summer by the sea with her Spanish family. Upon her arrival, however, she found that there was already an older Sahrawi girl, Aiza, living in 'her house'. She was surprised not by the girl's presence, but by Aiza's blue lips and thin frame. Her host-family explained that a group of Spanish doctors visiting the camps had seen Aiza there and had realized that she needed a series of operations which could not be completed in the camps themselves. The doctors had organized Aiza's trip to Tenerife, and the local Friends of the Sahara association had asked Zaynab's host-family to look after Aiza when she came out of hospital. Zaynab was told about Aiza's health, that her lips were blue because her heart was unable to pump blood around her body, and that she had put on eleven kilograms since her operation by enjoying the goats' milk and meat that her Spanish host-family fed her.

Zaynab had also come to Spain this summer for medical reasons, and having Aiza with her meant she would have someone else to visit her in hospital. Zaynab had suffered an accident in the camps, which had caused damage to her brain. While Aiza was due to return to the camps at the end of the summer, joining the other Vacaciones en Paz *children on their way back to their parents and siblings, Zaynab explained that the doctors had told her that she would have to stay in Tenerife for more medical treatment. Zaynab said that she would go to the airport to wave Aiza and the other children goodbye, but that she would be holding her host-mother's hand tightly, wondering when she would see her own mother again.*

Sahrawi refugee camp residents are provided with medical care by a variety of individuals and organizations in different settings. Pharmaceutical dispensaries and maternal/child-care units are available locally, and are run primarily by Sahrawis who either trained as doctors abroad or attended the camp-based nursing school. There are also a small number of non-Sahrawi workers in the camps providing medical attention to the population, including volunteers from the Red Cross/Red Crescent, and Cuban doctors who complete their (unpaid) work-abroad period in the camps.[10] Medical supplies are mostly provided via humanitarian aid programmes, although some types of medication are produced on a small scale in the pharmaceutical laboratory based next to the National Hospital. The national and local hospital/medical centres are attended on a daily basis by Sahrawi and Cuban doctors, as well as by non-Sahrawi doctors (primarily from Spain) who undertake short trips to the camps to examine specific sections of the population and identify those in need of further medical treatment.

Some of those identified are operated on in the National Hospital, with foreign doctors bringing most of the necessary medical equipment and staff with them (i.e. both anaesthetics and anaesthetists), while more serious cases are often referred for treatment outside the camps. Some of these cases, such as Aiza, are transferred to Spain directly via the sponsoring medical NGO. Others, like Zaynab, travel to Spain to obtain medical treatment via the *Vacaciones en Paz* programme. An additional group of pre-diagnosed children who benefit from *Vacaciones en Paz* are celiac children/youth who are invited by Spanish celiac societies, such as the *Asociación Nacional de Celiacos Saharaui* and the *Asociación de Celiacos de Madrid*. These associations have created a specific network of support for Sahrawi celiac children and their families, which is particularly important given the high incidence of wheat-intolerance in the camps. A World Health Organization study reported a 5.6 per cent prevalence of celiac disease, which is five to ten times the frequency in developed countries (Ratsch and Catassi 2001). Attending to this medical condition is especially difficult as the refugee families are unable to choose the kinds of food they receive from humanitarian aid groups.

The majority of children participating in *Vacaciones en Paz*, however, arrive without a prior diagnosis, and the summer visit provides them with the opportunity to have a thorough medical examination.[11] Host-families often take it upon themselves to cover the expenses of any follow-up treatment, such as dental work or prescriptions for glasses. Most of the children arrive in Spain with a degree of iron-deficiency and signs of malnourishment,[12] which host-parents try to remedy by providing well-balanced meals and vitamin supplements, thereby compensating for the limited nature of the humanitarian aid which reaches the camps. Some children are diagnosed with ailments such as kidney stones or eye irritations caused by sand exposure, and receive treatment accordingly, while others are diagnosed with more serious conditions, such as heart and thyroid problems. In these cases, host-families, local coordinators, the Polisario representatives and the child's birth-families in the camps decide upon the best course of action to support the child's well-being. In some cases, children diagnosed with serious conditions are invited to stay in Spain for a longer period of time, sometimes being fostered by the host-parents or by a new Spanish family.

Emotional Attachments and Proto-familial Bonds

– '*I love my daughter with all of my heart.*'
– '*It's been a very positive and enriching experience*' (*first time hosting*).
– '*For me it's been very satisfying because I have been able to help someone in need and it motivates me to be a better person.*'
– '*I wish we all would become more conscious of the needs of children throughout the world and everyone "add our grain of sand". The experience has been totally positive.*'

–*'Hosting a child is not charity. It's a privilege and an act of justice.'*
(Selection of quotes from Spanish host parents, 2005)

An emotional dimension frames the host experience, with both host-parents and children expressing different levels and forms of attachments. Sometimes these are strong attachments that mirror family relationships, especially in cases where children return summer after summer to the same Spanish families, or where cousins or siblings had previously been hosted in the same home. The young age of the Sahrawi children who go to Spain, coupled with the fact that they are far from home and family, may accentuate the proto-familial way in which these relationships develop.

Sahrawi children are integrated into their Spanish host-families in similar ways as their Spanish counterparts, that is, in positions of dependency in relation to adult household members.[13] Nonetheless, Sahrawi children are characterized by their Spanish hosts as socially independent. This independence was problematic in several cases because their actions challenged accepted family hierarchies in Spain. Ferida, for example, is an eleven year-old girl who travelled to the coast with her host-family for a camping holiday. On their first morning, her host-parents awoke to find Ferida missing from the campsite. After a frantic search they found her calmly exploring the beach, unaware that she had done anything wrong by leaving on her own and without permission. Jamal, a six year-old boy, walked out of his host-family's apartment and took the lift six storeys down. They found it difficult to convey to him that, for his own safety, they had to know where he was all of the time and that he had to ask permission to leave the family home. Sahrawi children are generally viewed by their Spanish hosts as relatively more curious, independent and mature than their Spanish counterparts.

Host-families integrate Sahrawi children into their homes in different ways. For some, it was crucial to treat them as 'one of the family', or as they would treat their own son or daughter.[14] In some homes, there were conflicts between the Spanish children and the newly-arrived Sahrawi children, especially when they were similar in age and were expected to share a bedroom and toys, as well as the affection of the Spanish parents. Many host-parents commented that Sahrawi children enjoyed being given family responsibilities, as it made them feel useful and part of that family. Seven year-old Mohammed therefore happily set and cleared the dinner table at family meals. Others assisted in the shopping and putting away of groceries. Host-parents often interpreted the children's enthusiasm as a reflection of the kinds of tasks children are expected to do within their homes in the refugee camps. Some host-parents took a different approach to integrating the children into their homes, believing that their role was to provide them temporary 'relief' from their lives in the refugee camps. They therefore refused to allow the children to carry out any household chores. 'She's on holiday' is how several host-mothers explained why girls in particular were encouraged to play and discouraged from carrying out domestic tasks while in Spain.

There were a few cases in which host-parents suggested that their emotional expectations were not met and it was clear that not all hosting experiences resulted in deep emotional bonds. Lola, a host-mother to seven year-old Ali, explained her ambivalent experience as follows. On the one hand, she felt 'responsible for him and everything has to be done right. It must be as if he were my own son'; she stressed that:

For me, he is a child in all the sense of the word, a child with dignity. That's to say, if I have to discipline him, I have to discipline him … And if he makes me happy I give him a kiss just as I would kiss my own son.

She insisted that her experience as a host-mother was 'very enjoyable in terms of feelings and in terms of love, because a boy, smiling at you when he has learned something new … it's lovely, it's something that makes it worth the effort.' On the other hand, she recognized that Ali was not a member of her family and that his stay was temporary. She was frustrated because for his first fortnight in Spain he refused to greet anyone in the family, not even to say hello, perhaps out of shyness or social unease. When she arrived in the airport on Ali's final day in Spain, Lola was clearly frustrated. Although Ali had evidently grown attached to her, he consistently refused to emotionally engage with her husband, refusing to say goodbye or kiss his host-father, as would be customary among Spaniards. Lola's emotional expectations were not met through the hosting experience, and she found that the practical workload outweighed the emotional compensation. Despite sharing a few tender moments, she doubted she was ready to host Ali or any other Sahrawi child in the near future. 'Maybe when my own son is older,' she decided.

In four cases, host-parents had relatively extreme reactions to the Sahrawi children. One parent wrote in the survey that 'there is a lack of respect towards the Catholic religion. We've really had it with so much "Allah"', and two children interviewed had reportedly been 'returned' to the organizers of the programme by their host-parents. In relation to the 'returned' boys, the organizers and other host-parents interviewed stated that this was wholly unacceptable, stressing that a child should only be 'returned' in the most serious of circumstances.[15]

When asked about their previous host-families, many of the children described them as 'alright,' but did not express deep emotional attachments to them. There were others who were eager to contact former host-families while in Spain and did so through telephone calls or personal visits. Host-parents were usually very willing to facilitate the contact and often used the opportunity to learn more about the children and their family background from their former host-parents.

While proto-familial relationships frequently develop within the hosting relationship, the Sahrawi children remain very loyal to their biological parents and speak tenderly about them, especially their mothers. When describing the differences between Spain and the refugee camps, one twelve year-old Sahrawi boy remarked:

> There are lots of differences … the parents, the things that they do to show their love, it's not the same… [H]ere, they're foster parents, and there, they're real parents who love you more. Here, even if they tell you that they love you, you're like the heart of your real parents. For the two months that you're away, they're already crying for you to return. Imagine a year…

Camp Visits

In addition to repeat visits to the same Spanish home, host relations are strengthened when Spanish families visit their host-children in the refugee camps. At key holiday periods, including Christmas, Easter and summer, solidarity associations organize trips to the camps that enable Spanish host-families to spend three or four days as guests with their host-child's family. This allows the Spanish and Sahrawi families to meet face-to-face and for them to see conditions of camp life at firsthand. While these encounters are generally positive, they sometimes entail emotional difficulties, as one host-mother indicated in her interview:

> Their behaviour there [in the camps] is completely different from their behaviour here [in Spain]… Here he's very open and caring, and we've never imposed anything, he's called us mummy and daddy without us having to say anything to him, it's been his own decision, he speaks about his [host] brother, he calls Alfonso 'my brother'… But when you get there, you're desperate to hug him and see him…forget it.

The range of children's and parents' emotional responses varies, with genuine bonds of affection developing in many cases, even in the more short-lived experiences. Indeed, as will be discussed below, the temporary host-relationship may transform into a longer-term fostering commitment, initiated by the Spanish hosts in some cases, and by Sahrawi families in others.

Economic/Material Support

Sisters Khadija and Salima were hosted by the Perez family for the second year in a row. The girls eagerly led the researcher by the hand, taking her upstairs to the bedrooms where they were sorting through the clothes and gifts accumulated over the summer. The dilemma: which items would be packed and which left behind? Salima was desperate to pack the oversized talking duck which they had bought for the newborn baby-sister the girls had yet to meet. Khadija slid behind the bedroom door to reveal their new matching winter coats, in addition to several winter outfits. There were gifts for each of the girls' family members – shoes for a brother, a watch for the father, perfume for the mother, and nappies for their sister. Various food items were to be shared with the family as well, such as cans of tuna, lentils, condensed milk, bars of chocolate and olive oil. In addition to what Khadija and Salima's host-family provides them, the local solidarity association provided each child in its group with a backpack full of school supplies, as well as a solar panel, the sole source of power for families living in the harsh desert environment. Like most of the other children in the programme, the girls returned with an envelope of cash, even though we suspect Salima would have preferred to return with the big yellow duck.

An economic network is embedded within *Vacaciones en Paz,* facilitating the transfer of goods and money to the camps for the benefit of individual children and their families. Although it primarily focuses on enhancing the physical and social well-being of the refugee children who participate, the programme's underlying economic benefits for Sahrawi families should not be ignored. One parent in the camps insisted that when 'a Spanish family helps one [Sahrawi] family, all the neighbours benefit... for example, if they help them to get electricity. According to Sahrawi tradition, if your neighbour sleeps comfortably, so will you.'

Host-Parental Survey

Of the twenty-six host-families who completed the host-parental survey, twenty-three reported sending their host-children back to the camps with between 40 to 350 euros. The average amount sent home was 150 euros. The three families who did not send cash sent material goods and gifts instead. One of these families stated that they were worried about money being stolen from the child before s/he could reach home. Conversations held with host-parents and the survey data indicated that some families customarily sent additional money to the camps for their host-children. Money was either given personally while visiting the camps or was sent with another host-family who relayed the gift on their behalf. The most any family reported sending money to the camps was three times within a given year (coinciding with the trips organized in summer, Christmas and Easter). However, there are many families who chose or could only afford to send money once during the year, at the end of summer.

As Khadija and Salima's story illustrated, the children also return to the refugee camps with up to twenty-five kilograms of goods. The host-parental survey indicated that all of the children in the sample were sent home with goods – with clothing and food the most frequently mentioned items. Other items, in order of frequency, were toys, school supplies, toiletries, medicine and gifts (in general) for the family. Many host-parents reported that the children had specific requests for items required by their families. Children therefore returned with pressure cookers, solar panels, sewing machines and sewing materials. One host-father explained his approach to sending goods:

> I send things that they need. I don't send mobile phones. I send solar panels or pressure cookers... But not everyone thinks like me. They started asking for mobile phones around three years ago. Eight years ago, it was bicycles.

Some host-families considered that their economic contribution to the child's family was the most important part of their hosting role. One host-mother indicated:

> Every year we take a collection from friends, family, and neighbours, even for Easter and Christmas we do the same. I feel very responsible. It's almost as if my greatest responsibility is economic.

After three summers hosting the same boy in her home, she decided to take a break from the programme, but felt guilty and worried about how the boy would perceive her choice:

> [I]t makes me sad to think he won't be with us next summer because we've really grown to care for him. What I do plan to do, and I assure his mom about this, is to help him economically every year that we are able to... I've tried to explain to him what might happen because I don't want him to feel bad... And of course I would continue to send him money.

Perceived Economic Impact

Some of the host-parents and local coordinators commented upon the impact their economic and material assistance has had on the refugee camps. On the one hand, they recognized that the money, food and goods they send have the potential to improve the well-being and socio-economic situation of individual children and their families. On the other hand, certain concerns surfaced regarding the development of a money-based market and socio-economic differentiation in the camps. The following examples capture these sometimes contradictory perceptions.

One host-mother who customarily sent 900 euros throughout the year to her host-daughter's family pointed out how a family with two or three young children who participate in the programme at the same time and receive similar contributions will live well during the year. Another host-father who has visited the camps on five occasions over the past decade suggested that the changes he had observed over the years were inevitable:

> If we consider that 10,000 children come to Spain every year and if every child returns with 100 Euros or even 50 Euros, you do the calculations… Eight years ago these little stores you now see didn't exist. Now, instead of going to buy from the Algerians who go to Tindouf, these families go to Tindouf to buy the products so they can set up their own stores [in the camps]… [A]s a consequence of the economic changes, the children are a bit more cared for (*atendidos*). You note it in their nutrition, and in their dress. The first years they came like [shaking his head] … my God.

Another child's family had used money sent to them over the years to open a small shop – 'Manolo's Store' – which they named after the host-father, who considered this a positive impact on the family. Children who were interviewed in the refugee camps supported the idea that the material benefits extend beyond the programme participants. Children who were unable to travel to Spain recalled being brought back sweets, toys and clothes by siblings who had returned from abroad. Others referred to gifts brought by visiting Spaniards which were often distributed beyond the host-child's family. Another boy, aged eight, looked forward to going to Spain for the first time because he wanted to bring back gifts for his mother and father. Children are both beneficiaries and conduits for the range of material contributions that are funnelled through the hosting network. Returning with gifts and money to the camps is a rare opportunity for them to express their agency as economic 'providers' within their families.

Community Support/Solidarity

As mentioned above, *Vacaciones en Paz* is one of many ways in which Spanish individuals and groups express their support and solidarity for the Sahrawi people. Other elements of the broader support network provide humanitarian (including medical) assistance in the camps, engage in consciousness-raising activities amongst their local communities or lobby for political representatives at local, regional and national levels to take a more proactive stance regarding the United Nations' referendum for Sahrawi self-determination.[15] Additional events include trips to the camps for municipal employees and Spanish youth to encounter the realities of camp life. These trips are often intimately connected to the summer hosting programme, as explained by Luz Marina in Tenerife:

> The Mayor had been bringing the children over several years, and one year he decided that he would send youth from here to see the reality in the camps. He wanted to do a project with the youth here and youth there,

for the groups to work together and run some activities there. So we went there, and when we saw what it was like ... [he] asked if we would like to foster a child, and we did.

Some NGOs focus on specific issues of concern to their members, such as the aforementioned *Asociación Nacional de Celiacos Saharaui* which supports Sahrawi celiac children and their families, or are formed by members who have a similar background, such as that composed of Spaniards who completed their military service in the Spanish Sahara (as the Western Sahara was known during the colonial era). Many other Spanish NGOs do not focus solely on the Western Sahara or the Sahrawi refugee camps, but complete either regular or occasional projects in the camps. These NGOs include the Spanish Red Cross, which frequently sends volunteers and equipment to the camps, or local Rotary International groups, which provide funding for smaller projects run by medical staff visiting the camps in a personal capacity. Many of these doctors and dentists run private practices in Spain and agree to complete free or discounted treatment for Sahrawi children participating in *Vacaciones en Paz.*

International NGOs also play an important role in the solidarity network, with pro-Sahrawi groups around the world, including in Switzerland, France, Germany, the United Kingdom, Australia and the United States. They not only organize local campaigns, but also lobby national and regional (especially European) NGOs, trade unions and individual politicians to focus their attention on the Western Sahara and the camps. They coordinate international events in the camps, including the annual Sahara Marathon, which is a desert sport event attended by international and local runners alike and is organized by the Sahrawi Sport Committee and NGOs around the world.[16]

On another level, many of these Spanish and international NGOs create and run internet sites which offer regular news updates and photographs of both the situation in the Western Sahara and in the camps, in addition to providing key resources for researchers and individuals interested in learning more about the Sahrawi situation. These sites include ARSO, Sahara Press Service and Western Sahara Online.[18] Given the serious difficulties encountered by politicians, NGO workers and journalists who attempt to travel to the Western Sahara, the internet and modern communication technologies play an increasingly important role in providing information about conditions in the territory and add another dimension to Sahrawi transnationalism, despite the remoteness and marginality of the camps themselves. Digital cameras, in particular, have made it possible to denounce human rights abuses, and to document demonstrations, sit-ins and hunger strikes held there. While these images are now available around the world via the internet, they are not accessible in Morocco or the Western Sahara, as most pro-Sahrawi websites have been blocked by the Moroccan authorities.[19]

Conditional Mobility and Attachments to Home

The relatively widespread support for the Sahrawi community has also created opportunities, though limited, for some children to be fostered long-term by Spanish families. It should be stressed, however, that nearly all of the children interviewed in Madrid expressed a strong desire, both in the short term (after the host-programme ended) and in the long term, to return home. Indeed, one seven year-old girl, when discussing the host-programme, responded, 'I would like to go, on condition that I return to my family.' Only three children from the research sample communicated a desire to stay on long-term in Spain. Even those who mentioned the possibility of returning to Spain in order to pursue higher education envisioned spending their adult lives, above all, near their mothers. The strong attachment to their mothers is likely a reflection of the fact that this particular research sample was comprised of young children (a median age of ten). The children's weak desire to emigrate to Europe may also reflect the interdependence and strong sense of family loyalty characteristic of their community-in-exile. The children accepted that they would be required to leave their families and the refugee camps in order to obtain an education. Nonetheless, this separation is conceived as temporary, and a return to the family is almost taken for granted. Although most of them aspired to work as adults, they intended to do so in the camps.

Other children linked any future 'emigration' from the camps with a return to the Western Sahara. As an adult, ten year-old Hassan wants 'to study, to work, to make money' and to live 'in the land of Sahara, where Morocco lives'. Other comments included, 'I wish we get our independence so that we have a homeland like the ones we see during the summer vacation' (eleven year-old girl), and another describing how Spain had 'many things I wish we had … I hope we get our independence and see the land that we have not seen so that our people can live free without anyone dominating over us' (thirteen year-old boy).

Rather than creating a desire to return to Spain, the novel encounters experienced through *Vacaciones en Paz* shape the way in which Sahrawi youth imagine 'home' and how they envisage an independent Western Sahara. One youth explained,

> We do not have many of these things now, but we will when we get our independence, and the holiday is useful because they [the children] see these things and get to know other countries and people with developed societies which will help them when we return to our homeland.

Sahrawi children's preference to stay with their families may therefore reflect the seeds of a more generalized political ideology that links remaining in the camps with the continued commitment to the independence struggle and hope for an independent Western Sahara. It is this collective hope for return that perhaps fuels the continued push towards educating the younger generations, despite the fact that every year educated youth return to the refugee camps, degrees in hand, with extremely limited possibilities for gainful employment. The interviews carried out in the refugee camps among different generations consistently returned to the notion of education as a collective investment, the full fruits of which will only come to bear when those Sahrawis currently living in exile return to an independent Western Sahara.

The Longevity of Child-centred Networks

Naima's Story
Naima is sixteen years old. When she was seven, a group of Spanish doctors visiting the Sahrawi refugee camps included her name on a list of children requiring urgent medical attention: there was something seriously wrong with Naima's kidneys. So, aged seven, she left her family for the first time and flew to Madrid to undergo surgery, living with the Gomez family until her doctors agreed that she was well enough to return home. When she was nine she qualified for Vacaciones en Paz *and returned to the Gomez home for two months that summer. She did not return to Spain again until she was sixteen, when she was again identified as requiring further medical treatment for her kidney condition. She returned to live with the Gomez family, which is where our interview took place. When asked about her plans for the future, Naima said that she wanted to remain in Spain, regardless of whether or not she required further medical attention, explaining:*

> *If I stay here [in Spain] I would like to study ... and to work. If I can, I want to find a job to help my family, since my dad can't work ... As for my sisters, when they go to Algeria and study they need to take a lot of things, but my dad doesn't have a lot of money to give them. They're in need of a lot of things.*

When Naima was nine, the Gomez family offered to foster her long-term but neither Naima nor her mother were prepared for her to remain in Spain. Seven years later, Naima now sees herself as a potential economic asset for her family and is considering applying for Spanish residency and a passport which would allow her to travel back and forth to visit her family in the camps. Naima wants to pursue a nursing career, but when asked where she wanted to work, she shrugged her shoulders and said, 'I don't know. I can't say where because I don't know what's going to happen with me. I don't know if I'll end up doing nursing or something else ... I don't know what's going to happen to me.'

Naima's story offers a glimpse into the life of an older child and the way in which her relationship to the transnational network of care connecting Spain and the camps evolved. Despite a seven-year gap between Naima's first and second visit to Spain, she and the Gomez family maintained contact via telephones calls and the family's frequent visits to the refugee camps. Naima's case illustrates the dynamic and multifaceted nature of the network which she was immersed in due to the serious medical condition diagnosed when she was seven. In this and her subsequent stay in Madrid she was able to enjoy the material benefits of living with a Spanish family and to gain new cultural knowledge and experiences. The medical network that allowed her to return to Spain as a young woman may ultimately provide links to educational or employment opportunities that will allow Naima to remain in Madrid and to transform her position within her family into their primary economic provider. Further qualitative research is needed to explore the views of older Sahrawi youth in the refugee camps in relation to their emigration intentions. If the slowly emerging money market continues to develop, the need for them to become financial providers for their families may become more widespread.

Medium- and Long-term Fostering

Like Naima, an unspecified, but relatively large, number of Sahrawi children are fostered by Spanish families on a medium- to long-term basis, generally to offer them a better quality of life (including medical treatment) than that available in the camps, or to enable them to receive a quality education in Spain. In these cases, as mentioned in chapter 1, specific agreements are usually made between the Sahrawi and Spanish families involved (RASD 2000) and signed before a Sahrawi judge in the refugee camps. Conditions include:

– The host-family is granted temporary custody and guardianship of the child and is responsible for all expenses related to his/her stay in Spain;

– The child is to return to his/her birth-family at their request;

– The host-family is responsible for maintaining the child's family and cultural ties and facilitating regular communication with the child's parents and family.

Most Sahrawi children who study in Spain are able to return to the camps with relative frequency, maximizing children's direct contact with their birth-families.[20] Flying to the camps is possible (although quite expensive) given the large number of charter flights which take thousands of Spaniards to the camps each year. Students can therefore either visit their birth-families for about a week, or may return to the camps during the summer holidays when other Sahrawi children travel to Spain.

Many Sahrawi students who are hosted for longer periods of time in Spain were reported to play a key role in the camps by teaching in the summer adult literacy programmes. Fostering arrangements tend to be conceptualized as temporary, with students usually being expected to return to the camps where they will use the skills they have learned abroad to help their families and community. Changes in the emerging camp economy may affect this trend in so far as remittances from Spain may replace or supplement the practical role played by youth upon their return to the camps.

During the interviews conducted in Madrid in 2005, several Spanish parents indicated their desire to foster the Sahrawi child they were hosting. Barbara, for example, has hosted ten year-old Hassan for the past three years, and his sister, Munina, aged twelve, for the past five. Since 2004, Barbara had discussed the possibility of fostering Hassan with his mother, who agreed that her son should stay in Madrid to continue his studies. However, although Barbara prepared Hassan's room and began the paperwork to make his stay legal, upon his arrival in 2005, Hassan broke the news that his mother was not prepared to have him stay on in Spain, at least 'not yet'. Barbara was annoyed that she had not been informed of the change of plans, and disappointed that Hassan would not be living with them, especially since she understood it was what his mother wanted for him.

On the other hand, a small number of Spanish parents felt pressured by the children or the children's family, who were keen for the host-family to adopt the Sahrawi child. Begonia did not feel comfortable with the idea of taking in Omar, her host-son, long-term, although this is what Omar's family wanted:

> I'm feeling a lot of pressure from his mom for him to stay here and study. She's had this idea in her head since the first year we took him in. But the truth is this was never our intention … our intention was for him to come to spend the summer with us. Then we did it again, because, as you can see he's a sweet boy. But his mother is really pressuring us (*agobiándonos*) … So I asked him, don't you want to see your mom and your brother and sisters, and he said he would. When the Sahrawi children come to Spain, he would go back to Sahara, and when they return to Sahara, he would come back to Spain.

An alternative concern regarding longer-term fostering was expressed by Sebastian, a host-father who spent seven years of his childhood in the Spanish Sahara.[21] Sebastian is torn between wanting to foster a child he has grown to love dearly over the last three years, and a belief that 'if each Spanish host-family were to take in a child, the Sahrawi community would lose their future and their identity'. We return to this concern regarding the compatibility and tensions of individual, family, and community desires below.

Aicha, Huria and Fatimetu

Three highly-visible cases documented and debated in the Spanish press outline some of the possible problems which may emerge as a result of long-term fostering. Between 2001 and 2003, three adolescent Sahrawi girls – Aicha, Huria and Fatimetu[22] – who had spent seven, four and three years respectively studying in Spain, became the centre of Spanish media scandals.[23] The girls' faces and names appeared frequently in the Spanish press and on the internet during the first years of this decade, since, despite their desire to remain in Spain to continue studying, their biological families requested that their teenaged daughters return to the camps.[24]

According to their public statements and those of their Spanish host-families, all three girls were determined that they wanted to stay in Spain and to complete their secondary and tertiary studies there. Their biological families in the Sahrawi refugee camps, however, decided that after between three and seven years of separation from their daughters,[25] they wanted them to return to the camps. Aicha's and Huria's families also explained that they needed their eldest daughters to return to the camps to support their families: Aicha's mother was seriously ill, and Huria's mother had just had a baby.[26] The girls and the Spanish host-families emphasized the medical and educational reasons why the girls should be allowed to stay in Spain, framing the situation in terms of the girls' individual human rights, especially their rights to health, and to an education.[27]

The conflicts that took place between the adolescent refugee girls and their respective Spanish and Sahrawi families highlight several difficulties which may accompany medium- or long-term fostering in this context. It appears that Sahrawi families, and the refugee community more broadly, consistently have to find a balance between temporarily losing touch with their sons and daughters for both the children's and community's good, and their fears that they might not only risk losing their children in the short term but also a more permanent dilution of their traditions and very cultural survival. The children and youth themselves are not only faced with a prolonged period of separation from their parents and siblings, but also with what may be rather radical culture shocks upon their arrival in their host-country and, again, upon their return to the camps. Furthermore, the youth's experiences in Spain may lead them to develop rather different expectations from those held by their parents and other members of the refugee community.

Sahrawi Parents' Views on the Host-programme

Thus far, this chapter has centred on the perspectives of the Sahrawi children and Spanish families who participate in the host-programme. Interviews carried out in the refugee camps provide some insight into what the children's biological parents and other family members think about the programme and its impact on its young participants.

When asked to comment on the younger generation, a forty-one year-old mother described them as 'educated, they have had the opportunity to study outside in different European countries'. As mentioned above, youth experiences of mobility are perceived by many parents to be a defining feature of Sahrawi childhood in the context of exile. Parents confirmed that one of the consequences of travelling abroad, first as young children in the host-programme, and later as teenagers in pursuit of higher education, is to introduce a range of new experiences and resources unavailable to them in the camps.

Another key dimension of the host-programme mentioned by parents was the medical attention children received in Spain. A thirty year-old single mother whose young daughter suffers from wheat-intolerance (celiac) found it difficult raising her children on her own, but 'endured this situation and remained patient until they grew up and went on the summer programme outside. After that, things got a bit better.' When her daughter joined the programme, the mother explained:

> The Spanish family where she stayed provided her with medical care … they stopped giving her wheat and spaghetti. If she returns [to the camps], I do not have what she needs and cannot control what she eats… Therefore, she stayed in Spain, the only place where she can be taken care of.

Another parent described how his son's kidney disease was discovered only as a result of the child travelling to Spain and undergoing the obligatory medical examination. Sahrawi parents in the camps therefore echoed the Spanish host-parents' and NGO members' belief that the medical benefits of the host-programme cannot be overemphasized.

In the refugee camps, the host-programme is generally accepted as a positive opportunity for children who must otherwise endure harsh living conditions all year long. As suggested earlier, the programme fills a very real resource gap. But filling this gap may have had some unintended negative consequences, as suggested by a twenty-five year-old Sahrawi woman interviewed in the refugee camps. Commenting on the programme, she pointed out the potential problems that emerge because 'the children go when they are very young and they do not know what they are seeing. They see customs that are not Sahrawi traditions, and they try to copy these. This is the negative aspect.' The concern that children will lose their sense of Sahrawi identity is especially applicable to cases of long-term fostering.[28]

As a way of mediating the cultural differences, however, another parent put the onus not on the Spanish host-families, but on the Sahrawi delegates and monitors who live in Spain and who form another link in this transnational network. She said:

> The Sahrawi delegates outside must pay attention to these children so that they maintain their links with the Sahrawi culture and its people... The Westerner, for example, does not eat couscous and does not pray. They have different traditions and customs.

Other parental concerns surfaced regarding the way they believe that the host experience may impact upon children's expectations. One forty-nine year-old mother poignantly stated:

> There, they get what they want; they have refrigerators, fresh vegetables and fruits and they take what they want. Here, we have a different standard of living, so when they return, they look at us and look down on our tents which for them seem small. They start to see things very differently ... they begin demanding things we cannot afford; sometimes we are forced to sell our rations to fulfil their demands.

Another parent reiterated this concern, claiming that 'some of the children who go on the summer holidays want to stay there longer because of what they experience, a life which is more luxurious than their own'. When they return, 'some of the children raise a problem because they begin to demand of their families things that the family cannot afford and which they had seen while in Spain'. The unintended consequence of the host-programme is therefore ironic. In attempting to compensate for the Sahrawi community's inability to meet its youngest generations' needs in exile, the programme may further expose and emphasize this powerlessness.[29] And in some cases, when children return with new and unrealistic expectations, parents go to great lengths, selling their own basic resources, in an attempt to demonstrate their agency as parents.

Concerns and Dilemmas

In addition to the parental concerns described above, some Spaniards also question the relative costs and benefits of the host-programme. One main concern is based on an assumed contrast between the children's experiences in the refugee camps (characterized by poverty) and their experiences in

Spain (characterized by wealth). A related assumption is that children exposed to life in Spain will naturally want to stay there, rather than return to the harshness of life in the camps. Some host-families worry that it may be cruel to expose the children to abundance knowing they will return to the camps at the end of the summer. Many host-parents saw the summer period as a time to 'fatten up' the children and stressed that their stomachs expanded whilst in Spain and allowed them to eat more than when they had arrived. However, the parents worried that in the refugee camps the children would return to a limited diet of food rations, and did not know how these expanded stomachs would be filled upon their return.

Indeed, as suggested above, the inability of Sahrawi parents to fill their children's stomachs is a major concern to them, and the recognition that Spanish parents can fulfil a function that they cannot may be distressing. However, as we also indicated, the majority of children interviewed both in Spain and in the camps did not express a desire to stay in Spain, nor did they describe their homes (the refugee camps) in negative terms: at the end of the summer they wanted to return to the camps, although they wished there were more food, trees and toys there. And despite their concerns, all of the Spanish and Sahrawi families interviewed believed that the overall health and social benefits of the children's participation in the summer programme predominated.

More information is necessary to fully evaluate the ways in which the programme is administered, particularly in terms of the screening process. The researchers suggest that the following issues are especially worthy of further examination. On a practical level, given the clear material advantages for the programme's participants, it would be important to ensure that all children participate at least once in the scheme, in order to produce the most widespread benefit for those living in the refugee camps.[30] Furthermore, with a limited number of slots, children lacking political capital may be at a disadvantage. Additional elements to consider in relation to the selection process would be whether children from all camps are given an equal opportunity to participate in the programme and whether more girls or boys are hosted in Spain (as a result of expressed preferences of potential host families). In this respect, it is worth noting that the Spanish families interviewed tended to prefer hosting girls than boys.

Another area of concern, which is based on the researchers' perceptions, centres on the process for screening potential host-families, the responsibility for which is assumed by the Spanish organizers. Interviews with local coordinators in Madrid revealed that there are currently no established guidelines for screening host-families. Potential hosts are usually interviewed and asked to provide copies of their national identification cards (DNI), and from there, coordinators seemed to rely on 'impressions' and 'gut instinct'. One coordinator insisted that anyone who volunteered to host a child for two months must be a good-natured person. If these are the bases upon which host-families are screened, we would strongly urge that a much more rigorous background check of all household members be put into place in order to ensure that the children will be housed in a safe environment, and that their mental, physical and emotional well-being will be guaranteed. It must be stressed that no major incidents of abuse were reported throughout our interviews, apart from two girls indicating that they had been slapped by their former host-parents, and the two boys who were 'returned' by their host-families to the local coordinators.

Conclusion

This chapter offered a case study of *Vacaciones en Paz*, a programme that each year enables thousands of Sahrawi refugee children to spend their summers in Spain. Based on interviews completed with children, host-parents and birth-parents, we argued that the host-relationship also allows for the transfer of goods and services between Spain and the refugee camps, especially those related to the nutritional, physical and social well-being of Sahrawi youth. While in Spain, the children establish valuable social networks in their host-families and gain knowledge and practical skills that may assist them in accessing higher education or work opportunities. The economic benefits referred to include the money, food, clothing and other goods taken back by children, together with contributions sent by host-parents to the children's families during the year.

Rather than a completely new form of care provision, we argued that the element of mobility that characterizes the host experience has deeper socio-cultural roots in Sahrawi society's pre-exile mobile practices. While the children expressed strong attachments to family and home, they also expected to leave the refugee camps temporarily, specifically for their education. We maintained that the children expressed a very weak desire to emigrate as adults or even in the short term; rather, they were eager to return to their families and the refugee camps at the end of the summer programme. We suspect this may reflect their particular life-phase and that older youth may be more willing to spend longer periods away from their families, especially when they can contribute economically to their natal households.

Finally, we suggested that the host experience may encourage both Spaniards and Sahrawis to reflect on their agency as hosts/hosted, citizens/refugees, youth/adults, children/parents. Through the programme, children act as both beneficiaries and conduits of valuable goods, information and services that benefit them individually, as well as their families. In this way, children's agency is enhanced. Some Sahrawi parents, on the other hand, expressed a sense of powerlessness to parent *materially* in the same way as the Spanish hosts and to meet some of the children's unrealistic expectations upon their return from Spain.

Raising healthy, educated and socially mature children is a high priority among Sahrawi refugees and one which is intimately tied to the hope and goal of returning to an independent Western Sahara. By transnationalizing the provision of care for children and youth, this goal is sustained by transcending the limitations of local resources and infrastructures. In so doing, children's mobility within these networks is reinforced as a necessary feature of Sahrawi family life in exile.

Notes

1. Fiddian-Qasmiyeh also conducted a number of interviews with Sahrawi youth and host-families based in Tenerife (the Canary Islands) in August 2006 – see below. We also drew from interview data collected in the Sahrawi refugee camps as part of the broader SARC study. The research team in the refugee camps was led by Randa Farah.
2. On the European Commission's involvement, see Horner (2006).
3. In the case of the Tenerife-based interviews, approval was sought from the local Spanish Town Hall which coordinated the children's visits, and who contacted host-families in order to obtain preliminary consent. The interviewer explained the background and purpose of the research project to the relevant Spanish authorities, host-families and children at each stage.
4. All of the interviews were carried out in Spanish, which is recognized as the second official language in the Sahrawi refugee camps. The youth interviews were digitally recorded and later translated and transcribed by the researchers.
5. Velloso de Santiseban (1993).
6. UNHCR's role in supporting the Cuban-based study-abroad programme has also changed over time. Since 1994, UNHCR has offered transportation assistance for Sahrawi refugee children enrolled in Cuban schools in or before 1996. UNHCR transports these graduating students back to Tindouf, although those who have enrolled since 1996 do not qualify for this form of assistance. In 2005 UNHCR also provided all Sahrawi students in Cuba (597 students) with a small stipend for clothing, shoes, hygienic items and school supplies. The UN body also monitored the programme, confirming 'the voluntary nature of participation in the programme of the children, the direct role of the parents in determining whether their child would participate, and the opportunity for the children who do not wish to continue the programme, to abandon it and return home' (UNHCR 2005).
7. Gaudio outlines the broad impact of sedentarization on Sahrawi social relations, including on women, stressing that 'nomadic life allowed them to be free and the mistresses of their tent. Sedentarized, they became secondary and confined individuals' (1978: 142-43, Fiddian-Qasmiyeh's translation).

8. See Perregaux (1987). Further, Chassey (1977) refers to *mahadras* based in what is currently Mauritania, but which fell within routes followed by Sahrawi tribes before and during the colonial era.
9. While not included in Parreñas' original definition of care (2005: 12), it may be possible to include 'spiritual well-being' as a form of care, and youth mobility to the religious *mahadras* could be understood as fulfilling this element of care provision.
10. Andrade (2003) refers to Cuban doctors spending two years in the camps, completing their institutionalized period of voluntary work abroad there. Cuban doctors' voluntary work abroad has been an integral part of Cuban internationalist aid from the beginning of the Cuban revolution.
11. It should be stressed that for the majority of children visiting Spain for the first time, this would also be the first time that they have such a medical examination.
12. According to a WFP/UNHCR/INRIN study conducted in the camps in February 2005, 38.9 per cent of camp inhabitants suffered from chronic malnutrition, with the prevalence of anaemia amongst children aged between six months and five years being 68.4 per cent, and with 39 per cent of children within the same age-range suffering from growth deficiency. Fifteen per cent of these cases were categorized as severe stunting (UN System Standing Committee on Nutrition 2005).
13. Spanish children of similar age to their Sahrawi counterparts (between seven and twelve) are considered as dependents and their parents are expected to ensure that their offspring's various material and emotional needs are met. Children are not expected to contribute to the household income, and it remains culturally acceptable for older, unmarried youth to continue living with their parents until they are married. The bulk of domestic chores are largely carried out by adult women in the family or by paid help, although the girls in the family may carry some domestic responsibilities, such as washing the dishes or assisting with food preparation.
14. In the host-parental survey, host-parents were asked whether the Sahrawi children called them 'Mum' and 'Dad' or by their personal names. Twenty-three respondents answered the question with nearly three-quarters of the children calling their host-parents by their first names (e.g. Antonio, Maria). Five respondents said their host-children call them by both, sometimes by their first name and sometimes as Mum or Dad. One parent clarified that their host-child calls them by their first name, but when talking to others describes the family members as mum, sister and so forth . One child calls the host-mother 'Mum' but the host-father by his first name. Another child calls everyone in her family by their first name, except the grandmother who she calls 'grandma' followed by her first name. One family reported being called 'Mamá' and 'Papá' , but the host-father said he and his wife would prefer to be called by their first names.
15. The reasons for the 'returns', as given by the observers were, in one case, because the original host-parents had been unable to accommodate their life to that of the Sahrawi child (the host-parents in question reportedly had no children of their own, and this was given as a reason for their not knowing how to 'deal' with the Sahrawi child), and in the second case, because the host-parent's biological child was so jealous that the host-mother had to choose between her own son and the

Sahrawi boy she had hosted for less than a month.

16. Indeed, the day after the 2005 *Vacaciones en Paz* children flew back to the camps, the researchers saw over a dozen Spanish host-parents who they had previously interviewed congregated in front of the Ministry of the Exterior in Madrid, participating in a hunger strike to lobby the Spanish government regarding the Western Sahara.

17. In 2006, the marathon raised 12,000 euros which the Ministry of Sport will use to create a sport centre in the camps, in addition to providing 1,000 euros of medicines for one of the camp's hospitals. For more information, see www.saharamarathon.org.

18. The email addresses are www.arso.org, www.spsrasd.info and www.wsahara.net respectively.

19. The websites which have been blocked include ARSO, SOS, Cahiers du Sahara and AFAPRADESA. More information is available from www.arso.org/index.htm.

20. This may be contrasted with children who study, for instance, in Cuba. Given the distance and travel costs involved, children who study in Cuba may spend up to a decade separated from their families in order to complete tertiary education, and therefore return as young men and women to the camps. Upon their return to the refugee camps, many of them have difficulties re-adapting to speaking in Hassaniya (the Arabic dialect spoken by Saharawis), and to traditions surrounding everything from clothing to interactions with members of the opposite sex.

21. Sebastian's father had been a member of the Spanish colonial army.

22. Two of the three girls had arrived in Spain primarily for medical reasons – Huria due to serious dental complications, and Fatimetu because of her condition as a celiac – while Aicha had wanted to complete her secondary and tertiary education in Spain.

23. For a more detailed analysis of these cases, see Fiddian (2006), Fiddian-Qasmiyeh 2009), and Fiddian-Qasmiyeh (2010 forthcoming).

24 A couple of the girls' cases, pushed by their respective Spanish host-families, even reached higher political institutions such as the Spanish Congress, Foreign Ministry and Senate.

25. As it was not possible to locate reliable information regarding the gender of Sahrawi children who are fostered in Spain, or the gender of those who are asked to return to the camps, it is difficult to identify whether or how such cases are gendered in nature. That these three cases should have adolescent girls as their central protagonists cannot be taken to indicate that girls are necessarily overrepresented in such cases, as it is unclear whether the story of a Sahrawi boy being asked to return to the camps would have attracted the Spanish public's imagination and so much media coverage.

26. On Aicha's family situation, suggesting that her mother was pregnant while suffering from hepatitis, see Castaño Boullon (n.d.); on Huria's baby sibling, see (n.a. and n.d.) 'Visita a los campamentos, engaño y retención'.

27. At least two of the three girls were finally allowed to return to Spain to complete their studies, following intensive Polisario negotiations with the girls' biological families.

28. While it may indeed be the case that the younger children 'do not know what

they are seeing', some youth become acutely aware of cultural differences, and reject some of these. For instance, a seventeen year-old girl who had been to Spain several times through the host-programme, and who was interviewed in the camps, maintained that she did not like Spain: 'The people have very different customs, they do not respect their elders, and they go out without any clothes on, naked (she laughs) … that is very difficult for the Sahrawis to do.' Refusing to return to Spain, she continued her studies in Algeria, 'where people have great respect for us,' the Sahrawi people.

29. It is worth noting that there may be a difference between children's expectations *per se*, and parental fears and insecurities regarding their inability to provide for their offspring. Hence, while all children interviewed in Spain stressed their desire to return to their 'real' parents at the end of the summer, highlighting that their biological parents love them and care for them in a way that their host-families simply cannot, many Sahrawi parents felt that their children might 'look down' on them and their way of life in the camps. The parents' fears may in this sense be a projection (i.e. what they imagine their children may feel), rather than a reflection of their children's actual feelings.

30. The researchers were informed that children are selected for participation following a combined medical, social and educational evaluation. We are under the impression, therefore, that not all children in the camps are offered places in the programme, and more information regarding the ways in which the selection criterion is applied would be welcomed.

References

Andrade. 2003. *El Territorio del Silencio: un viaje por el Sahara Occidental.* Tegueste, Tenerife: Ediciones de Baile del Sol.

Bryceson, D. and U. Vuorela. 2002. *The Transnational family: New European Frontiers and Global Networks.* Oxford: Berg.

Castaño Boullon, M.C. n.d.. 'Sr. Director'. Accessed at http://www.entender-sahara.com/articulo.php?sec=documentos&id=11 on 1 November 2005.

Chassey, F. De. 1977. *L'Etrier, la houe et le livre 'sociétés traditionnelles' au Sahara et au Sahel Occidental.* Paris: Editions Anthropos.

Fiddian, E. 2006. *Education and Representation in Exile: Gendered Dilemmas.* Seminar presented in February 2006 as part of the Theory and Methodology Seminar Series, Gender Studies Centre, University of Cambridge.

Fiddian-Qasmiyeh, E. 2009. 'Gender, Islam and the Sahrawi Politics of Survival', DPHIL in International Development Submitted to the University of Oxford April 2009.

Fiddian-Qasmiyeh, E. 2010 forthcoming. 'When the Self becomes Other: representations of gender, Islam and the politics of survival in the Sahrawi refugee camps,' in D. Chatty and B. Findlay (eds), *Dispossession and Displacement: Forced Migration in the Middle East and North Africa,* London: British Academy.

Gaudio, A. 1978. *Le Dossier du Sahara Occidental.* Paris: Nouvelles Editions Latines.

Goldring, L. 1998. 'The Power of Status in Transnational Social Fields', in M.P. Smith and L.E. Guarnizo (eds), *Transnationalism from Below.* New Brunswick: Transaction Publishers, pp. 165–198.

Horner, S. 2006. 'European Commission focuses on forgotten crises', *Forced Migration Review* 25: 56–57 (May).

Lippert, A. 1987. 'The Sahrawi Refugees: Origins and Organization, 1975–1985', in R. Lawless and L. Monahan (eds), *War and Refugees: The Western Sahara Conflict*. Refugee Studies Programme, London: Pinter, pp. 150–166.

Parreñas, Rhacel Salazar. 2005. *Children of Global Migration: Transnational Families and Gendered Woes*. Stanford: Stanford University Press.

Perregaux, C. 1987. *L'Ecole sahraouie. De la caravane à la guerre de libération*. Paris: L'Harmattan.

RASD. 2000. 'Acogimiento Provisional'. Accessed at http://www.elparchedigital.com/pags/huria/ on 1 November 2005.

Ratsch, I-M. and C. Catassi. 2001. 'Coeliac Disease: a potentially treatable health problem of Saharawi refugee children', *Bulletin of the World Health Organization* 79(6).

UN System Standing Committee on Nutrition. 2005. *Nutrition Information in Crisis Situations – Algeria*. NICS 7, August 2005. Accessed at http://www.unsystem.org/scn/Publications/RNIS/countries/algeria_all.htm on 1 March 2006.

UNHCR. 2005. 'Western Saharan refugee students in Cuba'. UNHCR – Information Note. September 2005. Accessed at http://www.arso.org/UNHCRCuba.htm on 12 May 2006.

Velloso de Santiseban, A. 1993. *La Educación en el Sahara Occidental*. Madrid: UNED.

n.a. and n.d. 'Visita a los campamentos, engaño y retención'. Accessed at http://www.elparchedigital.com/pags/huria/CASO_RETENCION.htm on 1 November 2005.

3
Food and Identity among Sahrawi Refugee Young People

Nicola Cozza

Preliminary Remarks

This chapter presents the findings of a sub-study on the relationship between food and identity among young Sahrawi camp refugees in Algeria aged from about eight to eighteen years. It is part of a wider research project on the relationships between food and identity among Sahrawi and Afghan refugee children (SARC project). In particular, this study complements the work carried out by Dr Alessandro Monsutti, who investigated issues related to food and identity among Afghan youth employing similar methodological instruments and approach (see chapter 6). The data collected and the analyses developed in the course of these two field-based studies were complemented by Professor Jeya Henry, who also played a central role in defining the methodology of the whole SARC sub-study on food and identity.[1]

Food and Identity among Sahrawi Youth

The role that food plays in the production and reproduction of social ties and collective identities has been the focus of much research within the academic disciplines of sociology and, notably, anthropology. The centrality of food as a means of communicating differences and similarities between individuals and groups was already expressed in some of the work of scholars such as Evans-Pritchard (1969) and Lévi-Strauss (1966). More recently, important developments in the anthropology of economic relations and consumption put food back under the spotlight (Godelier 1972; Appadurai and Breckenridge 1986; Douglas and Isherwood 1996).[2] Studies such as Mary Douglas' (1975) research on British food and Bourdieu's (1984) analysis of taste in France have helped to highlight the importance of food consumption in the production and reproduction of key social categories related to gender, age and socio-economic status. Far from being a mere source of nutritional elements necessary to human life, from this body of literature food emerges as an important constituent of all human social existence: caught between individual free choice and culturally determined practices, food is universally used as a means to express forms of inclusion, exclusion and a wide range of other social relations (Goodman *et al.*, 2000).

Although the social importance of food is now widely acknowledged, it appears to have been largely underplayed within the field of refugee studies. Without doubt, much research has been produced on the topic of nutritional requirements and deficiencies among camp refugees (see Keen 1992; De Waal 1997). Nevertheless, the social relevance of changing food habits among refugees and other forcibly displaced people has remained a largely neglected topic.

It is in this context that the SARC research on food and identity has taken shape. By focusing on Afghan and Sahrawi refugees aged between about eight and eighteen years, this research has aimed to explore:

1. How the conditions of forced and prolonged displacement may affect food practices and, above all,
2. How and to what extent changes in food practices – and possible resistance to such changes – play a role in the reproduction and change of social ties and in the construction of group identities among people who have been forcibly displaced for prolonged periods of time.

The present chapter explores these issues with reference to the Sahrawi camp youth. While the following analysis does not aim to be exhaustive (the complexity and relevance of the topic would certainly reward further investigation), it is intended to provoke debate on the relationship between food, displacement and identities.

Sahrawi Camp Refugees: a Brief Overview[3]

For almost thirty years Sahrawi refugees from Western Sahara have been living in four camps located in south-western Algeria, near the town of Tindouf, in a particularly harsh region of the Sahara desert. The first group of refugees fled Western Sahara in late 1975, when the Spanish colonial authorities withdrew from the territory and Moroccan and Mauritanian troops occupied it. Since then, and under the flag of a nationalist organization known as the Polisario Front, the Sahrawi refugees have fought a long war with the aim of fending off the occupying forces and achieving a fully independent state in Western Sahara.

After the withdrawal of Mauritania from the conflict in 1978, the war continued between Morocco and the Polisario. In 1991, under the auspices of the United Nations (UN), the two parties signed a cease-fire that is still in force. At the same time, the UN began the preparation of a referendum in which Sahrawi people would choose between an independent state of Western Sahara and the integration of the territory into the Kingdom of Morocco. Until now the referendum has not been held and it is unlikely that it will take place, at least in the next few years.

Firmly supporting the struggle of the Sahrawi refugees against Morocco, Algeria has been a key actor in the conflict. Since 1975 the government of Algiers has provided the refugees with considerable amounts of humanitarian aid and, no less important, it has allowed them to settle on Algerian territory. The Polisario Front has been given temporary jurisdiction over the land surrounding the camps, where this organization has set up the Sahrawi Arab Democratic Republic (SADR). Since 1976 the Algerian territory where the Sahrawi refugee camps have been located has been organized by the Polisario as a state-in-exile, with its president, elected parliament, ministries and judges. The SADR has been recognized as a legitimate state by over seventy countries across the globe and has enjoyed access to their bilateral aid. In addition, a number of European (mostly Spanish) non-governmental organizations (NGOs) have provided humanitarian aid to the Sahrawi refugees, together with the European Community Humanitarian Office (ECHO) and various UN agencies.

Nowadays there are about 165,000 Sahrawi refugees living in the four camps of the SADR in Algeria. Almost 60 per cent of this population is estimated to be aged eighteen or younger. Despite remaining largely dependent upon international humanitarian aid, since the early 1990s Sahrawi refugees have developed a range of economic activities, including trade within the refugee camps and between these and urban centres in Algeria and Mauritania.

Research on Food and Identity among Sahrawi Refugees: Methodological Considerations

The methodology adopted during my fieldwork in the Sahrawi refugee camps was based on four main tools:

Frequency of Food Consumption Survey

Forty-six Sahrawi refugees aged between eleven and sixteen completed individual survey forms in which they indicated all the food and drinks that they had consumed throughout the previous day. The survey was conducted among two classes of the primary and secondary school of the 27th February Women's School Camp. The students filled in the forms in their classrooms, ticking the boxes that they thought appropriate and adding the names of dishes that they consumed but which were not initially included in the survey form. In addition, the young refugees were asked to write at the bottom of the survey form their three favourite dishes and the three they most disliked. The forms were written in Spanish, a language that all students can read and understand, and were introduced and explained in Spanish and Arabic before the students filled them in. It was left open to students to use either Spanish or Arabic when they added their favourite and least favourite foods.

Daily Diet Diary Survey

Fifteen Sahrawi refugees aged between eleven and sixteen participated in this survey. Each young person was given a survey form and was asked to take note of all the food and drinks that she/he would consume during six consecutive days, writing them down as she/he ate or drank them (the participants were asked to start on the following day, but some decided to start later). The forms were introduced and distributed among pupils of the 9th June boarding school in their classroom on the penultimate day of school before the beginning of a ten-day holiday.[4] The completed forms were collected on the second day of school after the holiday. Consequently, the data collected convey the participants' diets when living at home and not during school time. The survey forms were written in Spanish but students could choose to fill them in either Spanish or Arabic. As an illustration of the data collected, three of the completed fifteen forms are included in Appendix 4.1.

Semi-structured Interviews

Ten Sahrawi refugees aged between twelve and sixteen were interviewed by Ms Fatimatu Mohammed Salem and myself. The individual interviews took place in the library of the 9th June boarding school and were tape-recorded. During the interviews, only the interviewee and the two researchers were present. The ten interviewed refugees had previously participated in the Daily Diet Diary survey. They were chosen for the interviews on the basis of their gender and age (the objective was to have a balanced sample of male/female and younger/older interviewees) and their willingness to take part in the exercise. The interviews focused on food habits – preferred food/drinks; food/drinks consumed in different contexts and in the company of different people; perceived changes in food habits between the past and the present; experiences of food/drinks consumed in Europe by the young refugees during the *Vacaciones en Paz* programme, etc. The guiding questions for the interviews were decided beforehand in consultation with Fatimatu Mohammed Salem and after reviewing the results of the two surveys mentioned above as well as other information and observations previously collected. The interviews were conducted in Hassaniya Arabic and were later translated into English.

Informal Interviews, Discussions and Participant Observation

Further important information and observations were collected during my fieldwork through informal conversations and discussions with a number of Sahrawi refugees. In most cases those who took part in these conversations were adult or young adult Sahrawi, both men and women. Many of them were parents of young refugees and all the interviewees had youth living in their household. More structured interviews with adult refugees were carried out on two occasions: one interview with the director of the 9th June boarding school, and a second interview with the person responsible for the shop located within the same school, where pupils regularly buy food and drinks. An informal interview was also carried out with the person responsible for the canteen services in the school, who gave information on the dishes usually provided in the school canteen and their ingredients. In addition, during my fieldwork I spent eight days in the Auserd refugee camp, living in the tent of the family of a personal friend who I have known since 2000: he was one of my key informants during my previous fieldwork in Nouadhibou (Mauritania). I had useful conversations with him and a number of his relatives (including some teenagers and children). Throughout my stay in the camps, verbal interactions were carried out in Hassaniya Arabic and in Spanish.

Young refugees participated in the surveys and interviews mostly with enthusiasm and showed a keen interest in the topic of the research. A few of them asked to have access to the final results of the study. It seemed clear that many young refugees regarded this research as a way of making their voices heard to far-away donors.

The choice of the two different schools – one in the 27th February camp and the 9th June School – was intentional. All pupils of the first school eat in their homes and live with their parents and relatives. However, the 9th June is a boarding school where pupils spend most of the year and where they normally sleep and have meals (a canteen in the school provides free meals). Furthermore, the first school is located within a refugee settlement where all pupils live (the 27th February), whereas the 9th June school is in an isolated position: the closest refugee settlement is the Aaiun camp, which is about ten kilometres away from the school, and is where the families of most of the students live. This said, pupils of both schools have easy access to shops where they can buy food and drinks.

In view of the scope of this research, the difference between 'usually eating at home' (pupils of the first school) and 'usually eating in school' (pupils of the second school) seemed a particularly relevant one. Furthermore, it was assumed that the choice of two different schools far apart from each other would help the triangulation of the data and observations collected.

A final note on the Frequency of Food Consumption and Daily Diet Diary surveys; these were based on questionnaires that Professor Jeya Henry had provided during a meeting held in Oxford in September 2003. The same two surveys were used by Dr Monsutti during his fieldwork in Iran and by myself during my research in the Sahrawi refugee camps.

Food and Identity among Sahrawi Young Refugees

Among Sahrawi camp refugees three categories of food were found to be frequently used when discussing dietary habits.

The first is traditional food which consists of dishes and beverages considered to be typical of Sahrawi people both in the past (before the beginning of the conflict against Morocco) and in the present. These dishes are regarded as the food usually consumed by Sahrawi nomadic camel-herders. All the ingredients have long been available locally, with fluctuations mostly due to seasonality, weather conditions and viability of trade routes. Among Sahrawi refugees there are popular stories about certain traditional dishes as well as common ideas that link some traditional dishes and other food habits to certain tribes and sub-tribes. In addition, a number of traditional dishes are believed to have curative properties while most of them are regarded as nutritious and healthy (Appendix 3.2).

Secondly, there is food-aid which consists of commodities freely distributed among camp refugees as humanitarian aid, such as pasta, vegetable oil, sugar and canned beans and vegetables. Food-aid differs significantly from traditional food, although traditional and food-aid ingredients may be combined in dishes prepared and consumed by camp refugees (for example, the traditional camel meat and the spaghetti of food-aid). Among Sahrawi and other Moors certain food-aid items (such as Spanish canned sardines, Italian tins of lentils and ECHO-marked sugar) have become symbols of the Sahrawi refugees, of their life in the camps and their struggle for national independence. As a young refugee explained: 'there are no Sahrawi refugees or soldiers who have not eaten the canned lentils of the camps'; then he added, joking: 'with all the lentils that we ate ... we must be all made of lentils by now'.

The third category is new food, largely a residual category, including food that is neither traditional nor food-aid. The availability of this food within the camps is relatively recent (starting from the early 1990s) and related to the end of the armed hostilities and the opening of shops within the camps. It includes items such as soft drinks, fruit yogurt, chocolate cream, flavoured sweets and biscuits as well as pizza, sandwiches and fried chicken.

Although the classification of certain food commodities under one group or another may be disputed at times (e.g. rice is traditional for many, but others see it as food-aid; eggs are traditional commodities but chicken categorization is less clear, although fried chicken is clearly regarded as new), the actual use of the three categories of food is accepted and common. Two features of this categorization need to be highlighted. First, the three categories are exhaustive and can accommodate all food items currently available in the camps. Secondly, there is a clear chronological relationship between these groupings. In particular, they are closely linked to and help represent successive historical periods that are socially important among camp refugees: traditional food is linked to the nomadic life of the past; food-aid represents the fight against the invaders from the hardship of exile; while new food represents the end of armed hostilities, the development of trade in the camps and the intercontinental travels of a significant part of the refugee population (mostly youth leaving the camps for study or holidays abroad).[5] Food items belonging to different categories are often combined during meals: a traditional dish of camel meat may be laid on a bed of rice from food-aid and accompanied by a soft drink from a shop in the camps. Similarly, the historical realities that the three food categories refer to (namely nomadic life, refugees' struggle for national independence and development of trade) are blended in the refugees' daily lives as different facets of the present. In fact, a large number of Sahrawi refugees (predominantly adult males) have become nomadic camel-herders and now spend most of their time away from the camps, often in the 'liberated areas' of Western Sahara. Sahrawi camp refugees persist in their political struggle and continue to receive food-aid, while many refugees sell 'new food' in small shops set up near their tents and others do trade between the refugee settlements and urban centres in Algeria and Mauritania. Nevertheless, we shall use the phrases 'traditional food', 'food-aid' and 'new food' with reference to the three categories mentioned above.

Between Traditional and New Food: youth, external influence and adult supervision

From the information and observations collected, it emerges that young Sahrawi refugees tend to prefer (arguably more than adults) food commodities and drinks that are usually regarded as new food among the refugee population. This preference was clearly voiced during interviews and then confirmed when examining youth's actual food choices. In particular, young refugees frequently opt for new food (such as baguette bread, chicken meat and fizzy soft drinks) when they are able to decide what to eat – a choice that they cannot always make. In effect, young refugees usually have limited control over the food that they eat at home during main meals with their families and relatives, and have virtually no control over the meals provided in the canteens of the boarding schools. However, it is clear that youth's preference for certain new food is far from being a total refusal of more traditional dishes. For instance, although the large majority of young refugees who participated in the surveys and interviews pointed to couscous (regarded as one of the most traditional dishes) as a food that they clearly disliked, virtually all of them eat it regularly, either during family meals or in the school canteens.

Young refugees' preference for new food is often emphasized by the adult refugee population. When talking about refugee children and adolescents, adults usually represented the camp youth as a group of people that strongly prefers new food and dislikes the traditional dishes – a preference that, in reality, does not appear to be quite so definite and uniform among young refugees. Table 3.1 presents this mostly *adult* categorization of food and drinks preferred and disliked by the youth.

Table 3.1: Adults' Representations of Youths' Food Preferences.

Preferred by youth	Disliked by youth
Baguette bread	Homemade bread
Chicken meat	Camel and goat meat
Fizzy soft drinks	Tea
Pizza/Burger	Couscous
Food purchased ready-to-use	Slow-cooking food
Quicker preparation	Longer preparation
Not-healthy	Healthy

Young Sahrawi refugees offered a number of different reasons for their general preference for new food, the most common being personal taste. Two other frequent explanations were first, the fact that new food tends to be consumed less often for main meals and therefore represents a change to the monotony of everyday dishes; second, that new food can be easily purchased and consumed without adult supervision (e.g. 'making tea takes a long time, is not easy and you can be told off if you don't make it well … buying a coke takes a minute … and nobody bothers you').

In contrast, when talking to adult refugees about youth's food habits, I was given two other reasons as to why young refugees have different preferences. Refugee children and adolescents were said to prefer new food because, first, this is the food that they eat in Europe during their 'holidays abroad' and, second, because 'they are young and still unable to choose what is best for them'.

A brief explanation of the 'holidays abroad' is necessary here.[6] This scheme for young Sahrawi refugees has been implemented since the early 1990s with considerable success. Every summer no less than 6,000 Sahrawi camp refugees, aged mostly between nine and thirteen years, spend about two months in Europe, predominantly in Spain, as guests of European families. All the Sahrawi teenagers whom I met in the refugee camps told me that they had spent at least one holiday (more often two and sometimes three) in Europe. I was repeatedly shown pictures taken during summer holidays abroad and was told the names of Spanish or Italian locations where the young refugees had spent their vacations.[7]

Adult refugees often emphasized the effects of the 'holidays abroad' on youth's food habits. Far from their parents, young refugees were said to be easily 'enchanted' and 'fascinated' by European food and to be prone to change their food preferences after only a few weeks abroad. Furthermore, it was stressed that while in Europe young refugees could eat and drink (often unconsciously) foodstuff and drinks that are forbidden to Muslims. This supposedly strong European influence is presented as stemming not from any special 'power' of the host-families, but from a 'weakness' of all non-adults. Children and (in varying degrees) young refugees were portrayed as easily influenced by adults: this would be the reason why the holidays in Europe (far from the supervision of adult Sahrawi) can have a deep effect on the food preferences of the youth.

In other words, adult refugees tend to associate youth's preference for new food with the fact that they are inclined to be influenced by others and are not yet adult. Becoming an adult Sahrawi seems to entail a somewhat stable taste and a change of preference from new foodstuffs to more traditional ones. It was explained to me that as the young refugees develop into adults, they become able to control and motivate their decisions and preferences: they would gradually leave the new food and come to appreciate traditional food for its healthy properties and original taste. While adults tend to associate the choice of new food with childhood and docility to external influence, a steady preference for traditional food tends to be perceived as the choice of an independent adult.

It is important to underline that this common adult understanding of youth's food preferences appears to be given little importance by Sahrawi young refugees, who do not attribute their general preference for new food primarily to their contact with Europeans during summer holidays, but rather to their own taste. Commenting on this topic, many young refugees explained to me that when they were in Europe they tried a lot of different dishes that they did not like and others that they enjoyed better, and while some of these young people liked certain European dishes, others liked different ones. Taste – rather than European influence – was given as the key reason behind their food preferences.

Adults' common explanation of youth's preference for new food reveals how food practices have taken part not only in the social construction of adulthood and childhood but also in inter-generational relationships. The representation of youth's preference for 'new' food as stemming from the influence of others (that is, the Europeans) reinforces an understanding that youth require constant adult control and supervision. Being allegedly unable to choose what is supposed to be best for them and easily seduced by 'others', children and young refugees are represented as in need of mature overseeing.

This theme is also present in common adult attitudes towards 'eating at home' and 'eating at school'. As clearly emerged from formal and informal interviews and discussions with young refugees, they generally prefer eating at home rather than having meals in the school canteen. At home food tastes better, is better cooked and is eaten in a more relaxed environment.[8] In addition, if the youth do not like their home meal, they may avoid it by visiting a neighbouring friend and being offered a meal there, or they may purchase food in nearby shops.

Although virtually all adult refugees agreed that home food is better, they also emphasized that eating in school is healthier for the youth. It was often explained to me that, although home food is better, children and young refugees are less controlled when they are at home; they can easily eat a very small quantity of the family meal and then go to a shop and buy food and drinks that they prefer. In their own home the young refugees can decide more easily when, where, what and how much they are going to eat. At school, on the contrary, students are closely supervised during meals by staff and are expected to eat all the food that they are given. For this reason, the adult refugees explained, students residing in the boarding schools look 'healthier' than young refugees who eat at home. In other words, adult refugees tend to agree that more closely supervised meals are beneficial to the youth when compared with weakly or non-supervised meals. Again, adult control over youth's food habits is portrayed as leading to better health and is therefore to be preferred.

It is also important to stress the symbolic value of traditional food, particularly among the adult camp population. During informal interviews with adult refugees, it emerged that they used to have a much more limited food choice than the present camp youth, at least till the early 1990s when the first food shops were opened in the camps. They relied almost entirely on food-aid and had very limited access to traditional food for which they longed. This desire has also been an expression of their longing for the 'Sahrawi nomadic life of the past' and a means to remember and define it. Indeed, the ingredients of traditional food are intimately related to the nomadic life and its economy, hinged on camel-herding and trading. As an adult refugee explained, 'a Sahrawi is not a Sahrawi without his desert and his camels ... the *ader* [wooden bowl for camel milk] and the *tichtar* [dry camel meat]. All this was stolen from us and we must take it back.' In this context, youth's preference for new food and their dislike for traditional dishes (possibly over-emphasized by adults) could be read as a refusal of what many adults regard as an essential aspect of 'Sahrawiness': the traditional life-style of nomadic camel-herders.

From all the above it is clear that food preferences play an important role in the social construction of childhood, adulthood and generational change. Sahrawi camp refugees of different ages appear to share a common representation of adults and youth as having different food preferences. In this context, generational status and change are mediated also through the use of food. Preferring new food can be a powerful means of stating one's resistance to adult supervision, a challenge to socially influent forms of knowledge and an assertion of non-adult and peer group identities. On the other hand, 'becoming adult' is expected to entail a switch towards traditional food, a change reflecting the fact that young refugees gradually acquire an 'adult' knowledge of themselves (knowing what one *really* likes) and of nature (knowing what is good for the body, what is healthy). Meanwhile, by gradually adopting some adult preferences, the growing youth also gain a lower degree of parental (or, more generally, adult) supervision.

This process is, nonetheless, far from being linear and has required changes from both sides of the child/adult continuum. In particular, the management of youth's food preferences has induced significant changes in the behaviour of the adult refugee population with reference to their control over household resources. It is clear, in fact, that youth's preferences have become an important economic concern at the household level where, to some extent, they have been accommodated within the limited resource allocation of the family unit (see chapter 1 by Chatty, Crivello and Fiddian). It is significant that almost all the young refugees interviewed explained that they receive some pocket money from their carers on a rather regular basis and spend a large part (often most) of it on food and drinks.

Food, Beauty and Gender

The female refugees who were interviewed usually emphasized that there were no significant differences between what boys and girls eat and drink. They often explained that, allowing for individual taste, boys and girls eat the same food. Nevertheless, other observations collected and the analysis of food and drinks consumed by the two groups reveal a more complex picture. Four aspects appear to be prominent:

When compared with males of the same age, female teenagers tend to show less interest in food. This emerged from the analysis of boys' and girls' interviews as well as from their diets and shopping preferences. In particular, girls tend to spend a significant lower percentage of their pocket money on food and to purchase more non-food items (e.g.: beauty products, non-food gifts for relatives and girlfriends);

Female teenagers tend to consume more dietary products such as milk, yogurt, soft cheese and fruit;

Among Sahrawi camp refugees, there are many common notions (at times contradictory) concerning what girls and young women should or should not eat. Nevertheless, no specific notions on boys' diets were noted;

Girls' diets are more thoroughly supervised by adults.

From the information and observations collected, girls' food habits appear to be more often and consistently affected by certain concerns about 'beauty'. Of course, more research is needed to improve our understanding of how 'beauty' (i.e. individually and socially defined standards of body appearance) influences the social construction of genders. Also, further research is needed to better understand the perceived relationship between food, body and beauty, as well as the meanings of 'beauty' among Sahrawi refugees. Nevertheless, the observations collected allow a tentative understanding of some connotations of 'beauty' and of certain relationships between this and food practices among Sahrawi female youth.

Sahrawi young refugees tend to associate 'female beauty' with 'white skin' and a 'slim body'. The first of these ('white skin') is by far the less disputed one: among Sahrawi and other Moors a fair skin is generally much appreciated by both men and women. In this context, girls' food choices appear to be affected by the common belief that certain foods can help one have a fairer skin. This seems to be the main reason why girls, more than boys, consume food and drinks that – as emerged during interviews – are believed to have a 'whitening' effect on the skin: milk, yogurt, soft cheese and certain types of bread and fruit.

The second connotation of beauty (a 'slim body') is more controversial among Sahrawi refugees. Plumpness has long been an important aspect of female beauty among Sahrawi and other Moors.[9] Notions concerning what, when and how much women should eat are numerous among Sahrawi refugees and they usually emphasize that women should eat more and more often than men (particularly when they have reached child-bearing age) and should habitually consume animal fat (especially in the form of traditional dishes based on camel fat; Rguibi and Belahsen 2006).

Nevertheless, a plump body appears to have lost much of its appeal among younger female generations and is often seen as part of the old and the 'bad side' of the traditional life. While several factors may have contributed to this change in the standards of female beauty (including exposure to dominant Western paradigms of the attractive female body, e.g. during holidays in Europe), it can also be argued that a role has been played by the propaganda of the Sahrawi Arab Democratic Republic (SADR). In particular, since 1998 the SADR has promoted campaigns in the camps against the idea of 'fat is beautiful'. These have focused on the medical pathologies that tend to accompany obesity and, in particular, on the cardio-vascular risks associated with a high-fat diet.

This authoritative backing for the 'slim body paradigm' has certainly not eliminated social tensions surrounding the definition of what women should eat and how they should look. For example, young female refugees tend to control what and how much they eat in the light of their desirable standards of beauty (above all 'white skin' and a 'slim body') and on the basis of their notions of the relationship between food and body. In so doing, female teenagers and young women often find themselves in a particularly difficult position, caught between more intense adult supervision on their dietary habits (arguably as part of a wider political economy of gender relationships and social control) and their wish to achieve a non-traditional, 'slim body' beauty.

If, as argued above, food practices provide a ground for the social definition of adulthood and maturity, they are also a privileged terrain on which the struggle for control over the female body (in the form of standards of female beauty) is conducted. Female teenagers bear most of the burden of achieving a 'slim' body while under the close supervision of a 'fat-fancy' adult population. Thus, girls' apparent lack of interest in food – and their emphasis on the fact that boys and girls eat the same things – can be seen as a defensive strategy, an attempt to underplay common social concerns surrounding changing standards of female beauty and girls' dietary habits.

Sahrawi Youth and the Political Economy of Food-aid

It has been argued above that individual food preferences are socially important and carefully managed in the social environment of the refugee camps. Preferences and attitudes towards food (but arguably also choices concerning how, when and where food is consumed; for example, adults, unlike children, hardly consume any food on the road) are imbued with social values and beliefs defining the individual's gender, age, knowledge, maturity and social status. While food may play similar roles in other societies, it can be argued that in the Sahrawi context it has acquired a distinctive importance, rooted in the political economy of the Polisario Front and the Sahrawi Arab Republic.

Among Sahrawi refugees food-aid is a frequent and delicate topic of discussion. The primary reason lies in the fact that it has come to play a critical role in the political economy of the camps. Following the end of the armed hostilities between Morocco and the Polisario Front, since the early 1990s a food-aid economy has developed, centred in the refugee camps but reaching far into Algeria and Mauritania. A significant share of food-aid is diverted before being distributed to the camp refugees and is then sold in large quantities in Tindouf (southern Algeria), Zouerate (northern Mauritania), Nouadhibou, Nouakshot and other urban centres. Only a limited number of Sahrawi refugees have been benefiting from this state of affairs. For this minority, the food-aid economy (which Sahrawi refugees often call *el comercio*, a Spanish word meaning 'trade') has generated significant economic resources. For the majority, however, *el comercio* has meant, above all, a considerable reduction in the quantity and quality of their food-aid rations.

The development of the food-aid trade is intimately related to the creation and strengthening of local and transnational networks of a predominantly tribal and sub-tribal character. These networks have also functioned as a contract enforcement system, reducing the risk of commercial misbehaviour and fraud in an environment characterized by weak state structures (Cozza 2004). In patent contrast with the 'no tribes, one nation' propaganda and the egalitarian nationalist doctrine of the Polisario, a number of Sahrawi political leaders have unofficially supported *el comercio* as a means to gain economic resources and gather political support (Garcia 2001). It is clear that *el comercio* remains a rather uncomfortable issue for the political establishment, which officially portrays it as an illegal activity carried out by a handful of refugees.

El comercio has been a complex social, political and economic reality with which Sahrawi have been dealing for almost two decades. It is important to note here that the refugees largely perceive this trade as a major cause of loss of solidarity among camp inmates and a critical factor in the rise of tribal politics and economic inequalities among the refugee population. As one adult Sahrawi put it: 'if some people were not stealing our food, certainly we would all be better off … and food would not be the problem that it is today. Too many [refugees] live with too little [food].'

The food-aid trade, together with its economic, social and political consequences, is a frequent topic of discussion within refugees' households and among relatives, friends, rivals and enemies. On limited occasions it has been openly discussed at public gatherings, although the delicate and conflictive nature of *el comercio* has made it more suitable to smaller venues of a more domestic or private character. While it is not regarded as a forbidden topic for younger refugees, it mostly remains an adult business: children and youth have been exposed to it often as casual witnesses, although there have also been cases of young male refugees directly participating in the food-aid trade.

It is against this daily background of political complaisance, economic opportunities and growing inequalities centred round food-aid that the new, distinctive alimentary preferences of the youth have sounded as a strident note to many adults. It is interesting that adults seem most worried about youth's food preferences. The reason lies perhaps not only in the fear of losing tradition and a sense of Sahrawi identity, nor in justifying the need for adult supervision, but also in the challenge posed to the centrality of the Sahrawi state and its food-aid-based economy in the lives of refugees. Youth's food preferences, in fact, are an unremitting assertion of individual free choice and difference vis-à-vis both the state-controlled food-aid and the nationalist connotations of 'Sahrawi traditional food'. Above all, their preferences are a constant reminder to adults that, after more than thirty years of state history, the Sahrawi national socio-economic and political system is poorly suited to satisfy the demands of youth. In this regard, a young refugee interviewee made a pertinent point before I could put my first question: 'We children have a right to good food. I will tell you about this and what I eat and what I like. But I will not tell you anything about the other food and *el comercio* and so on... That is not my business and I thank God.' The promise was kept and the topic was not mentioned again.

Concluding Remarks

Three main findings have emerged from this study of food habits among the Sahrawi camp youth. First, this research has suggested that among the camp refugees food plays a central role in remembering socially important events and periods. Changes in food availability, procurement and use have accompanied the refugees from their flight, through the armed hostilities, to the present time of no-war-no-peace and intensified contacts with outsiders. In this context, food has contributed to the representation of a shared history among camp inmates and has acquired connotations that are socially and politically important. Certain food, for instance, has been closely associated with a pre-war, ancient Sahrawi identity,[10] while other provisions have become a symbol of the refugees' armed resistance against the invaders. Indeed, virtually every food item consumed by the camp refugees has become embedded in their collective history and its consumption can easily transcend individual momentary choice and acquire symbolic connotations.

Secondly, food has been an important element in the social construction of gender, childhood and adulthood as well as in the management of generational change among Sahrawi refugees. In particular, it has been argued that differences in patterns of food consumption have been a powerful means in the hands of individuals and groups to state, challenge and change their generational status within the community. Also, given the important symbolic connotations that food can assume at the community level, youth's distinctive food preferences have acquired an unexpected political significance. Within the current political economy of food and trade in the Sahrawi camps, such preferences can become a vivid expression of the new interests and demands of the camp youth, some of which can hardly be accommodated within ongoing economic and political processes and constitute an important challenge for the whole Sahrawi community.

Besides these considerations, it is clear that relationships between food, age and gender cannot be reduced to the aspects that have been examined here. Food certainly plays a significant role in other important aspects of refugees' lives which remain beyond the scope of this research. In particular, additional research is needed to explore the relationship between food and socio-economic status among Sahrawi refugees.[11] Also, further studies would benefit from a closer focus on the demands and expectations of the Sahrawi youth and how they are affecting social and political processes among the camp population – a topic that emerged as a major concern among many young and adult refugees in the course of the present research.

Appendix 3.1: Examples of Weekly Intake, Daily Diet Diary (Period: 30 January–4 February 2004)

Chart 1. A male child, 11, living in the 27th February Women's School Camp with his family (father, mother and one brother)

The informant has lived in the Sahrawi refugee camps since his birth, in the settlement called 27th February Women's School Camp. Both his father and mother are unemployed. He went to Spain twice with the *Vacaciones en Paz* programme and is quite fluent in Spanish. His favourite foods are tuna, fresh milk, chocolate, pizza and coke; he dislikes sugar, powdered milk and chick peas, which are all part of the food-aid basket, unlike his favourite foods.

Time		Food / Drink	Amount
Day 1	8.36 am	Tea; Bread	2 glasses; 1 piece of bread
	12.53 pm	Lentils	1 tin
	6.11 pm	Tea	1 glass
	9.33 pm	Spaghetti with tomato sauce and meat	1 dish (shared with one person)
Day 2	8.36 am	Tea	3 glasses
	11.10 am	Couscous; Milk	½ dish; some milk from bowl
	5.00 pm	Tea	2 glasses
	10.06 pm	Spaghetti with tomato sauce	1 dish
Day 3	7.57 am	Tea; Bread	1 glass of tea; 1 piece of bread
	12.23 pm	Lentils	1 dish (shared with one person)
	9.46 pm	Rice with vegetables	1 dish (shared with two people)
Day 4	8.30 am	Tea; Bread; Water	2 glasses; 1 piece of bread
	10.10 am	Bread	1 piece
	12.21 pm	Rice with meat; Water	1 dish (shared with one person)
	9.40 pm	Couscous; Meat; Onions; Tomatoes	1 dish (shared with two people)
Day 5	8.26 am	Salad with vegetables	1 dish (shared with one person)
	12.30 pm	Rice with vegetables; Milk	½ dish; some milk from bowl
	5.20 pm	Tea	2 glasses
	9.20 pm	Bread; Meat	2 pieces of bread with some roasted meat
Day 6	8.30 am	Bread; Milk; Water	1 piece of bread; 1 tin condensed milk with water
	12.48 pm	Bread; Meat	2 pieces of bread with some roasted meat
	9.45 pm	Bread; Meat; Banana; Coke	1 pieces of bread with some roasted meat; 1 banana; 1 can of Coke

Chart 2: A female adolescent, 14, living in Aaiun camp with her grandmother (father's side) and one sister. She has one more sister and one brother who live with her father and mother in another district of the same camp

The informant lived with her father and mother until she was ten. Her father is a soldier of the Sahrawi Liberation Army. Her mother works in the agricultural garden of Aaiun camp. She went to Spain three times with the *Vacaciones en Paz* programme and is fluent in Spanish. Her favourite food is roasted chicken, French fries and omelette while she dislikes fried and boiled eggs, rice and couscous. She explained that she is more comfortable living with her grandmother than with her parents; in this way she can decide more often what to eat.

Time		Food / Drink	Amount
Day 1	10.09 am	Bread; Tea	1 piece of bread; 3 glasses of tea
	2.10 pm	Bread; Water	1 piece of bread; ½ glass of water
	7.27 pm	Bread; Milk	½ piece of bread; 1 glass of milk
	9.40 pm	Bread; Tea; Water	½ piece of bread; 3 glasses of tea; 1 glass of water
	11.00 pm	Bread; Potatoes; Water	1 piece of bread; 1 dish of potatoes; some water
Day 2	9.10 am	Bread; Butter; Tea; Milk	1 piece of bread; 3 spoons of butter; 3 glasses of tea; 2 glasses of milk
	3.12 pm	Rice with vegetables; Tea; Milk	1 dish of rice; 3 glasses of tea; ½ glass of milk
	8.40 pm	Bread	1 piece of bread
	10.00 pm	Bread; Potatoes	1 piece of bread; 1 dish of potatoes
Day 3	9.14 am	Tea	3 glasses of tea
	11.20 am	Meat	Some meat
	12.53 pm	Meat; Bread	1 dish of meat; 1 piece of bread
	1.00 pm	Meat; Potatoes; Coke	1 dish of meat; ½ dish of potatoes; 1 can of Coke
	3.53 pm	Sweets; Biscuits	2 sweets; 3 biscuits
	6.00 pm	Bread; Butter	1 piece of bread; 2 spoons of butter
	10.00 pm	Rice; Meat; Water	1 dish of rice with some meat; 1 glass of water

Time		Food / Drink	Amount
Day 5	8.00 am	Bread with butter; Milk	1 piece of bread with butter; 1 glass of milk
	11.00 am	Yogurt	1 glass
	2.00 pm	Rice with sauce; Soft drink Meat; Couscous; Coke	1 dish of rice with meat sauce; 1 glass of soft drink
	9.00 pm		1 dish of couscous with meat; 1 glass of soft drink
Day 6	8.00 am	Tea; Bread	1 piece of bread; 1 glass of tea
	11.00 am	Sweets; Chewing-gum; Twins (snack)	5 sweets; 4 chewing-gums; 2 twins fingers
	2.00 pm	Meat; Couscous	1 dish of couscous with meat
	9.00 pm	Bread; Lentils	1 piece of bread, 1 dish of lentils
Day 4	8.00 am	Bread with honey; Milk	2 pieces of bread; 2 spoons of honey; 1 glass of milk
	1.00 pm	Roasted meat; Bread; Soft drink	1 dish of meat; 1 piece of bread; 1 glass of soft drink
	9.00 pm	Meat; Rice; Soft drink	1 dish of rice with meat; 1 glass of soft drink

Chart 3: A male adolescent, 15, living in the Auserd refugee camp with his parents and three sisters

Apart from the two sisters with whom he lives, the respondent has one more sister and two brothers from his father's side who live with their respective mothers. His father is employed at the camp telephone post. His mother is an active member of the women's group of the camp. He speaks Spanish with difficulty. He spent one summer in Spain under the *Vacaciones en Paz* programme. His favourite food is bread (the type made in the camps), lentils, *mjefisa* (dish made with bread and meat stock), goat milk and fruit. He enjoys traditional food (such as dates, camel milk and meat): it is prepared in his household whenever there is enough money to buy it.

Time		Food / Drink	Amount
Day 1	9.12 am	Bread; Milk	1 piece of bread; milk from bowl
	3.00 pm	Potatoes; Bread	1 dish of fried potatoes; ½ piece of bread
	9.30 pm	Potatoes; Bread	1 dish of fried potatoes; 1 piece of bread
Day 2	7.00 am	Dates; Meat	Some dates; 1 dish of meat
	7.00 pm	Rice with lentils	1 dish shared with two people
	9.30 pm	Bread; Lentils	2 pieces of bread; 1 dish of lentils
Day 3	8.30 am	Milk; Dates	1 glass of milk; some dates
	2.00 pm	Beans; Bread	1 dish of beans; 2 pieces of bread
	11.00 pm	Rice; Pasta	1 dish of rice with vegetable (small quantity eaten); 1 dish of pasta with sauce (small quantity eaten)
Day 4	9.00 am	Biscuits; Milk and coffee	5 biscuits; 1 glass of milk with coffee
	1.00 pm	Rice with meat; Coke	1 dish of rice with meat (shared); 1 can of Coke
	6.00 pm	Sandwich with chocolate cream; Fanta (soft drink)	1 sandwich; 1 can of Fanta
	9.30 pm	Bread; Lentils; Water	1 piece of bread; 1 dish of lentils; 1 glass of water
Day 5	9.00 am	Biscuits; Milk and coffee	2 biscuits; 1 glass of milk with coffee
	1.00 pm	Pasta; Coke	1 dish of pasta; 1 can of Coke
	6.00 pm	Sandwich with chocolate cream; Fanta (soft drink)	1 sandwich; 1 glass of Fanta
	9.30 pm	Lentils; Water	1 dish of lentils; some water
Day 6	9.00 am	Biscuits; Milk and coffee	3 biscuits; 1 glass of milk with coffee
	1.00 pm	Rice; Meat; Coke	1 dish or rice with meat; 1 glass of Coke
	6.00 pm	Sandwich with chocolate cream	1 + ½ sandwich
	9.30 pm	Bread; Lentils; Water	½ piece of bread; 1 dish of lentils; some water

Appendix 3.2: Food Glossary

Al 'iish: dshisha with sweetened milk or fat (sometimes oil or butter).

Al-makla: toasted barley flour.

Al-rkid: water, milk, oil and barley

Al-zammit: *al-makla* with water, sugar and camel fat; similar to *bulaghman* but lighter and fast to prepare, it is regarded as effective against digestive disorders, particularly excessive acidity.

Attay: green tea, prepared with sugar and *nana* (mint); consumed several times during the day, it is always available in every Sahrawi household and at virtually every private gathering.

Bulaghman: *al-makla* with water, sugar, salt and camel fat (or oil); quick to prepare, it is regarded as nutritious and healthy and particularly suitable for the traveller.

Couscous al-ghobba: couscous without meat, with milk and sugar.

Dhan: melted butter.

Dshisha: toasted barley.

Echwa: meat of a sacrificed animal cooked in the stomach of the animal.

El couscous: couscous with meat.

Ftur laayalat: roasted liver and meat of camel; eaten for breakfast.

Galiat: roasted grains of wheat served with fat or butter.

Labsis: barley flour, *dhan*, water and sugar; it is regarded as a healthy breakfast.

Laftir: bread made with barley flour and water; often eaten in pieces with meat stock in a combination regarded as a healthy dish.

Lajli'i: dish based on pounded dry meat; regarded as highly nutritious and healthy, with curative properties and suitable for both adults and youth.

Lamriss: a drink prepared with toasted barley flour and water.

Maru-o-lham: rice and meat; a common dish among Sahrawi.

Maru: rice.

Mrifissa: bread, *dhan* and camel meat; regarded as a simple but nutritious dish.

Tbija: meat (camel or other) cooked with only oil and salt; meat from the back of the animal is usually served to men while meat from the sides and ribs is served to women.

Tichtar: dry meat (mostly camel).

Tidguit: soup of dry meat (mostly camel); regarded as one of the best dishes to offer to guests and also used when trying to obtain favours or support from older or influential people.

Tmar: steamed dates served with fat or butter; regarded as a good dish to welcome guests.

Notes

1. The following analysis stems from information and observations collected mostly during a three-week fieldwork period (24 January to 14 February 2004) spent in the Sahrawi refugee camps in south-western Algeria. Preliminary findings were discussed during a meeting of the SARC Project team held in Damascus, Syria, in March 2004. A number of suggestions and observations that were raised on that occasion were taken into consideration during the final stages of the analysis and in the preparation of this chapter. Furthermore, during the research process important insights were developed through discussions on methodological and analytical issues with Dawn Chatty, Jeya Henry, Alessandro Monsutti and Randa Farah, whom I would like to thank for their contributions. I am also grateful to Gina Crivello both for her critical suggestions and for her administrative support. I thank Fatimatu Mohammed Salem and Bachir Radhi Saghaiar for their collaboration and kind hospitality during my fieldwork in the Sahrawi refugee camps. Last but not least, I would like to express my gratitude to the Minister of Education of the Sahrawi Arab Democratic Republic, Bachir Mustafa Sayed, for logistical and administrative support, including the authorization to carry out surveys and interviews in two of the schools in the Sahrawi refugee camps. I remain, of course, solely responsible for the views expressed in this chapter.
2. Although not focused on food, the formalist/substantivist debate helped explore economic and cultural aspects of consumption. Among the vast literature related to this debate are Polanyi *et al.* (1957), Godelier (1972), Cook (1973).
3. This brief history of the conflict between Morocco and the Polisario Front is based on Hodges (1983), Pazzanita and Hodges (1994), Barbier (1982).
4. At the time of writing, the 9th June school is no longer operative, having been severely damaged during heavy floods in 2006.
5. On the role of food in shared memories among camp inmates, see Malkki (1995; 1997).
6. For more detail on the 'holidays abroad' programme, see chapter 2 by Crivello and Fiddian.
7. Despite the efforts made by the research team in this direction, it was not possible to meet young refugees who had never taken part in the 'holidays abroad' programme. Although they appear to be a minority in the camps, the absence of their voices in the data represents a limitation that future research should hopefully overcome.
8. When the fieldwork for this study was conducted, school meals were still prepared by 'dubious Moroccan cooks' – as some interviewees put it – who were Polisario's prisoners-of-war. This situation may have changed following the release of a large number of Polisario's prisoners-of-war in 2005.
9. Cf. Caro Baroja (1990), Munilla Gomez (1974).
10. The word 'Sahrawi' first appeared in written testimonies just a few years before 1975, when the post-colonial conflict in Western Sahara began (Cozza 2004).
11. In the apparently uniform social environment of the refugee camps, food appears to have become an important symbol of relative wealth and education. Only well-off refugees can afford to eat meat more than twice a week, while the preparation of varied meals is normally regarded as a symbol of education. However, education and wealth do not necessarily coincide. For instance, eating meat every day may well be

evidence of wealth but it is also regarded as a sign of lack of education: educated people are supposed to know that a varied diet is important for one's health.

References

Appadurai, A. and C.A. Breckenridge (eds). 1986. *The Social Life of Things. Commodities in Cultural Perspective.* Cambridge: Cambridge University Press.

Barbier, M. 1982. *Le Conflit du Sahara Occidental.* Paris: L'Harmattan.

Bourdieu, P. 1984. *Distinction.* London: Routledge and Kegan Paul.

Caro Baroja, J. 1990 [1955]. *Estudios Saharianos.* Madrid: Jucar.

Cook, S. 1973. 'Economic Anthropology: Problems in theory, method, and analysis', in J. Honlgnlan (ed.), *Handbook of Social and Cultural Anthropology.* Chicago: Rand McNally, pp. 795–860.

Cozza, N. 2004. 'Singing like Wood-birds: Refugee Camps and Exile in the Construction of the Sahrawi Nation'. Thesis submitted for the degree of Doctor of Philosophy in Development Studies. Oxford: University of Oxford.

De Waal, A. 1997. *Famine Crimes: Politics and the Disaster Relief Industry in Africa.* London: James Currey.

Douglas, M. 1975. *Implicit Meanings.* London: Routledge and Kegan Paul.

——— and B. Isherwood. 1996. *The World of Goods. Towards an Anthropology of Consumption.* London and New York: Routledge.

Evans-Pritchard, E.E. 1969. *The Nuer.* New York: Oxford University Press.

Garcia, A. 2001. *Historias del Sahara. El Mejor y El Peor de los Mundos.* Madrid: Catarata.

Godelier, M. 1972 [1965]. 'The Object and Method of Economic Anthropology', in M. Godelier (ed.), *Rationality and Irrationality in Economics.* New York: Monthly Review Press, pp. 243–319.

Goodman, A., D. Dufour and G. Pelto. 2000. *Nutritional Anthropology: Biocultural Perspectives on Food and Nutrition.* Mayfield: McGraw-Hill.

Hodges, T. 1983. *Western Sahara. The Roots of a Desert War.* Westport: Lawrence Hill.

Keen, D. 1992. *Refugees: Rationing the Right to Life – The Crisis in Emergency Relief.* London: Zed Books.

Lévi-Strauss, C. 1966. *The Savage Man.* Chicago: Chicago University Press.

Malkki, L.H. 1995. *Purity and Exile: Violence, Memory and National Cosmology among Hutu Refugees in Tanzania.* Chicago: University of Chicago Press.

——— 1997. 'Speechless Emissaries: Refugees, humanitarianism and dehistoricization', in K. Olwig and K. Hastrup (eds), *Siting Cultures. The Shifting Anthropological Object.* London and New York: Routledge, pp. 223–244.

Munilla Gomez, E. 1974. *Estudio General del Sahara.* Madrid: Instituto de Estudios Africanos.

Pazzanita, A.G. and T. Hodges. 1994. *Historical Dictionary of Western Sahara.* Metuchen, NJ and London: The Scarecrow Press.

Polanyi, K., A. Conrad and H. Pearson (eds). 1957. *Trade and Market in the Early Empires.* New York: Free Press.

Rguibi, M. and R. Belahsen. 2006. 'Fattening Practices among Moroccan Sahrawi Women', *Eastern Mediterranean Health Journal* 12(5): 619–24.

AFGHAN SECTION

4
Refusing the Margins: Afghan Refugee Youth in Iran

Homa Hoodfar

After security, educating the younger generation is the single most important concern of Afghan refugees in Iran (Hoodfar 2004).[1] While such concerns are not unusual for those, such as Palestinians, who live with insecurity and in a conflict situation, this is a remarkable development considering that the initial large-scale wave of Afghans migrating to Iran in the 1980s was predominantly illiterate, and many of the refugees cited the introduction by the Soviet backed of compulsory schooling (together with the new marriage law), as the major reason for becoming refugees (Hoodfar 2004; Dupree 1984). At that time, schooling, particularly for girls, was often considered undesirable, and many Afghan families chose exile rather than face the shame of sending their daughters to school (where they might interact with boys or engage in immoral activities such as writing love letters). Two decades later, however, schooling and formal education emerged as such an important priority for Afghans in Iran that the Iranian government, weary of having to accommodate millions of refugees, attempted to force Afghan refugees to repatriate by making it virtually impossible for the majority of Afghan refugee children in Iran to attend school.[2]

The Afghan community was sufficiently convinced of the importance of formal education and schooling that in response to these restrictions, and despite much legal harassment by the Iranian authorities, they developed the informal, self-directed and self-funded Afghan schools that became a common feature of many Afghan communities in Iran. The policy of banning Afghan children from Iranian schools, as I will argue below, has had far-reaching and unintended social, economic and political consequences, far beyond what could have been foreseen by either Afghan community leaders, the Afghan and Iranian scholarly community or the Iranian authorities. Moreover, the findings have important implications in terms of policy design for international organizations such as UNHCR whose mandate is to protect and oversee the well-being of millions of refugees, the majority of whom are children.

Although education of the refugee youth and children has sometimes been mentioned as an important element, there is little indication of a well argued education policy, particularly for long-term refugees.[3] What is largely missing from the refugee studies is a discussion of the role and the kind of education that should be provided for these long-term refugee children. Such a policy would have to consider whether the host country intends to integrate the refugees in their midst or whether the refugee community is expected to be repatriated. Clearly formal education has to take its direction from this larger and longer-term perspective. Formal education can be a tool for the integration of the youth into the host society or it can be a means of preparing them for repatriation by immersing them in the history and culture of their community and country of origin and by developing a sense of identity and belonging. Our findings in this research provide a particularly relevant case study of long-term refugees facing shifting educational policies: preparing the youth for either integration or a planned exclusion from Iranian society.

This chapter analyses the political and social conditions that led to the emergence of formal education/schooling as a priority over the last decade, and explores how the attendance of Afghan students in Iranian schools led to their developing a sense of 'Muslimness' as their primary identity, legitimizing their entitlement to education, security and equity. The easy access of Afghan youths to Iranian schools during the 1980s did not particularly support the development of Afghan identity or solidarity among Afghan youth refugees. However, this changed when the Iranian government banned undocumented Afghan children (who comprise the majority of Afghan children in Iran) from Iranian schools in an attempt to encourage the repatriation of Afghan refugees. Exclusionary practices also targeted documented refugee children who continued to attend Iranian public schools. These policies and practices led to the emergence of informal/clandestine Afghan schools established by parents and community leaders, mostly women, who refused to accept the denial of education to their children (Hoodfar 2007). These exclusively Afghan spaces have played an important and unexpected role in the creation of a previously non-existent supra-Afghan youth identity which largely overrides ethnicity. This is particularly significant considering that one of the consequences of the deliberately uneven and discriminatory economic and social policies of consecutive Afghan governments since Abdur Rahman (1880–1901) has been strong distrust, and at times outright hostility, between different Afghan ethnic groups, which has prevented the development of an Afghan identity corresponding with Afghan citizenship (Mousavi 1998; Rubin 1994). Thus, a second focus of this chapter is the importance of the long-term educational policies of the host (and international community) in preparing refugee youth, whether it is the integration of refugee youth into the host society or their repatriation once condition were appropriate in their home society.

The informal Afghan schools have provided youth with the opportunity to collectively re-assess their culture and history, their ethnicity and citizenship, their refugee experiences, their relationship to their Iranian host society and the world at large, the meaning of 'Muslimness', and finally the various ways of being Muslim they have encountered as a result of their experiences in Iran, which do not always correspond with the norms of their various ethnic Afghan cultures or their lives. Most Afghan refugees before coming to Iran thought of themselves as Hazara, Tajic, Pashtune, etc. Few identified themselves as Afghan and had little knowledge of other ethnic groups. However once in Iran they were referred to as Afghan regardless of their ethnicity. This helped to develop a sense of collective Afghan supra-identity and a corresponding Afghan nationalism which was rare in the identity matrix of fragmented and diverse Afghan society. This new sense of collective identity can have far-reaching, positive consequences for Afghanistan's social and political development if policymakers and Afghan leaders can capitalize on it. These developments also have important implications for policies concerning the general and educational needs of long-term child and youth refugees, at the national (host and country of origin) level as well as for humanitarian organizations and international agencies.

The Iranian Context and Social Location of Afghan Refugees

The movement of large numbers of Afghan refugees to Iran in the 1980s had less to do with conventional politics than with the concern of ordinary people in villages and small towns that their new Soviet-backed government was intent on interfering with their customs and 'causing them to lose Islam'. Many were worried about the government's introduction of a marriage law (Decree 7) which legislated the consent of the bride as essential and designated the minimum age of girls for marriage as sixteen (Moghadam 1993; Dupree1984; Tapper 1991). Many Afghans saw this as proof of communist Russia's desire to destroy Islam and Muslims. Our research, and interviews with the older generations (both in Iran and Pakistan from 1998 to 2001), clearly indicate that most Afghans believed compulsory education and the new marriage law provoked the popular uprisings that followed these policies, as both were perceived as threats to girls' honour; public reaction to compulsory schooling even led to the killing of some teachers (Dupree 1984; Moghadam 1993). In interviews I conducted in recent years, older Afghans refugee said they believed the Soviet Union tried to undermine Afghanistan's moral fabric after the occupation; they pointed out that for example in poor villages, free school uniforms were easily available and youths had access to any school supplies they wanted, provided they went to school. The villagers felt that the Soviet Union was trying to buy their compliance, and undermine Islam through compulsory education and the marriage and divorce reforms. Many interviewees said that at the time they did not realize that universal education was entirely consistent with Islam – something they came to recognize after living in Iran. Others pointed out that even those who realized that such changes were in accordance with Islam questioned the government's intentions, as the new schools were not segregated like those in other Muslim countries such as Iran.

The popular understanding of formal/modern schooling/education as 'un-Islamic' was used by leaders of anti-government groups to mobilize the public into armed resistance against the Soviet-backed government in Kabul. In actual fact, the real concern of opposition leaders was the proposed land reforms put forth by the government, but rallying the public against land reform would have been difficult if not impossible, since such reform was obviously beneficial for the majority of Afghans. Compulsory education and the new marriage law were used as rallying points instead, to destabilize society and bring younger men into anti-Soviet guerrilla warfare that was called *Jihad* (holy war), despite their frequently unholy tactics.

But, more than twenty years later, when we conducted the last phase of our fieldwork research with Afghan youth in Iran from September to December 2003, education was viewed as an Islamic obligation by the Afghan population in Iran and refugees felt increasingly compelled to show that they were good Muslims by finding ways to send even working children to school. A minority of households among our interviewees had earlier returned to Afghanistan upon the withdrawal of Soviet forces in the early 1990s, but returned to Iran after the massacres at Mazar Sharif established Taliban control over most of Afghanistan (Rashid 2001: chapter 3). Our interviewees explained that although they had stayed in Afghanistan through civil war and massacres, the closure of schools and the extreme limitation of education for girls was a major factor in their decision to migrate to Iran in the second half of the 1990s. The extent to which lack of education for girls in Afghanistan was truly a force in their moving to exile is hard to assess, as such decisions involve a complex matrix of interrelated variables and priorities for different households. What is significant is that presenting lack of access to education for their daughters as a major cause indicates a drastic ideological change. It is also possible that since our interviews followed on the heels of the Iranian government's crackdown on schooling for Afghan children, the education issue had gained increasing prominence even in retrospect.

What lies behind this drastic change in Afghan attitudes towards education is in itself an area deserving considerable investigation. While I will present some of the factors that I believe contributed to the reversal of perceptions of (especially girls') schooling, it is outside the scope of the present work to analyse the complexity of the Afghan diaspora experience over the twenty-year period in question. I believe that there are many, subtle forces at work in Afghan refugees' decisions: it is not necessarily true that all the Afghan families who came to Iran would have sent their children to school had the Taliban not closed the schools. Their decision to move was to a large extent an ideological one similar to the resistance to compulsory education, or decree 7 on marriage law in the 1970s; not everyone would have married off their daughters without their consent, but everyone was against a law which required a bride's consent. Perhaps it was the fact that as parents they were being denied the power and right to decide what constituted a proper Muslim upbringing for their children that drove Afghans to migrate to Iran from Afghanistan, whether because of the imposed compulsory education of the 1970s or because of the Taliban's closure of all girl's schools (and many boy's schools) in the 1980s.

Ironically, given their reasons for exile, by the mid-1990s the Iranian authorities made it increasingly difficult for Afghan children to attend school, creating a dilemma for Afghan parents who were committed to their children's education. The situation in Iran has contrasted sharply with the Afghan refugee experience in Pakistan, where international organizations have helped support the hosting of Afghan refugees, including the provision of education. This has allowed many Afghan families in Pakistan to send their children to Afghan schools, which have operated much like the informal Afghan schools in Iran. As there is no financial support from the Pakistani government, international organizations often support these schools, though when it is possible parents also pay a small tuition fee. At least some of these schools do have legal status, or at least they are not illegal. The schools operate in both Dari and Pashtu, which means that the Afghan students are prepared to eventually continue their schooling in Afghanistan. Furthermore, the Afghan community was able to establish an Afghan university in Peshawar, funded in part by Norway, in which many displaced Afghan university professors were teaching. However, in an attempt to suppress anti-Taliban forces, Pakistan closed this university in the late 1990s and finally the Afghan University of Peshawar was relocated to Afghanistan.

The Research

The study presented here is part of a larger project on 'Children And Adolescents In Sahrawi And Afghani Refugee Households: Living With The Effects of Prolonged Armed Conflict And Forced Migration', organized by the Oxford University Refugee Study Centre.[4] The bulk of the fieldwork was carried out in suburbs of Tehran and Mashhad, cities with the largest concentration of Afghan refugees where we helped set up two Afghan youth clubs. The youth club in Tehran was located in Sarollah School, which also functioned as our base for the research project. In Mashhad the difficult political situation and the authorities' rigid control of Afghan schools, together with their intention to shut down all thirty-five of them, meant the club there could not be based in a school, as originally intended. Instead we operated out of a rented space in the neighbourhood of Golshar, which probably has the largest concentration of Afghans in Iran outside the few refugee camps (for more detail see the introduction in this volume). The data was collected over a period of more than a year; the core of the fieldwork involved organizing composition and photograph competitions, several formal and informal discussion groups, individual in-depth interviews with youths, and interviews with parents. We interviewed seventeen youths and their households in Mashhad, and thirty-four in Tehran. The sample was divided between boys and girls, and into various age categories.

Table 4.1: Location of Household vs. Gender.

Gender	# of boys	# of girls	Total interviews
Tehran	13	21	34
Mashhad	8	9	17
Total	**21**	**30**	**51**

Table 4.2: Location of Household vs. Age.

Age	8–11 years	12–15 years	16–18 years	Total interviews
Tehran	1	16	17	34
Mashhad	4	7	6	17
Total	**5**	**23**	**23**	**51**

We were also careful to include youths with diverse backgrounds and experiences, in terms of country of birth, age of migration if migrated, and whether parents were born in exile (table 4.3). We assumed these factors would be relevant to the subjects' feelings about their Afghan identity. We also paid attention to the question of ethnicity, as in Afghanistan this tends to be a much more significant social and political force in an individual's or family's circumstances and experience than nationality or citizenship.

Table 4.3: Refugee Generation.

Pattern	Mashhad	Tehran	Total
G1 Born in Afghanistan	2	13	15
G1.5 Migrated before age 5	0	7	7
G2 Born in exile	15	13	28
G3 Parents born in exile	0	1	1
Total	**17**	**34**	**51**

Table 4.4: Ethno-religious Identity*.

*Please note that although we had several Uzbeks in our larger sample, none were included in the in-depth interviews that provided the data presented in these tables.

Ethnicity	Sunni	Shi'a	No response	Total	%
Hazara		15	4	19	37%
Pushtun	2			2	4%
Seyyed		12	4	16	31%
Tajik	2	3	1	6	12%
Other*	2	5	1	8	16%
Total	**6**	**35**	**10**	**51**	**100%**
%	12%	68%	20%	100%	

Table 4.5: Youths' Educational History.

Experience	Total
Iranian school in Iran only	17
Afghan school in Iran only	6
Both Iranian and Afghan schools in Iran	20
Literacy classes only	1
School in Afghanistan, now no schooling	1
School in Afghanistan, now Afghan school in Iran	1
School in Afghanistan, Iranian school, Afghan school in Iran	4
None	1
Total	**51**

Changing Heart: Afghan Refugees Revaluating the Value of Schooling

Unlike in Pakistan, where the majority of Afghan refugees were settled in camps composed of large kin groups, to all intents organized according to ethnicity, Afghan refugees to Iran dispersed widely in search of a livelihood and settled where they could find jobs; this was all the more important as Iran received negligible international support for the refugees, and given the economic conditions and the ongoing Iran-Iraq war (1980–1988) could not support its more than two million refugees.[5] The children of the first wave of Afghan refugees attended public school in Iran during the 1980s. No restrictions were placed on their access to educational institutions regardless of whether or not they had a refugee card. While middle-class and urban Afghans took advantage of this opportunity immediately, the rest, who formed the majority, were slower to send their children to school, but within a few years, urban refugees at least did so in large numbers.

Several older refugees explained that when they first arrived in Iran, they believed schooling would be a corrupting influence on their children, undermining their development as good Muslims and dutiful sons and daughters. However, the new refugees, especially those in Mashhad, were astonished to encounter the very opposite perspective on the part of the Iranian government, which for many represented the ideal Muslim state. Large billboards in the streets declared that all parents had a responsibility as pious Muslims to educate their daughters, and flocks of Iranian girls of all ages could be seen on their way to school in Muslim uniform, fully covering their bodies and hair.

Figure 4.1: A special ceremony in a girls' school in Iran.

This was shocking for many of the older Afghan women who had been raised to believe that schooling was a terrible thing for a woman. One said that as a child she had longed to learn to read, but believed that a female reading was as sinful as looking with desire at a male neighbour. Such attitudes initially prevailed among older refugee women (in their fifties and sixties), but over time in Iran they gradually came to embrace the idea of Islamic education, especially at the primary level where the basic skills for reading the Quran were taught.

Almost all local mosques in urban Iran offered literacy and Quranic classes for adults, and many refugees, particularly Shi'a women (mostly Hazaras), gravitated to them. In these classes, as they listened to lectures and met ethnically and culturally diverse Muslim women from different parts of Iran, Afghan women began to expand their religious perspectives. The ideologues of the Islamic Republic, then just a few years into its history, viewed the expansion of education as a major vehicle for the construction of their envisaged Islamic society. Accordingly they emphasized reforming the educational system to reflect the regime's ideology, which was to stress Islam and 'Muslimness', as a common bond between all Iranians and the wider Muslim community (*ummeh*). The Iranian government thus allocated a generous budget (an average of over seventeen per cent of government expenditures during the 1980s) to facilitate educational expansion (Hoodfar 1998). The programme was very successful and literacy grew at a much faster rate during the Iran-Iraq war than it had done under the liberal regime of the Shah (1941–1979), before the Islamic Republic. Moreover, the gap between male and female literacy narrowed considerably, an attainment few expected under the Islamic Republic (Mehran 1991, 2002).[6]

The regime's adult literacy campaign particularly attracted women, in part because adult literacy classes were very flexible in terms of scheduling and also because many were located in the local mosques so women could attend without social stigma. The religious leaders used radio and television, and the mosque pulpit, all of which remain under their monopoly, to promote education. Popular posters carried such sayings as the Prophet's 'a Muslim should go as far as China [the most distant civilization known to Muslims in the Prophet's time] in search of education', and Ayatollah Khomeini's pronouncement that 'a good Muslim is an educated Muslim'. There was great emphasis on Quranic literacy for all. All this presented a new religious horizon for many less educated and more conservative Afghan refugees, particularly the Hazaras, historically the most disadvantaged group in Afghanistan, who as racially distinct Shi'a Muslims were subject to severe social and economic discrimination.

What made acceptance of girls' education not only palatable but even desirable as a buttress of Islam was the idea that girls would grow up to be the mothers of the next generation of Muslims. The notion that only educated and *momen* (bound by Muslim morality) women could engender strong Muslim nations was heavily promoted by the Islamic Republic and was internalized by many Afghans living in Iran. 'I am too old to fight against the Taliban, but I can work hard to educate my granddaughters so that they can help to make a just Muslim society in Afghanistan or in Iran or wherever fate and God will take them', said a grandfather who supported his deceased son's family of four females.

It is important to remember here that a significant strategy for the mobilization of the general public in Afghanistan against the Afghan government in the late 1970s and in the 1980s was criticism of compulsory education of girls. However, Iran's free public education system, with its Islamic ethics and curriculum, gendered-segregated schools (at least in the cities and towns) and the Islamic dress code for girls, made the transition to accepting education for their children relatively unproblematic, at least for households which had the means. All these factors created a climate that also encouraged many older women, and to a lesser extent men, to join literacy classes (Hoodfar 2004).

Iran's emphasis on Islam and Islamic morality encouraged the Afghan community to examine and revise its views on the role of education. The shared language of Farsi/Dari helped this process. Many Afghans, particularly those who had found jobs in Iran, increasingly desired (and at times felt social pressure) to send their children to school: either public schools, or at least literacy or Quranic classes. Before long educational attainment became a major desire for Afghans in Iran, particularly for those living in urban areas.

There were other reasons why education and various aspects of the Islamic Republic's ideologies were particularly appealing to Afghan refugees. The Iranian curriculum's emphasis on 'Muslimness' as a major source of unity, particularly in the 1980s, had a strong influence on the emerging social organization of the refugee community. This was particularly evident in the frequent quoting by informants of all ages of the statement that that 'Islam has no borders'. Religious unity had been generally under-emphasized in Afghan custom; in practice Afghans historically have given priority to their ethnic and tribal affiliations in terms of cooperative ties. Many Afghan political leaders, even at the early stage of the creation of Afghanistan as an independent state, saw the question of ethnic rivalry and the suppression of minorities as a major reason for Afghanistan's political instability (Mousavi 1998; Rubin 1995). Political developments in the 1990s (the civil war and the ascendance of the Taliban to power) only increased ethnic divisions. However, in Iran the Afghan community's claim to membership in the *ummeh* (community of Muslims, undifferentiated by race, gender, language and ethnicity) has been the main justification for, and legitimization of, their demands for refugee status and protection. Most of the benefits reaching Afghans (particularly during the so-called 'Khomeini Era' of the 1980s), such as ration cards, jobs, short-term small loans and so on, were distributed from the local mosques and religious centres. It was therefore important and in the best interest of Afghan refugees to emphasize their 'Muslimness' and their accord with the Islamic Republic's views on education and dress code. This complex context suggests some of the reasons for the change in Afghan refugee views on education.

One significant aspect of this change is that it is not only the elite or younger generations who have come to view education as important, but Afghans from all walks of life. While there may remain some differences in desired levels of education or what is considered suitable learning for men versus women, Hoodfar's research (1998–2002) in Afghan communities in Tehran, Mashhad and Zabul found agreement across class, ethnicity and gender that education was food for the mind and spirit, and the tool of choice in the struggle for justice.[7] The view of one older, illiterate Hazara Afghan female interviewee captured the essence of this idea:

> Now I think every Muslim who can walk and talk has to struggle for the good of all Muslims. They have to take a *sangar* [literally rampart: a front, a position, an entrenchment] to fight against injustices imposed on Muslims. The *sangar* of youth are their schools and education. Those who close schools and thus deny Muslim youth their ability to struggle are the enemy of Muslims. That is what the Taliban were.

Such powerful imagery is telling. On the one hand it indicates that the Afghan population is very much concerned with issues of war and justice, and on the other hand it criticizes the Taliban, and more recently the Iranian government's denial of schooling to Afghan children, which, as I mentioned and will elaborate on shortly, became a government tactic for 'encouraging' the 'forced-voluntary' repatriation of Afghans from 1996 onwards.

The Iranian School Curriculum and Afghan Students

Afghan youth attending Iranian schools during the 1980s followed the Iranian curriculum; given their similar histories, culture, and in most cases language, this was not viewed as problematic either by Afghan community leaders and intellectuals or by Iranian authorities. It was assumed that Afghan children would be schooled in Iran until the conflict in Afghanistan ended and would then return home. The fact that primary education is an important political tool with which states shape their citizens and inculcate its world-view did not concern the Afghan community, particularly since during this era the great emphasis was on 'Muslimness' rather than on national and cultural history. This aspect of education was particularly appealing to the Afghan community, since it not only emphasized what they have in common with their Iranian hosts but also legitimized their claim for protection and hospitality based on their membership in the community of Muslims, *ummeh*.

The Iranian curriculum included substantive material and teachings on Islam and religion, though it did not address anything pertaining to Afghanistan. The curriculum was designed to create devout Muslim citizens for the Iranian state. There were no lessons on the history or geography of Afghanistan, nor were there community educational institutions that took it upon themselves to fill this gap. Perhaps the most significant shortcoming, in light of Afghanistan's official bilingual status, was the lack of Pashtu language teaching. Moreover, the urban Afghan refugees, especially outside Mashhad, lived in small colonies that were very fluid and unstable. This meant that the mechanisms of learning informally through the community did not work well. Thus the younger generations gained minimal knowledge of their homeland, especially since many of their parents had known little beyond their immediate villages or cities. Moreover, most refugee parents were concerned that their children 'fit in' and not feel like outsiders, and thus tended to focus more on their children's Muslim identity, as opposed to instilling a sense of Afghan identity.

The little exposure that Afghan youth in Iran did have to Afghanistan came primarily through Iranian media, and was usually concerned with war and destruction. These negative images of Afghanistan, along with the general devaluation of Afghan identity in Iranian society, engendered a tendency among Afghan refugees in Iran to focus on their Muslim, as opposed to Afghan, identity. In Iranian schools many Afghan youths learned Iranian cultural chauvinism at the expense of their own nationalism. Some of the younger interviewees told us their understanding of Afghanistan evolved through fights and arguments with their Iranian schoolmates, who told them Afghans were backward and uncivilized, lacking great poets or intellectuals, and capable only of war and construction work.[8] After one group interview in 2001, participants told us if we wished to support Afghan youth we should produce a brief 'Afghan pride booklet' to provide a positive picture of Afghan history, Afghan intellectual life and Afghan contributions to human civilization. 'Nothing else is as important as this', another youth added, 'It is painful (*dardnak*) when we can not say anything in response to our Iranian adversaries, who constantly put us down by repeating that Afghans have nothing.' It appears that the best Afghan students in Iranian schools were most victimized in this way, or, as one fourteen year-old told us, 'psychologically tortured'.[9]

Despite this, interviews with community leaders and an examination of

Afghan community publications in Iran produced by political and religious organizations did not indicate any concern, prior to the mid-1990s, about the lack of 'national pride' among youth, or the absence of curricula on Afghan culture and history. In fact, there was an emphasis on the languages and histories shared between the refugees and their host community, for at that stage, the Afghan refugee communities still saw their stay in Iran as temporary (though this was soon to end), and were not too worried about the long-term consequences of Afghan youth immersion in Iranian culture and education. Yet others felt that could be an asset.

Shifting Policies: The Adoption of Exclusionary Measures

This changed in the mid-1990s (Rajaee 2000), almost fifteen years after the Iranian revolution, as the Iranian state stopped emphasizing its ideology of Muslim unity. Like many modern states the government was more concerned with responding to the needs of its citizens – who had the power to elect or dismiss them – than with ideological rhetoric. The end of the eight-year Iran-Iraq war meant that more people were in search of jobs. The population explosion resulting from the pro-natalist policies of the 1980s meant that Iranians needed more schools and other social services, the delivery of which was beyond the limited resources of the government (Hoodfar 1994, 1995). As is the general rule, government cutbacks first targeted those with the least power and influence – in this case the non-citizen and refugee populations. Furthermore, shortages were blamed on the refugee population, given that Iran had been hosting one of the largest refugee communities in the world for a decade with very little international support. The Iranian government began shifting its refugee policies in an effort to move the refugee population out of the country, claiming that coping with millions of refugees was simply no longer within the means of the state. In its attempt to discourage more migration from Afghanistan, the Iranian government in most cases refused to issue refugee cards, or issued temporary cards (Rajaee 2000). The majority of Afghans in Iran became illegal refugees, and the Iranian government frequently used the term 'economic migrants' to refer to its Afghan population.[10] Although it was never quite clear whether or not Afghan refugees had the right to work, in the absence of any other form of financial support they often entered into the informal urban economy. Others disappeared into rural areas where their labour was badly needed to fill the gap caused by young Iranians migrating to cities.

The Afghan community began to face strong and concerted official and social hostility in Iran, and this had a big impact, first on the economic well-being and later on the education and self-esteem of Afghan youths. The government began limiting the economic activities of Afghans, prohibiting them from entering the labour market (Rajaee 2000; Frelick 1999). However, the state did not always have the means to impose controls, particularly in the informal labour market. Also, with the unstable political situation in Afghanistan, the Iranian government would periodically ease its pressure. On the whole, while the Iranian government's strategies made the lives of Afghan refugees very difficult and insecure, there is no evidence that these policies persuaded them to return, in part because many were from rural areas and drought had destroyed their land, gardens and animals, making a return to their villages untenable. Additionally, since the majority of refugees in Iran were Hazara, a religious and ethnic minority historically subject to severe hostility by the Pashtun states and in particular the Taliban, return was often not a logical option for them (Mousavi 1998; Rubin 1994).[11]

When the tightening of economic opportunities did not yield the results the Iranian government was hoping for, it implemented other means. First, the state made it very difficult for Afghan refugees to enter into universities. Later, the right to education for Afghan youth was removed for all those who did not have valid refugee cards and for those whose cards were issued in cities other than where they were resident. This applied to the majority of Afghans in Iran, as no refugee cards have been issued since 1996. This was a major catastrophe for the Afghan community as the education of their children was a major reason why many had fled the Taliban regime. While the community tended to be more forgiving of the prohibition against Afghans working, exclusion of their children, from even primary school, was viewed as a betrayal not only of Afghans but of the principles of the Iranian revolution. The refugee community was incredulous that the regime which had played such a major role in convincing them that education was the gateway to a just and moral Islamic society was now prohibiting their children from attending school. Seeing education as the means to ensuring their children's futures, they believed the Iranian government to be acting immorally in denying children access to schooling.

Community leaders scrambled to find a solution. Some tried to mobilize the more liberal members of the government, and lobbied them to reverse the policy. Others tried to lobby UNICEF and Iranian charities. Afghan and Iranian intellectuals tried to mobilize the public in support of the right to education for all children in Iran, particularly since Iran had signed the UN Convention on the Rights of the Child, though it was not a signatory to the Refugee Convention. But the powerful BAFIA (Bureau of Alien and Foreign Immigration Affairs) office just wanted Afghans out of Iran, and the lobbying had little effect, despite some intervention from the president's office.[12]

Responses of the Afghan Community

The Afghan community adopted various strategies in response to the closure of schools to their children. These included individual strategies such as borrowing Iranian birth certificates to register for school, and borrowing cards from Afghans who had legal rights to education and who were registered elsewhere. Others pleaded with teachers and principals whom they knew to be sympathetic. In some cases, teachers agreed to allow Afghan youth to sit in class so long as they did not participate in exams and went home immediately if official observers came to visit. However, these small strategies clearly could not solve the community problem.

The most effective strategies evolved out of the initiatives of Afghan women, who turned their homes, usually located in and around Afghan colonies, into 'informal' neighbourhood schools (Hoodfar 2007). This was very similar to the clandestine schooling women provided for girls in Afghanistan under the Taliban. Gradually a structure developed: some women taught younger children, while others took older students. Informally organized networks of Afghan women took on the job of finding second-hand schoolbooks so that the Afghan students could follow the Iranian school curriculum. For the first time in the experience of most members, the Afghan community came together regardless of ethnicity, religious sect, political affiliation and class to mobilize on behalf of their children's education. Prior to this concerted effort, those involved in communal activities had come together on political platforms that more often than not were tied to ethnicity. Many had also been involved in creating income-generating activities, but these efforts too were organized around ethnic and kinship ties. The common goal of educating Afghan youth finally brought the community together; as one woman noted, the need for schooling was not confined to Hazaras or Tajiks or Uzbeks: it was a concern of all Afghans. The fact that the informal school movement was started by women, generally unconcerned with any personal political ambitions, also meant that internal rivalries, characteristic of community efforts by male groups, did not emerge as an obstacle.

These home-based, informal schooling initiatives became very widespread in Tehran and major cites, where government policies had the most impact. However, because most Afghans lived in one- or two-room apartments in multi-family dwellings, Iranian landlords started to complain about the numbers of children coming and going, the noise, and the wear and tear on their buildings. The Afghan home-based schooling strategies clearly were not a long-term solution.

Resourceful Afghans sought permission to set up privately-funded schools for Afghan children. They soon discovered that this was not a legal option either, as by law pre-university education in Iran is publicly funded and even in cases where no funding or official recognition is requested, it is forbidden to set up private schools.[13] The only legal channel open to the Afghan community was to set up schools under the pretext of Quranic classes, which could raise few objections in Iran. Therefore 'Quranic' schools were set up, often consisting of one or two rooms with several shifts of students in different grades taught by a single teacher. Children simply sat on the floor next to one another and opened their books to study.

Figures 4.2 and 4.3: While all Iranian schools are segregated, Afghan schools in Iran are usually mixed.

A small fee was charged for each child in order to help cover rent and provide small salaries for teachers. For families with several children this often meant deciding which of their children could be educated.

The Ministry of Education indirectly supported these initiatives and subverted the home-office policies, by providing informal Afghan schools with second-hand or new textbooks for a small fee, albeit sometimes weeks after school started and only after numerous trips to various ministry offices by school principals. It appears that such liberality stemmed from the fact that not all government officials approved of the government's policies, and certainly the Education Ministry felt there were alternative ways to reduce the costs of the Afghan refugee population to the Iranian government. Our formal and informal interviews with officials in the Ministry indicate that most viewed the government's exclusion of Afghan children from school as short-sighted and having severe consequences for the Iranian as well as the Afghan populations. Most Ministry officials recognized the limited window of opportunity for reaching the hearts and minds of children through education, and for promoting self-confidence and values of peace and co-existence at a young age. These views made it possible for many Afghan schools to gain some access to Iranian schoolbooks.

It is impossible to ascertain how many of the schools were functioning at any given time through the late 1990s and how many continue to operate (because of the schools' illegal status community members are not inclined to discuss them or their whereabouts with outsiders). Most of the informal schools provided primary and middle education; some went on to provide high school education as well. The problem has continued to be that certificates given by the Afghan schools are not recognized by the Iranian government. This has meant that their high school graduates could not continue on to Iranian universities. Regardless, the number of informal Afghan schools continued to grow through the spring of 2004. They were usually located on the outskirts of urban centres, where most Afghans were living.[14] By 2002, we had compiled a list of 46 schools in the immediate neighbourhoods of the Tehran suburb where we were conducting our research, with the number of students in each varying between 60 and 1,100 (the larger schools were housed in several buildings and often had three to four shifts). However, all involved in the field agree that this number probably represents a small percentage of the clandestine schools in and around Tehran, not to mention the other major cities where there are large Afghan populations, such as Mashhad and Isfehan.[15]

Over the last eight years, the pressure placed on these schools has varied in conjunction with political developments and the Iranian government's preoccupations. While the situation for Afghan refugees in Iran eased slightly after the attacks on the US on September 11th 2001 and during the US war against the Taliban, once the Karzai government was in place and particularly since the inauguration of the president and parliament in 2005, the pressure on Afghans to leave Iran has increased considerably.[16] As usual this has translated into pressure on Afghan schools to close, which often results in the schools changing location and paying higher rents. At the same time, Afghan families are reluctant to go back to Afghanistan because of the lack of security and educational and medical services. Most Afghans currently living in Iran have no capital with which to start their own business, and the employment prospects are very limited for the less skilled and less educated, who tend to be members of minority ethnic groups like the Uzbek and Hazara. These groups are deeply suspicious of new polices that involve foreign military personnel building schools and roads, taking jobs away from Afghans who are perfectly able to perform these tasks, but lack the capital and security need to return to Afghanistan. So despite pressures from the Iranian government most Afghan schools in Iran were still functioning in 2005–2006, and according to several school directors we talked to, there has not been a significant drop in the number of students; those who have left Iran are replaced by those who have been expelled from the Iranian schools.

Afghan Schools: 'A Space We Never Had'

The primitive state of many of the informal schools, located in poorly ventilated, poorly lit basements with no heating or cooling facilities, and sometimes without tables or chairs, washroom facilities, courtyards, or even drinkable water, was shocking to students who previously attended Iranian schools. Many told us they were initially so ashamed that they avoided telling friends they were going to an Afghan school, preferring to say they were not attending school at all. Some students told us they dreaded waking up to face another day at the Afghan school. Students said they felt anxious and demeaned and wondered if somehow they deserved this inferior schooling because they were Afghans. The choice 'was between these primitive schools or no education', said one student. Many of the teachers were not professional and lacked the self-confidence of the Iranian teachers. As sixteen year-old Mohammed told me:

'When you are young your teachers are the most important authority over your soul and your mind, and you need to see them as self-possessed and confident. But our Afghan teachers were not confident and that troubled us, and at first made learning more difficult.' Indeed many of the teachers told us that initially they had trouble seeing themselves as teachers; most had not planned to teach and many had not completed high school. But circumstances moved them to volunteer to meet what they saw as a crucial need for Afghan youth and the future of the community. Many of the youths we interviewed said it was not long before they learned to appreciate the commitment and dedication of their teachers and began to establish a rapport with them which was very different from the relationship they had experienced with their previous Iranian teachers.

Despite the tenuous status of the schools they became firmly established in the Afghan community, and advantages emerged which many of our interviewees said far outweighed the substandard facilities. Initially set up in response to the educational needs of the community, it soon became clear that the schools were providing other important functions. Many students told us that their initial dismay over the poor conditions gave way to a proud sense of ownership. 'This is a space we never had, even if to you it may not look worth having', said one seventeen year-old, full-time student who also worked up to nine hours a day in various jobs. What follows describes what Afghan youths seem to most appreciate about their Afghan schools.

A Safe Haven

Despite the large number of Afghan youth in Iran, no Afghan youth centres had ever been set up; as one community leader explained, 'the basic needs have been so huge that to even consider a rudimentary youth center seemed to us almost sinful'. The schools became de facto youth centres, providing safe spaces where young Afghans could take refuge from the constant social harassment and discrimination they felt on the city streets and in Iranian schools. Our inquiries indicate that young refugees did not experience harassment in the 1980s, when the Iranian host community was for the most part hospitable and accommodating, reflecting the state ideology of the Khomeini era.[17] However, in the 1990s a very different ideological climate had emerged in Iran where there was little sympathy for non-citizens, or for Muslims beyond Iran's borders.

This new situation was very distressing for the Afghan youth, raised in Iran within an ideology which emphasized the unity and equality of all Muslims and achievement through proper action and moral conduct, and which underplayed nationalism on the premise that citizenship was a matter of luck and fate. Many Afghan youths deeply internalized the ideology of the pre-eminence of their Muslim identity over all other sources of identity. They had grown up with a strong sense of belonging to the *ummeh*, 'the community of Muslims', and felt that their membership in this community entitled them to equal treatment in a Muslim host country.[18] Their exclusion from education, and the general discrimination they began to encounter from the mid-1990s came as a great shock; they felt that their hopes for a better future, for which they considered education key, were being denied. Many said they felt deeply hurt and depressed but had nowhere to turn.

'Ironically these primitive Afghan schools have given us a space that is ours. This is something we didn't have before.' Variations of this statement were frequent, especially from students aged thirteen to eighteen. The schools have afforded young Afghans in Iran a safe space, where they need not watch what they say, and where they do not have to pretend not to have heard the condescending comments made by teachers and students about Afghans. The Afghan youths chat, share stories about their experiences of discrimination in the Iranian schools and try to analyse and understand the reasons and the mentality behind their treatment. These kinds of conversations do not take place between Afghan youths and their Iranian friends for a variety of complicated reasons articulated by the students, having to do with pride, and, for girls especially, not wanting to make their Iranian friends 'feel bad' or responsible. Many of the girls recognized that the discrimination they experienced had more to do with social and political ideology than with the true sentiments of individuals. As one of our more articulate and reflective participants put it:

> A nation does not turn racist and chauvinist in one generation. You would not hear from Afghans complaints about discrimination in Khomeini's era. Not that they did not have problems or everybody treated them well. But when it happened they did not feel it was part of a collective discriminatory and exclusionary approach, but things have changed now. The government does not want us here. We, the Afghans are blamed for every thing that that goes wrong here, from serial killings to high unemployment, to spread of diseases. But the problem is that most of us have no where to go back to ...

A male student busy studying overheard us discussing discrimination against Afghans and commented: 'The government of Iran would really be in trouble if they did not have America to blame for what went wrong at the political level, and Afghans for what is not working at the society level.' Other students overheard us and joined the conversation and stories of discrimination poured out. In reviewing our notes and interviews it is clear that the Afghan youths have come to greatly value their schools, despite the inadequate facilities, and many of them feel happier in these schools though they worry that their educational certificates may not be recognized as they move on to higher education in either Iran or Afghanistan.

Afghan Schools and the Creation of an Afghan Identity

An unintended consequence of the informal schools and of the growing social rift and educational segregation between Iranian and Afghan youth has been to bring Afghan youth of different ethnicities together. Many interviewees discussed at great length how they have just begun to understand what it means to be Afghan, as opposed to being a member of a particular ethnic or kin group.[19] Generally their parents have always identified themselves as Hazara or Tajik or Sayyed, etc.; this is particularly true of families originating from the rural areas of Afghanistan, who refer to themselves as Afghani only when dealing with Iranian neighbours or the authorities, since Iranians are generally unaware of the ethnic diversity of Afghans and the huge differences, if not hostility, between Afghan ethnic groups. Many parents of urban Afghan origin said that even in the city in Afghanistan they lived among their own ethnic group, shopping in their own ethnic shops, attending mosques led by clerics of their own tribal affiliation, and if their children went to school these tended to be practically segregated as well. A few more educated parents noted that the government of Davod Khan (1973–78) and subsequent governments talked about trying to break down ethnic barriers in Afghanistan, but after civil unrest, the eruption of war (1978) and the Russian invasion (December 1979), ethnic divisions escalated as mobilization against the Russians occurred through ethnic/tribal affiliation.

The question of citizenship in Afghanistan has been a thorny one. The governments of modern Afghanistan (from 1880 to 1978), except for a brief period of Tajik rule in 1929, have been Pashtun-led, deriving support from the various Pashtun tribes (Griffiths 1967; L. Dupree 1973: 415–658). In practice, this meant that Pashtuns were privileged in all political, economic and social spheres. This also meant that other ethnic groups have been alienated by the state to varying degrees and thus cling even more strongly to their own ethnic and tribal organizations for protection and support. Even the more urbanized Tajiks, the second largest ethnic group in Afghanistan, suffered much discrimination under the exclusionary practices of various governments until 1973. Hazaras, a religious, racial and ethnic minority, have especially suffered from formal and informal discrimination since the 1880s (Mousavi 1998; Rubin 1995).[20] In more recent times, they were particularly targeted by the Taliban and were massacred in the thousands in Kabul and Mazar-i-Sharif in 1996 (Rashid 2001).

Ethnic boundaries in Afghanistan have pervaded economic, political and social arenas, so even in large cities such as Kabul people have tended to live, work, study and pray within segregated, insular neighbourhoods and thus have had little to do with Afghans of other ethnic groups. Except among the very poor and sometimes very rich, inter-ethnic marriages have been rare, particularly for Hazaras, who have been the most disadvantaged of Afghan ethnic groups. Even in the 1970s and the post-Davod Khan era (1973–78), and despite revolutionary slogans, inter-ethnic marriage was considered radical; such marriages have led to deadly blood feuds going on for generations.[21]

Since any sense of shared Afghan nationalism has tended to be insignificant or non-existent for older Afghans currently in Iran, younger generations have had little impetus or encouragement to develop inter-ethnic Afghan solidarity. In Iran their primary interaction has been with their own kin and ethnic groups, and many of our young interviewees had their first experience of 'Afghan-ness' not through some sense of shared history and culture, but because they were all subject to the discriminatory regulations of the Iranian government, which tagged them as unwanted Afghan refugees and barred them from educational institutions. Even documented Afghan refugees who have not been subject to as much legal discrimination share the outsider status, insecurity and precariousness of undocumented Afghans. This shared experience of exclusion has fostered a type of unity and a sense of cohesion that transcends ethic divisions (McDonough and Hoodfar 2004, Hoodfar 2008).[22]

For many of the youths their first interaction with Afghans from other ethnic groups occurred in the context of the Afghan schools, where students have been exposed to each other's languages, dialects, customs and food.[23] For many students this eye-opening process has diminished prejudices and increased inter-ethnic respect. Having experienced exclusion and discrimination from the Iranian government and society, many of the students tend to be critical of their parents' biases toward Afghans of other ethnicities. The phenomenon has generated great interest among some of the Afghan school directors in Tehran, and a survey of Afghan students in Tehran and nearby towns to assess students' perspectives on ethnicity was carried out by one of the coordinating educational bodies.[24] The preliminary results indicate that while children under ten still hold negative views of Afghans of other ethnic groups, older children talked about being a diverse nation of unified Afghans.[25] The issue of learning to think of Afghanistan as a unified nation of diverse people was very prominent:

> Being with different ethnic Afghans here in the school helps us to accumulate more information about Afghanistan and its people. This helped us to learn about our culture and learn to respect each other. In the Iranian schools the teachers only talked about their own country. Our teachers have changed our attitudes. Our teachers are Afghans and they talk more about Afghanistan to encourage us to be proud of our country. [sixteen year-old living in Tehran]

> Some Afghans have thought about us, and our future, and they have started these schools so that we can study and make a better future for ourselves and Afghanistan, and this makes us feel very good. We have come to understand that if we are educated and united then Afghanistan will be reconstructed, but if we stay as our ancestors were then

Afghanistan will remain as it is now, divided and burning in civil war, and we remain like beggars pleading with Iranians and Pakistanis. We know that politics is a big game and our leaders and outsiders have put Afghanistan and our generation in this position. [fourteen year-old female living in Tehran]

For me the best part after being in Afghan school, is that I am studying with my own people, even if they were not Hazara. I learned that I have to cooperate and sympathize with other ethnic Afghans and we should help each other in everything. This is not what our parents think. I am learning so much here about Afghanistan, life, and politics, and I feel the education level here is even higher than Iranian schools. [fourteen year-old living in Tehran]

It is significant that the development of a sense of supra-Afghan citizenship among the youth, and to a lesser degree within the larger Afghan community in Iran, was expressed not only by Hazara and Uzbek (who as disadvantaged minorities have the most to gain from an emphasis on the unity of the Afghan nation), but by the historically economically and politically privileged and dominant Tajiks and Pashtuns as well.

This considerable shift has occurred in part because Hazaras, the most socially and economically disadvantaged group in Afghanistan, form the majority of the refugee population. Most school founders and teachers have been Hazara, which contrasted sharply to the past pervasive stereotype of Hazara as unskilled workers and servants to urban Afghans. The majority of students in most classes were also Hazara and this has contributed to Hazara youth's growing sense of social esteem in the Afghan community. The Hazara's impoverishment in Afghanistan was often blamed, without explanation, on their Shi'a religious affiliation, rather than on legal and social discrimination. However, in the Iranian context this assumption has been rendered highly illogical, given that Shi'a is the religion of the majority in Iran; there is little dispute by Afghans of any group that Iran is more 'developed', modernized and peaceful than Afghanistan. Non-Hazara Afghans in Iran can no longer point to religion as the downfall of the Hazaras; indeed, some of the Tajik students we interviewed said they were Shi'a because their parents, raised in the Sunni tradition, had converted to Shi'a due to its emphasis on social justice. Given the size of the Afghan youth population in Iran, such inter-ethnic developments will have considerable social impact in terms of addressing ethnic inequalities in a reconstructed Afghanistan; Hazara youth will not accept unequal treatment at the hands of other ethnic groups that have historically monopolized Afghanistan's power structure.

It should be noted that such expressions of 'Afghan-ness' are more concerned with issues of social justice and less applicable in the more private, domestic arena. When we asked students to think about future marriage partners, the majority said they would prefer to marry someone from their own ethnic group. Though most explained that theoretically they have no personal objection to marrying a compatible partner from outside their ethnic group, they said their parents, who will play an important role in their marriage arrangements, would have trouble accepting an 'outsider', and thus for the sake of their elders they would prefer to marry inside their ethnic group (see table 4.6). A few said that as long as their partner is Muslim, ethnicity does not matter, while a few of the boys said that honesty and morality are most important, even if the bride were not Muslim. In fact, the largest single category in terms of marriage preferences were those who said any 'good person' would be an appropriate spouse, regardless of ethnicity or nationality.

Table 4.6: Youth Preference regarding Marriage Partner.

Preferred Ethnic Identity of Future Spouse	Number of Respondents
Definitely the same ethnicity	10
Prefer the same ethnicity	10
The same religion	4
Any good Afghan	3
Only Tajik or Pashtu	4
Sayyd Iranian or Afghan	3
Any good person regardless of ethnicity	14
Not sure	2
No marriage (female)	1
Total	**51**

Given that ethnic relations and inter-ethnic marriage have been delicate issues among Afghans, the expressed openness towards other ethnic groups is recent and markedly different from older generations. The great majority of parents in our study insisted that their offspring would marry within their own ethnic group, and even within the kin group (table 4.7). And parents and some of the youth were adamant, though often for different reasons, that the younger generation – particularly girls – would not marry Iranians, who they believe treat Afghans with disrespect and take divorce very lightly (Hoodfar, forthcoming). This is interesting given that the UN puts the official number of marriages between Afghans males and Iranian women at 50,000, while unofficial estimates are much higher, particularly since the figure does not include marriages of Afghan women to Iranian men (Sadr 2007).

Regardless, this figure indicates the highest rate of inter-ethnic/inter-group marriage on record for Afghans.

Table 4.7: Parent's Preferred Marriage Partner for their Children by Ethnicity.

Preferred ethnicity	Number of respondents
Their own kin and ethnic group	27
Other Afghan ethnics	13
The same religion	5
Maybe other tribes	2
Only Tajik or Pashtu	2
Refused to be interviewed	2
Total	**51**

Introducing Afghanistan into the Curriculum

As students become more conscious and proud of their identity as Afghans they crave more information about Afghanistan and its history, and become increasingly critical of the lack of material pertaining to Afghanistan in their curricula. Though they appreciate the importance of Iranian content they also feel that if they are to go and help with the rebuilding of their country they need to know more about Afghanistan. This is a complaint I have heard from the youth since 1998 when I began research with Afghan refugees in Iran.

In April 2002, while participating in a workshop in Mashhad on the reconstruction of Afghanistan, I met a young woman who had finished Iranian high school and after graduation spent a year, at great cost to her and her parents, going to the Mashhad library several times a week to research and prepare a geography book for young people, to be used in the informal schools. She said that as a student she had longed to know more about her country, but her Iranian teachers knew nothing about Afghanistan, and though her parents spoke of the war and their neighbourhood in Mazar-i-Sharif, like many Afghan refugee parents they were reluctant to talk about the past. After a year of diligent work she had completed her manuscript, but had no resources or experience with publishing (she was raised in a poor Afghan colony since arriving with her family in Mashhad as a baby). She made an appointment with the UNHCR office in Mashhad to ask for their help to publish her book, but they refused. In tears she recounted her story:

> they insulted and humiliated me and threw me out of the office like a dirty thing. They told me I had got too big-headed and I should always

remember that I am just an Afghani. After crying my eyes out for a week, I tried the Iranian Ministry of Education. They did nothing either, but at least they did not insult me. The old man told me that Iran is trying to send Afghans back to Afghanistan and therefore it is highly unlikely that they would pay for the publication of a book to be used for Afghan children in Iran.

I examined the book, which was handwritten and decorated with postcards from Afghanistan. Since I knew that a basic book on Afghanistan was something many youth were longing for, I managed to raise some funds and get some technical assistance from other Afghan experts, and published the small book, which was adopted by some Tehran schools as a textbook for primary grades four and five.[26] By the time the research on which this paper is based was concluded there was at least one other similar book, and a few very committed teachers in Tehran and Mashhad had helped their students start newsletters, some of which ran to 2,000 copies,[27] and which were no doubt were widely passed around.

With the pressure on the Afghan community to leave Iran, many youths are anxious about 'returning' to a home they have never seen or do not remember. One interviewee told me that it was 'kind of strange' to be nationalistic about a country you have no image of. To address theses anxieties, an Afghan children's publishing company (Taravat), with support from one of the larger Afghan schools in Tehran, prepared a simply written book called *The Return* (*Bazgashat*), and published several thousand copies in cheap print without any financial support from outside sources.[28] The book depicts a young Afghan raised in Iran, returning for the first time with his family. Each chapter describes the region as the family passes through different provinces, and each chapter focuses on a different ethnic group. This book circulated widely and was so successful that at the suggestion of students it was adopted for use in several schools in Tehran. Even though the students are not tested on it, teachers told me that many students say it is their favourite part of the curriculum. Reflecting on the policies of the Iranian authority, UNHCR and UNICEF, and the 'forced-voluntary' repatriation policy, one wonders why there is not more support for initiatives that might help make the transition easier for youths.

Social Justice and Inclusive Practices

Being subject to exclusionary practices by the larger community has sensitized many Afghan youths in Iran to issues of social justice. Many of them have become determined not to practice discrimination themselves. Given that Iranians generally seem more inclined towards a 'tit for tat' attitude, the behaviour of Afghan youths in this regard caught my attention on several occasions as youths showed that they have chosen not to discriminate against others. This became clear when the research participants were reflecting on their experience as refugees:

> Having talked about our experiences of being discriminated against outside our school I learned not to be concerned only about myself, and to consider others. My patience has increased by seeing all these problems we had to endure. Seeing how Afghans have suffered and yet have not given up their dignity. And these problems have made me what I am now and I try to be fair with others. [sixteen year-old female living in Tehran]

Initially I took little notice of this frequent claim of social consciousness by the youth, which I viewed primarily as a critique of their Iranian host community. However, as the research progressed I noticed that many of them are truly committed to this position. As part of our research and after consulting with the youths in Mashhad we helped to set up and fund a volleyball team for young girls (aged twelve to sixteen) in summer 2003. I had insisted that the volleyball team be exclusively Afghan girls, and when the two young organizers objected, I argued that Iranian girls have many other options while the Afghan girls do not. In a meeting a few weeks later to finalize the team plan, fourteen year-old Bashireh engaged me in a long discussion, arguing for the inclusion of Iranian girls, several of whom were very keen to participate. She reasoned that the team would be Afghan, with an appropriate name, but that Iranians willing to be on an Afghan team should able to join. Seeing that I was not giving in, Bashireh said:

> Dr. Homa, how can we be critical of Iranians for their discriminatory treatment of us as Afghans and then we do exactly the same thing to them as soon as we get half a chance? I would rather not have a volleyball team, even though you know this has been my dream for the summer, than have one and tell some girls they can't join because they are Iranians.

Clearly she won, as there was not much I could say to such a well-argued case! After much debate the team was named *Doukhtaran ayendeh saaze–i-Afghanistan* which literally means 'girls/daughters who are the future makers of Afghanistan'. It was evident that the girls' sense of identity and nationalism derives from self-confidence and not from a sense of supremacy over or marginalization of others. Despite their experiences of discrimination these girls are not out for revenge; at their young age they seem to have learned to distinguish between Iranian government policies and Iranian individuals.

Figure 4.4: The last day of volleyball the girls held a small celebration and took a few pictures, but given the conservatism of the neighbourhood not everyone wanted to be in the picture.

Our project agreed to help set up newsletters for Afghan youth in Mashhad and Tehran, primarily by covering basic costs and providing a computer. The newsletter in Tehran was school-based and produced through the student club, with the idea that it would take contributions and content from other Afghan schools, and the community at large, to attract a broader Afghan readership, which it did to some extent. The content of these publications reflected a concern not just with Afghanistan, student life and students' immediate communities, but with youth movements globally and other broad, international political issues. At one point police closed all the Afghan schools in Mashhad and the youth club had to operate from outside school; the newsletter continued to be published and was a key channel for keeping youth connected. Many readers sent letters to the editor after each issue. There had been long debate about the name of the Mashhad newsletter – World of Youths (*donyay-i- jawanin*). I was surprised that nothing in the title indicated it was an Afghan youth publication, however the youths involved insisted they wanted their newsletter to be for everyone, even if the focus was on Afghan youth issues. Clearly these young Afghans in Iran reject exclusivity, and see themselves not only as Afghan, but as citizens of the globe and members of the world community of youth. They fiercely proclaim this membership and refuse to be marginal in any sense. Their experiences in Iran have rendered them inclusive, and loathe to accept political divisions such as nationality and ethnicity as reasons to exclude others. Again, this has important political implications, as so many Afghan leaders today continue to operate within the old oppositional mind set, and fail to appreciate the global vision that these youths seem to have incorporated into their own visions and identities.

Figure 4.5: Newsletter working committee, Mashhad.

Although many of the surveys and studies carried out in the Afghan community (Hoodfar 2004; Frelick1999;) indicate that the majority, for economic and security reasons,[29] would prefer to remain in Iran at least for the near future, the youths we interviewed all expressed a desire to go to Afghanistan, but only after completing their studies. They do want to participate in Afghanistan's reconstruction in whatever small way they can, but they are fearful of being forced to return while there is no educational opportunity or security for them, though they do feel that skilled people should return immediately to help to reconstruct the country. They expressed hopes for a strong, united Afghanistan where they and their future children will never experience the violence of war and ethnic strife. Two fifteen year-old girls, reflecting on their dreams for a advanced Afghanistan, told me they think Iranians who so choose should also be allowed to live in Afghanistan, and that everyone should study together so that in the future all Muslims can support one another and improve the world for Muslims and all humanity.

It appears that the Iranian authorities, through their exclusionary practices, have inadvertently helped sow the seeds of a humanistic Afghan nationalism. Despite their youth, the students we interviewed demonstrated considerable awareness of and bitterness over recent Afghan history, observing that Afghans have been the pawns of various world powers. The students discussed the American preoccupation with Russia and how America (as they referred to the US) wanted to fight a cheap war without losing American soldiers, so used and then abandoned Afghans. They talked about Pakistan hoping to use a puppet Pashtun government to sign away the claims of Afghans along the Pakistani border. Chinese and Iranians were seen to be primarily concerned with securing their trade interests and selling as much as possible to Afghanistan. They were highly aware of how each of these countries has used Afghanistan's ethnic divisions to its own advantage, arming their own favorite groups in return for political favours. Having lived as refugees, these young Afghans have developed a more global vision and believe they can help unite Afghans and prevent further civil war. 'Maybe it would have been good to come together because of love and caring, but even coming together due to harassment and discrimination is still valuable, and maybe, only maybe, we can help prevent our children from suffering the way we have', one participant said thoughtfully.

Conclusion

The foregoing discussion and the data presented in this chapter indicate that in cases of prolonged conflict and forced migration it is important to pay attention to the education and identity needs of youth who are being brought up in societies other than their own. Formal and semi-formal schooling is particularly important because the informal socialization processes and customary avenues of identity-makers are often interrupted in situations of forced migration. In situations where refugees are subject to social and/or legal discrimination, attention to schooling or the formation of other institutions and building a safe environment for boosting the self-confidence of refugee youth become of paramount importance. Ideally policies should be directed toward eliminating such discrimination; however, taking into consideration the limited resources that are made available to refugees and a possible lack of political will, at least some resources should be directed for the refugee youth to collectively share and learn from each others' coping strategies and limit their alienation in the host societies.

Schooling remains a powerful tool for forging a shared identity and citizenship anywhere. Thus the nature of the educational institution and its expressed and implied goals are extremely important. Iranian authorities have long realized the significance of early schooling and have jealously guarded the right to establish schooling by making primarily and secondary education the monopoly of the government in facilitating the ideological inoculation of the new generation of citizens. Thus it is ironic that they have paid little attention to formal schooling for Afghan youth as a means of preparing them to repatriate, although they have been more open to allowing Iraqi refugees to provide schooling for their youth.

Youth schooling plays an even more significant role when the displaced intend to return to their country of origin, or when the host society does not have a policy of refugee integration. There are some studies on the way in which immigrant communities adjust and integrate into their host societies, and on the role of schooling, but there are few that examine the situation of the refugees or that problematize the educational policies (or the lack of them) dealing with the refugees. The case of Afghan refugee youth in Iran is particularly important for illuminating some of the major issues that are overlooked by policymakers dealing with long-term refugee situations. In the context of Iran, Afghan refugees were initially allowed to attend Iranian public schools, where the youth, perhaps more as a coping strategy, privileged their Muslim identity over their national identity. While this helped them to feel connected to their host society and the larger Muslim world, the absence of any initiatives to familiarize them with Afghan history, culture or the Pashtu language proved to be a major disadvantage when the Iranian government distanced itself from its earlier ideological rhetoric of a borderless Muslim world and moved towards more nationalistic and exclusionary practices.

Barred from Iranian schools and severed from much of their Afghan background, Afghan refugee youth have, since the mid-1990s, had few tools at their disposal to deal with their rejection and the denial of what they had come to understand as their basic rights. For years, the Afghan community in Iran was told that education, particularly the education of the youth, was a basic requirement for being a good Muslim, and that an obligation of good Muslim parents was to educate their children. Faced with rejection by the only society most of them knew, Afghan youths lacked the tools with which to construct a new identity, and a safe space in which to try and make sense of their fate and their identity.

In the struggle to create a school system for its youth, the Afghan community unwittingly created much more, thanks to the creativity of Afghan youth. Despite their limited resources, the Afghan schools provided a safe space for Afghan youth to reflect on their shared experiences of exclusion and social discrimination and to reflect on the context of their lives as refugees. They have come to recognize how ethnic divisions, lack of democracy, regional politics and Afghanistan's manipulation by super powers have contributed to their circumstances. They have reflected on the kind of Afghan society they would like to create, having learned through bitter experience about the opposite of the value of inclusiveness and accommodation.

The development of informal Afghan schools in Iran over the last decade shows that even with limited resources, it is possible to prioritize the needs of refugee youth through community programmes to a much greater extent than is generally the practice in such cases. In part, the larger vision of the refugees as victims and passive recipients of support, as Harrell-Bond (1990, 1999) has eloquently critiqued, has influenced the refugee policies, and intervention has been formulated in such a way that it effectively discourages the refugees from taking the sort of constructive steps that Afghan refugees in Iran have taken, according to their own priorities, to improve their condition. Moreover, this case indicates the extent to which a culture of self-reliance can help refugee communities evolve to a degree beyond that which policymakers have tended to acknowledge. Furthermore, this study suggests that creating a supportive space enables mutual aid for emotional and psychological needs without much help from mental health experts.

The crisis of exclusion and identity faced by many Afghan refugee youths had gone un-addressed by older members of their community until the education crisis and the advent of the informal schools. It was a comparison of data from interviews with Afghan youth in both Afghan and Iranian schools that focused our attention on the significance of Afghan identity and the newly formed sense of belonging and cohesiveness that emerged through the Afghan schools, along with young Afghan refugees' growing desire to go 'back' to Afghanistan.

While the development of a collective Afghan identity is an unintended consequence of the Iranian government's policies and the Afghan community's reaction to them, our data speaks to the need for unambiguous educational/schooling policies to deal with long-term refugees, particularly in cases of large-scale exodus. Host communities and/or international agencies such as the UNHCR must devise appropriate policies for the basic needs of refugee communities, including and prioritizing education and the development of a positive sense of identity. Clearly if the host country is reluctant to incorporate the refugee population, it should provide institutional support for education geared toward the needs of refugees' country of origin in order to facilitate their return home. Such schooling should not necessarily separate long-term refugees from the main educational system of the host country, but should at least provide some enrichment programming and curricula, and the establishment of youth centres or clubs where refugees can develop a sense of shared identity and belonging.

Notes

1. By 'education' our interviewers were referring to formal schooling. Often obtaining a formal certificate was also implied when mentioning access by youth to better jobs such as teaching, engineering and so on. At times, women and the older generation talked about becoming literate; this indicated that being able to read and write was seen as important, while the ability to read religious texts was presented as justification. Informal education and learning life skills, while obviously important to them, were not what they were concerned with here.
2. This chapter focuses on the formal and clandestine schooling as opposed to other formal or informal training and education. However, throughout I use the term schooling and formal education as interchangeable terms since that is the way in which the research participants understood schooling.
3. International instruments and declarations proclaim the right of all individuals to have an education. This is believed to set a foundation for the promotion of all human rights, which, while widely discussed in various institutions dealing with refugees, has remained largely theoretical. Indeed, not enough research has been done to be able to meaningfully put into action those ideas and broad policy guidelines that are set in various United Nations documents (see UNHCR 1999, 2002).
4. The study presented here is a sequel to a study of informal schools and the development of civil society among Afghan refuges in Iran (1998–2002).
5. One can argue that the Iranian style of indirect support is a healthier policy, particularly in cases of prolonged conflict, as opening the labour market to Afghan refugees promotes a sense of self-reliance and allows refuges to use and update their skills.
6. There were some restrictions on women entering some of the engineering faculties, but places for women in medical schools were increased as a gendered-segregated society was possible only if there were enough female doctors, teachers and so on. Various restrictions were later removed because of women's demands, and because the Islamic Republic realized that organizing and maintaining a totally segregated society was not cost efficient.
7. This was a sequel to an earlier study (2001) on Afghan informal schools and the development of civil society among Afghan refugees in Iran.
8. A number of Afghans work in the construction industry, which is one of the most dynamic economic sectors in Iran.
9. This was in some ways in contrast to the situation of Afghan refugees in Pakistan, where Afghans lived in camps or more stable colonies in cities like Peshawar or Karachi, often working and shopping in their own communities. They frequently organized their own schooling either through local initiatives or more commonly through the UN and other international agencies. The curriculum was Afghan, though often with a particular version of history. Both Pashtu and Dari languages, though at different levels, were used in Afghan refugee schools in Pakistan, which meant that Afghan children were familiar with their country, languages and history. In many ways, refugees in Pakistan lived as though they were in an Afghan city outside Afghanistan.

10. Although there were also at least half a million Iraqis in Iran, also without much international support, they never became a subject of public discussion, in part because they lived in camps or designated areas away from major cities, and in part because they did not enter the labour market thereby competing with the Iranian unskilled and semiskilled workers. Moreover, the Iranian government saw them as a potentially valuable source of future political influence given the shaky situation in Iraq following the first Gulf war.

11. Some Afghans told us that notwithstanding drought and discrimination, life was just better in Iran, with good running water, better healthcare and a functioning infrastructure. Afghan refugees in Pakistan returned because life in Pakistan was not as good for most Afghans, who lived in camps and had very few job opportunities except for those they created for themselves. In contrast Afghans in Iran could live quite comfortably and felt they were in a 'developed' country, though they had to put up with discrimination. Those who lived in urban centres knew they would have difficulty reverting to their previous lives. This was especially true for Uzbeks and Hazaras, subject to discrimination by the more powerful Tajik and Pashtu ethnic groups.

12. Various liberal groups and organizations wrote to President Khatami, bringing the issue to his personal attention. He did write to the Budget and Planning Committee, which subsequently talked to BAFIA and then issued a letter stating that opening Iranian schools to Afghan youth would be against the national interest. Later, celebrity filmmaker Mohsen Makhmalbaf and lawyer Shirin Ebadi (who was recently awarded the Nobel Peace Prize) championed the refugee education cause and while they managed to open up the public discussion, the events of September 11th brought a close to much of the debate. Subsequent preoccupation and discussion shifted to the reconstruction of Afghanistan rather than the education of Afghan refugees in Iran.

13. This was in sharp contrast to the situation facing the Afghan community in Pakistan where a large percentage of educational institutions are privately funded, even if the state has an overseeing role.

14. More marginalized people tend to live on the edges of cities, where informal housing tends to sprout. This was certainly the case with the rapid imposition of so-called 'volunteer' repatriation, which is more accurately described as forced. As Afghans were evicted or squeezed out of more central urban areas, they gravitated toward the edges of the cities.

15. In fact those most closely involved with the Afghan schools estimate that there are over 200 relatively 'organized' schools, with many more smaller-scale, less organized versions as well.

16. Pressure on the refugee community to leave, including raids on informal schools, increased even more once it became known that up to one million Afghan refugees had repatriated from Pakistan during a period when only 30,000 Afghans returned from Iran, in the immediate year after the fall of Taliban. While there was an agreement between UNHCR and Iran to begin repatriating all Afghans following the Afghanistan presidential elections of October 2004, it is acknowledged that the logistics of moving this huge number of people will require at least two years to implement. Nonetheless, the pace of expulsion has hastened again since the beginning of 2005.

17. While many male interviewees said they did not experience discrimination as children, some men said that as adults they felt like outsiders. Thus, for instance it was stated that while they had cordial relations with the Iranians they worked with, few Iranians would invite them to their homes. Some also stated that that Iranians did not consider them suitable marriage partners for their daughters. However, in general the situation of Afghans in Iran was much better in the 1980s.

18. Zohera (an interviewee) asked about the status of Afghan refugees in Europe and Canada, and if they were treated unequally in the schools. Afterwards she said 'Isn't it ironic that infidels treat their Afghan refugees as equals and Muslims treat them as lesser beings'.

19. There is no agreement on the relative percentages of Afghanistan's different ethnic groups. A CIA country study estimates that in 1996 various Pashtun tribes made up approximately 40 per cent of the population, Tajiks 25.3 per cent, Hazara 18 per cent, Uzbeks 6.3 per cent, Turkmen 2.5 per cent, and 7.9 per cent 'other' (Afghanistan Country Study, CIA 2001); however, a CIA fact sheet (Fact Sheet: https://www.cia.gov/library/publications/the-world-factbook/geos/af.html) has different numbers. In any case demographic information is very political and Pashtun-dominated governments have had a vested interest in inflating the Pashtun numbers.

20. Since Hazaras are agriculturalists they became an easier target for the levying of heavy taxes and many lost their lands, which were transferred to the Pashtun tribes. Others were sold into slavery because they could not pay their taxes or repay the loans they had taken in order to pay their taxes. Their leaders were suppressed and their political structures were dismantled (Mousavi 1998).

21. Among interviewees in both Iran and Pakistan we heard several mind-boggling stories of feuds and killings rooted in inter-ethnic marriages that forced families into exile or hiding.

22. Immigrant minorities who are seen and discriminated against as one undifferentiated group have responded similarly, coming together and trying to support one another. For example, because American society in the 1920s and 1930s discriminated against Jews regardless of their origins, Jews from both eastern and western Europe responded by putting aside their own prejudices against each other, in a sense accepting society's definition of them as a community, and working together to improve their social status.

23. This process has not always been smooth; some children, particularly younger ones, often brought their familial prejudices to the classroom, sometimes creating an uneasy atmosphere, but teachers told us that over time a considerable change in attitude tends to occur.

24. The directors of Amir-al-momenin School and Taravat Youth Educational Publishing Center carried out a joint sociological study in 2003 with 3,000 students aged eight to eighteen. A large part of the questionnaire focused on questions regarding ethnic relations and identity. The preliminary result of this study replicates the result of our study in terms of the dynamics of ethnic relations among this population.

25. Some older youth said they should be referred to as Afghanistani (similar to Pakistani, Hindustani, etc.) since Afghan is usually understood as synonymous

with Pashtun, while Afghanistani refers to collective citizenship without denying ethnicity. This appeared to be a hot topic as they wrestled with issues of citizenship and how they should refer to themselves. Some even objected to Iranians referring to them as Afghans or Afghanis.

26. *Geography of Afghanistan* (Tehran: Shocria Rezabaksh, 2003).

27. Some of the newsletters circulating among our interviewees were: *Rah Kamal*, Tehran; *Afghan Youth Newsletter*, Tehran; *Taravet*, Tehran; and *Donya- e- javanan*, Mashhad.

28. Sayyed Nader Mosavi, 2003. *The Returned*, Tehran: Travat Children's Publishing House. Financial support is not usually available to the very people who know the community best and invest their time and energy. To connect to international agencies one needs to know English and generally be familiar with NGO systems and protocol. Neither the UNHCR, UNICEF or UNESCO have time for this small Afghan publishing house for youth publications , even though it is carrying out the very task that these agencies are paid handsomely to accomplish.

29. Hazaras in particular feel it is not safe for them to return given their experiences of massacre during the civil wars and under the Taliban regime.

References

Boyden J. and P. Ryder. 1996. *The Provision of Education to Children affected by Armed Conflict*. Oxford: Oxford University Press.

Centlivres-Demont, Micheline. 1994. 'Afghan women in peace, war and exile', in Myron Weiner and Ali Banuazizi (eds), *The Politics of Transformation in Afghanistan, Iran and Pakistan*. Syracuse: Syracuse University Press, pp 333–364.

Christensen, Hanne and Scott Wolf. 1988. *Survey of Social and Economic Conditions of Afghan Refugees in Pakistan*. Geneva: United Nations Research Institute for Social Development.

––– 1990. *The Reconstruction of Afghanistan: a Chance for Rural Afghan Women*. Geneva: United Nations Research Institute for Social Development.

Dupree, Louise. 1973. *Afghanistan*. Princeton: Princeton University Press.

Dupree, Nancy Hatch. 1984. 'Women and emancipation before the Saur Revolution', in Nazif Shahrani and Robert Canfield (eds), *Revolution and Rebellion in Afghanistan*. Berkeley: Institute for International Studies, pp.306–340.

Frelick, Bill. 1999. 'Refugees In Iran: Who should go? Who should stay?', *Refugee Reports* 20(6) (June 1999). Available at http://www.reliefweb.int.

Griffiths, John C. 1967. *Afghanistan*. New York: Fredrick A. Praeger.

Harrell-Bond, B.E. 1990. *Imposing Aid: Emergency Assistance to Refugees*. Oxford: Oxford University Press.

––– 1999. 'The experience of refugees as recipients of aid', in Alastair Ager (ed.), *Refugees: Perspectives on the Experience of Forced Migration*. New York: Pinter, pp. 136–68.

Hoodfar, Homa. 1998. *Volunteer Health Workers in Iran as Social Activists: Can 'governmental non-governmental organizations' be agents of democratisation?*, Occasional Papers No. 10. France: WLUML.

--- 2004. 'Families on the move: The changing role of Afghan refugee women in Iran', *Hawwa: Journal of Women of the Middle East and the Islamic World* 2(2): 141–71.

--- 2007. 'Women, Religion and the "Afghan education movement" *in Iran*', *Journal of Development Studies* Vo. 43(no. 2) 265–293.

---2008. "The long Road Home: Adolescent Afghans in Iran contemplate "Return" in Years of conflict: Adolescent, political Violence and Displacement edited by Jason Hart. Oxford: Berghahn Books, pp. 165–187.

McDonough, Sheila and Homa Hoodfar. 2004. 'Muslims in Canada: From ethnic groups to religious community', in Paul Bramadat and David Seljak (eds), *Religion and Ethnicity in Canada*. Toronto: Pearson Education.

Mehran, Golnar. 1991. 'The Creation of the new Muslim Women: Female education in the Islamic Republic of Iran', *Convergence* 23(4): 42–52.

--- 2002. 'The Presentation of self and other in post- revolutionary Iranian school textbooks', in Nikki R. Kiddie and Rudi Matthee (eds), *Iran and the Surrounding World*. Seattle: Washington University Press.

Moghadam, Valentine. 1993. *Modernizing Women: Gender and Social Change in the Middle East*. Boulder: Lynn Reinner Publishers.

Mousavi, Sayed Askar. 1998. *The Hazards of Afghanistan: An Historical, Cultural, Economic and Political Study*. London: Curzon Press.

Rajaee, Bahram. 2000. 'The politics of refugee policy in post-revolutionary Iran', *Middle East Journal* 54(1): 44–63.

Rashid, Ahmed. 2001. *Taliban: Islam, Oil and the New Great Game in Central Asia*. London: I.B. Tauris Publishers.

Rubin, Barnett R. 1994. 'Redistribution and the State in Afghanistan', in Myron Weiner and Ali Banuazizi, *The Politics of Social Transformation in Afghanistan, Iran and Pakistan*. Syracuse: Syracuse University.

--- 1995. *The Search for Peace in Afghanistan: From Buffer State to Failed State*. New Haven: Yale University Press.

Sadr, Shadi. 2007. 'Demand for Mother citizenship Rights: Legal Policies on Marriage between Iranian women and Afghan men', *Gul-v-Gu (dialogue on Culture and society)* 50: 61–81.

Tapper, Nancy. 1984. 'Causes and consequences of abolition of bride price in Afghanistan', in N. Shahrani and R. Canfield (eds), *Revolution and Rebellions in Afghanistan*. Berkeley: Institute of International Studies.

--- 1991. *The Bartered Brides*. Cambridge: Cambridge University Press.

UNHCR. 1999. Emergency Educational Assistance Unit. Education in Situation of Emergency crisis. Paris: UNESCO.

--- 2002. Education Sector Policy and Guidelines. Geneva: UNHCR.

5
Afghan Refugee Youth in Iran and the Morality of Repatriation

Sarah Kamal

The 'Children and Adolescents in Sahrawi and Afghani Refugee Households: Living with the Effects of Prolonged Armed Conflict and Forced Migration' (SARC) research project studied coping strategies and issues of belonging and identity among long-term Afghan and Sahrawi refugee youth in 2003. Our participatory research in Iran attempted to encourage the Afghan youth in our study to engage with and learn from the research, develop their skills and knowledge base, and build trust with the research team at a time of relatively high instability. In Tehran, over 100 Afghan youth became involved in SARC activities, such as generating video footage, producing a youth newsletter, interviewing each other, and organizing and participating in essay and photography competitions.

In one participatory research exercise, an eighteen-year-old Afghan refugee trained a video camera, slightly tilted, on the face of his fifteen-year-old male schoolmate for an off-the-cuff interview in the middle of the bustle and noise of an informal Afghan school. The two youth, Afghan refugees who had spent most if not all of their lives in Iran, were acutely aware of their uncertain futures in the face of the Iranian government's increasing pressure on Afghan families to repatriate to Afghanistan. As classmates crowded around and made faces for the camera, their exchange proceeded as follows:

Youth 1: You were born here [in Iran]?
Youth 2: Yes.
Youth 1: Which province are you from?
Youth 2: From Mazar-e-Sharif [in Afghanistan].
Youth 1: In your opinion, is it better here or in Afghanistan?
Youth 2: It's better here.

Youth 1: Why?
Youth 2: Because Afghanistan is in a terrible state.
Youth 1: From the standpoint of...?
Youth 2: From the standpoint of safety.
Youth 1: So from the standpoint of comfort-
Youth 2: [interrupts] For comfort, Afghanistan is better.
Youth 1: Afghanistan is better?!
Youth 2: For comfort, yes.
Youth 1: But you just said it was at war, so how is it better?
Youth 2: Well, um, from the ... [looks away, stutters] uh, you know, from
a different kind of comfort.
Youth 1: You mean like ... spiritually?
Youth 2: Yes.
Youth 1: Ah...

The video clip captures how one long-term refugee youth framed and
conceptualized his conflicting loyalties, stumbling somewhat as he
impulsively vocalized an unsettled, untested opinion fraught with emotional
resonance. With the aid of his older researcher-peer, the young man chose
to place 'the spirit' firmly in Afghanistan, a place he had never known
personally – perhaps speaking to the hope of finding wholeness upon
reuniting with his family's land of origin, or indicating his muted protest over
what many youth saw as the Islamic Republic of Iran's un-Islamic tactics for
divesting itself of its Afghan refugee population.

The SARC project was primarily interested in issues of identity and
belonging for refugee youth, and youth perspectives on religion, work,
education, gender and their larger social world. The timing of the project,
however, coincided with a concerted effort by the Iranian government and
the UNHCR to press for Afghan repatriation. Consequently, one of the
most immediate sources of anxiety and hope for the youth, as well as their
reflexive interrogations of themselves as moral beings, centred on
repatriation decision-making and prospects for a future in Iran or
Afghanistan.

Many of the youth and their families left for Afghanistan after the end of
the project's data collection period, in many cases as a response to the
growing inhospitality of their environment in Iran. In this chapter I will
discuss notions of morality in repatriation, especially as seen from the
perspectives of refugees, then I will describe some ways in which youth
experience refugee life and repatriation. I will present the context and
repatriation decision-making concerns of fifty long-term Afghan refugee
youth during the 2003 SARC project. I will then offer a 2006 follow-up
study on the decisions and outcomes of eight youth, four of whom
repatriated and four of whom remained as refugees. In doing so, I hope to

present a comparative, long-term account of 'return' (a problematic term that I use with caution since the majority of the youth were born in exile) from the youth's perspectives as embedded in their household and social contexts. I will focus particularly on the youth's evaluations of repatriation and coalescing constructions of self and moral adulthood as seen across the three-year time span following a coercive repatriation programme.

Morality in Repatriation

With voluntary repatriation presented as the optimal, durable solution in international political and legal frameworks since the early 1980s, much refugee research has been directed towards the legal, political and logistical issues in facilitating refugee repatriation. Social and economic concerns have also gained ground as research literature on return has increased, leading to an increasingly sophisticated understanding of repatriation as more than an unproblematic end to the refugee cycle (Cornish et al. 1999; Koser and Black 1999). A lack of clarity on the implications of repatriation programmes on the lives of refugees has brought about calls for more longitudinal investigations of refugee perspectives on repatriation (Bradley 2006; Eisenbruch 1997; Chimni 2002; Zetter 1994) especially among refugee youth with little or no experience of their family's country of origin (Cornish et al. 1999).

The plight of the refugees and their right of return is often debated and framed in moral terms, and this has been seen as problematic in a number of ways. Nader (2006) argues that the assumption that human rights paradigms are universal is 'moral imperialism' and dangerous for instilling 'normative blindness' (2006: 6). Chimni (2002) criticizes legal analysts' and academics' use of human rights discourse as promoting premature repatriation and legitimizing coerced return. Support for repatriation programmes has waned with growing awareness of their less than exemplary methods, with some programmes being seen as harassing their refugee population into returning (Blitz et al. 2005; Stigter 2006). Indeed, the coercive nature of some state-sponsored 'voluntary' repatriation programmes and the unstable 'post-conflict' conditions awaiting returnees has prompted ambivalence on the ethics of assisted return (Bakewell 2000; Bradley 2006; Chimni 2002; Stein 1997).

Debates on the morality of return have also extended into connections between identity and place. Drawing inspiration from critiques of anthropological localism, academics have focused attention on the commonsense notion that a 'natural' identity is anchored in an 'original' place or community (Ferguson and Gupta 1997; Malkki 1997; Black 2002). The assumption that identity is 'rooted' in place, they argue, makes dislocation unnatural – in the case of refugee flight, a violent and deeply painful wrenching. As a consequence, the ethical valence of return would outweigh that of any other outcome in a refugee crisis, with healing understood to begin with the 'popping' back into place of repatriation. In contrast, when identity and place are decoupled, and presuming that physical origin allows for a 'construction, rather than merely a discovery, of difference' (Ferguson and Gupta 1997: 13), the moral weight of repatriation becomes less intrinsic, as displacement indicates mobility rather than rupture.

Nevertheless, from the standpoint of the refugees themselves, the notion of return can carry a moral weight and is often considered as a central objective, albeit at times a symbolic one, in their lives. Roger Zetter (1994) conducted a long-term study of Greek-Cypriot refugees in protracted exile, and felt that an important outcome of their two decades of forced transience was an ambiguous sense of identity. Zetter argues that displaced Greek-Cypriots kept themselves separate from their host community because of the 'myth of the return' (citing Cruise O'Brien 1972), maintaining hopes of one day reconstituting their often idealized and fictionalized past homes even as they constructed lives for themselves in a new setting. As their exile extended into the future indefinitely and their prospects of return became increasingly remote, the Greek-Cypriots faced some ambivalence over whether they saw themselves as 'returnees or settlers, migrants rather than refugees?' (Zetter 1994: 314). Their 'profound conviction' in the need to repatriate, driven by the desire to recapture the past through returning to sites of nostalgic longing, was mediated by concern over changes to the physical locales to which they might be returning, and the realization that they themselves had changed in diaspora and would be unlikely to return to their prior existences.

In another study, Bisharat (1997), writing about Palestinian refugees in the West Bank, describes the shifting of longing for return for long-term forced migrants from the specificity of villages and houses to an idealized, romanticized homeland. Loyalty to particular communities transformed into strong nationalism, especially as long-term displacement saw the physical locales to which the refugees had strong ties changed and removed by occupying forces. As with the Greek-Cypriot refugees and the myth of the return, the Palestinian refugees' quest for return had political implications that imbued repatriation with a moral force – the righting of a violent wrong, and the restoration of natural order.

Black (2002) suggests that the moral case for return was particularly emphasized in the case of Bosnia-Herzegovina. He argues that in Bosnia repatriation was understood as offering a means for reconciliation and redress for ethnic cleansing. Such claims regarding ethnic 'homelands' were problematic, however, as they had been the basis for ethnic division and cause of forced migration in the first place.

Refugee Youth and Repatriation

Assertions regarding an ethnic 'homeland' and connections between identity and place can be challenging in the case of long-term refugee youth. Youth born in the middle of the refugee 'cycle' often inherit some aspects of the confluence of nostalgic longing, political claims, social rights and moral obligations of enforced exile from their elders. They can also, however, have some basis for claiming naturalization in their host nation. How might youth born as refugees weigh the morality of return against their right to belong in the only land they have known? How might youth contribute to household decision-making regarding repatriation, if at all?

Forty-four per cent of the world's 21 million refugee population is comprised of youth aged eighteen years or younger (UNHCR 2005). Youth in exile have been characterized as conflicted and burdened: enduring a loss of cultural pride (Vargas 1999; Blitz et al. 2005), feeling marginalized in the host community (Vargas 1999, Zetter 1994, 1999), and facing constant uncertainty over their futures (Anderson 2001). Bash and Zezlina-Phillips (2006) argue that the 'neither here nor there' psychological limbo of refugee identity, together with the transition into adulthood, can make the emotional instability of refugee adolescence fraught with turmoil. They suggest that within such uncertainty, refugee youth do demonstrate resilience in that they can 'act as managers of their own, many sided, frequently fluid, identities in their search for cultural anchors' (2006: 126). Such resilience is not without cost, however: in maintaining and proclaiming the multiple identities required by their context, refugee youth risk undermining the personal cohesion for which they strive.

Refugee youth are often differentiated from the older generation by both their ability to cross cultural boundaries more fluidly and their looser affinity to their country of origin. Refugee youth, in more easily absorbing the host country modes of being, can represent a demarcation in refugee families between 'before' and 'after' relative to their parents (Rousseau et al. 2001). Seen within their family networks, refugee youth have been described as a vehicle for the retention of their parent's culture and memory (Dhruvarajan 1993) or a conduit for the interpretation of and connection with the host community (Anderson 2001).

For refugee youth, the prospect of the 'return' to a land in which they have never been or barely remember can evoke multiple anxieties. Refugee youth can face rekindled uprootedness (Eisenbruch 1997), loss of prosperity and mismatched skill sets when engaging with their new, often rural, environments (Bradley 2006), and risk becoming reverse refugees in their country of origin (Zetter 1999). Given their limited experience of the family's country of origin, youth at times distance themselves from the older generation's nostalgic longing to return (Kakoli 2000; Zetter 1994; Rousseau et al. 2001) even though they can be influenced by those discourses into visualizing an idealized home (Cornish et al 1999). Refugee youth's reasons for wanting to return are often different and more politicized than the sentimental discourses of their parents, reflecting claims to rights and property (Zetter 1994, 1999; Rousseau et al. 2001) or more idealistic desires to rebuild their country (Blitz et al. 2005).

Dona and Berry's (1999, in Cornish et al. 1999) model of re-acculturation posits that long-term forced migrants' difficulties upon return are similar to their struggles adapting to life in their host country. Cornish et al. (1999) used the re-acculturation model to study the experiences of Malawian refugee youth upon repatriation. They found that young Malawian refugees experienced 'acculturative stress and ambiguity regarding self and national identity' after repatriating from Zambia (1999: 281). Their study investigated a sample of youth refugees born in exile and brought up in the knowledge of their difference without having experienced transition from their family's original context. They found that for many of the youth, feelings of being outsiders did not abate upon return, but in some cases were actually exacerbated. Some of the youth became unsure of their nationality, and some seemed to identify themselves with a returnee identity. The study authors suggest that the returnee youth's unfavourable comparisons of Malawi with their former host country indicate that the refugee experience continues to be difficult after repatriation.

Refugee youth, then, can experience repatriation with greater confusion than and in a different way from their parents. Adolescent notions of the morality of repatriation may also differ significantly from those of adults. As suggested by the fifteen-year-old Afghan interviewee's quote regarding spiritual comfort, despite the generally accepted belief among many Afghan households in our study that the Islamic Republic of Iran represented a more 'pure' form of Islam, Afghanistan became a mystical-moral destination for a number of youth. I will provide some context of Afghan refugee life in Iran and describe our study of repatriation in detail before returning to a discussion of the logic behind and implications of this point of view.

Afghan Refugee Youth in Iran

Unlike Pakistan, which has received significant support for its refugee population, Iran has hosted Afghans as one of the largest refugee populations in the world for over twenty years with very little international support. Most Afghan refugees in Iran are integrated with the local population, with only a small percentage living in refugee camps. With the fall of the Taliban, Iran renewed the efforts it had made since the 1990s to discourage the inflow of refugee and promote repatriation. In 2003, the

Iranian government signed a tripartite agreement with the government of Afghanistan and UNHCR to facilitate the voluntary repatriation of Afghans. Iran also passed eleven articles entitled 'Regulations on accelerating repatriation of Afghan nationals' which outlawed employment, administrative services, banking, participation in civil society and accommodation for Afghans without valid residence permits (Abbasi-Shavasi et al. 2005). In the same year, the government implemented the mandatory registration of all Afghans in Iran. While the state had conducted repeated campaigns to repatriate Afghans since the 1990s, the more stringent enforcement of its 2003 initiatives instilled anxiety in the Afghan population.

Access to formal education was a central factor in the decision of many Afghan families to migrate to Iran. Over the years, the Iranian government gradually withdrew free Iranian educational services from the Afghan refugee population. Informal Afghan-run schools were organized by the Afghan community, often operating out of people's homes before shifting to larger venues (see chapter 4 in this volume, for a detailed historical account of Afghan refugee education in Iran). Many of the Afghan youth who were forced out of Iranian institutions felt the decline in the quality of teaching and resources in Afghan-run schooling keenly. Using second-hand Iranian textbooks, Afghan-run schools had neither the facilities nor staff to provide the quality of education available in mainstream Iranian schools. 2003 was a pivotal year for the youth, as the Iranian government made clear its intention to (and gradually implemented) the forced closure of many informal Afghan-run schools. For many youth, Afghan schools represented their final link with educational prospects in the country. The closure of most if not all informal Afghan schools (although some reopened after a few months' closure), together with highly curtailed economic prospects, became a juncture for decision-making regarding return for many families.

The SARC Project in 2003

I spent nine months in 2003 at an informal Afghan school in Tehran, working to set up and collect data for the SARC project.[2] The school we had chosen as our main data collection site in Tehran was Afghan-run and Afghan-funded, and located in a small, fairly poor southern Tehran suburb sometimes called 'little Kabul' due to its high Afghan population. The air was hot, dusty and polluted from the smog of Tehran and the oil refineries a few miles away. Children in slippers were often seen kicking stiff pink and white striped plastic balls in the streets. Unlike the fashionably dressed women in north Tehran, women in the suburb were almost invariably dressed in the more conservative black *chador* (large, all-enveloping Iranian

Islamic covering for women) and men often seen fingering prayer beads. The area had a utilitarian, industrial feel to it with little investment in greenery or architectural beauty.

Life for most Afghans in the suburb was highly transitory, with many Afghan households moving once or twice every year due to steep rent increases by landlords against whom they had no legal protection. Afghan schools were even more vulnerable as recognizable centres of Afghan activity. The school's lack of money, fear of vandalism, its more or less yearly displacement, and legally unrecognized status led it to maintain an anonymous exterior and low profile. Indeed, students were instructed not to cluster in obvious groups when entering the dank, dark, noisy and overheated basement housing the school's five classrooms.

Figure 5.1: 'Little Kabul' in the south of Tehran.

Afghan youth felt the insecurity of their schooling and living quarters keenly, and negative encounters with Iranians also added stress to their lives. As a researcher and participant observer in the SARC project I occasionally experienced[3] the routine discrimination facing Afghans travelling around Tehran, including calls of 'Afghani Afghani!' in the streets, rudeness and dismissive behaviour in markets, and muttered propositions by men walking beside or behind me. Four months into my fieldwork, I had become so conditioned to negative attention from strangers that if people treated me poorly, I often assumed it was because they thought I was Afghan.

Political instability in Iran was another pervasive source of tension. In June 2003, university students protesting against the privatization of universities spearheaded nightly demonstrations in the streets of Tehran that were also an outlet for more generalized discontent with the Iranian regime. While the majority of Afghans had little to do with the protests, many felt vulnerable in the face of angry mobs wandering the streets, as easy targets for harassment and beatings by bands of frustrated Iranian youth.

At the start of the SARC data collection period, the youth knew very little about Afghanistan. Its flag, map, the location of Kabul, and the sound of the Kabuli accent were unknown to almost all our interviewees. For many, footage of ruins and devastation on the television vied with their parents' nostalgic memories of stunning natural beauty and fertile land. In involving the youth in data collection processes and asking them questions about their identities and lives as forced migrants, the project catalysed some soul-searching and collective inquiry into Afghanistan, the meaning of migration and repatriation.

The SARC project's participatory research captured some of the youth's early attempts at conceptualizing and voicing their conflicting views on Iran and Afghanistan. The possibility of remaining in familiar but unfriendly Iran evoked ambivalence, with the youth saying they would enjoy a greater standard of living and benefit from a 'higher' culture at the expense of continued discrimination and feelings of not belonging or being second-class citizens. Also often present in their discourse was a strong justification for not repatriating in the near future: 'we would go, but ... our lives would be at risk because the country is insecure/my family would not survive economically/my studies would be disrupted.'

As time progressed and the youth grew more comfortable navigating and vocalizing their often contradictory feelings to us, pride, defiance and concern over Iranian discrimination emerged more frequently in their discourse. The SARC project supported enrichment activities for the youth which included the establishment of a student-run school newsletter. The youth decided to include pictures and investigative articles on the Iranian government's 2003 mandatory registration for all Afghan refugees, including 'person on the street' interviews with newly registered Afghans highlighting the injustices and mistreatment of the process.

In another activity, a photography competition, the youth chose to highlight the menial, poorly paid jobs which were often the only employment opportunities available to Afghans in Iran. I was particularly struck by an encounter I had with a pair of boys who walked into the research office and asked me to accept two photographs they had taken as entries to the competition. I downloaded the digital photos they had taken onto the computer, and saw that the photos showed two young men collecting garbage. In all the photographs, the faces of the garbage collectors were not visible – either because their faces were turned away or blocked strategically. I thought the photographs were good, and said so, then teasingly added, 'Hey, I know that guy!' as I could tell that one of the faceless garbage workers was the youth submitting the photograph. The boy took my teasing graciously as the other boy laughed and punched his shoulder. I then asked the boys if they could explain why they had chosen to take the picture they had. They asked for some time to think about it, and I nodded. They came back later: the boy who was not in the photograph deferred to the one who was, and he looked me straight in the eye, a thin, dark-haired handsome boy with deep lines on his face that I associate with old age, and said, 'we took this picture because we want people to know what Afghan youth have to do'. There was an honesty and dignity in his straightforward gaze. 'This is what I do when I'm not in school. I'm a garbage collector.'

I smiled and thanked him sincerely for an excellent entry. And later as I thought about it, I knew what it was that had made this moment so striking to me: I cherish the memory of that other boy, the one who was not in the picture, smiling as his garbage collector friend spoke to me, quietly leaning an arm on his friend's shoulder and seeming as though his chest might burst with pride.

Figure 5.2: Two youth's submission to the 'Afghans at work' photography competition.

The youth's feelings about their status relative to Iranians were often tinged with battered self-esteem mixed with the defiant pride I have illustrated above. Most working Afghans were relegated to the low-income, informal economy as labourers or unskilled workers – difficult, low-paying jobs that few Iranians would accept. Their hard-earned self-sufficiency, however, as well as the contribution they believed they made to the Iranian economy, were sources of dignity. Likewise, while often ashamed of their poverty and the poor conditions of their school, the youth circulated stories of Afghan students scoring higher than Iranians in Iranian schools and competitions and being denied their rightful place. In general, the youth seemed vulnerable and defensive about their refugee status and the backwardness of their country, but also characterized themselves as more morally upright, resourceful, academically gifted and hardworking than the 'soft' Iranians who were accustomed to the many privileges Afghans lacked.

The youth, described by their long-time teacher as being generally apathetic and pessimistic in classes, embraced the SARC project's enrichment activities enthusiastically, perhaps in part because they finally felt their school's activities rivalled those of better-equipped Iranian institutions. The students gradually began to feel as if they had some control over their environment, and their teachers noticed the change in their confidence level in classes. One committee of youth became responsible for looking into ways of improving the school's conditions. They installed ceiling fans that made the heat in the school more bearable, painted and repaired rusty school benches, and provided ice-cold drinkable water to the school.

Students at a nearby informal Afghan school also set up an extra-curricular youth club. With very limited adult supervision, they replaced broken panes of glass, cleaned out a well that had been filled with litter, painted and cleaned out a storage room (which they later turned into a student-run library), and even repaired a broken, uneven step and floor with cement. Shortly thereafter, however, the municipal government sent notice that that school's premises were to be demolished to make way for a park. Approximately two months after their youth club activities began, the local authorities sent bulldozers to tear down the walls around the school. The teachers were forced to evacuate their students in the middle of class.

For many SARC youth, the bulldozing incident at their neighbouring school and subsequent forced closure of Afghan schools by the Iranian state fed anger over what they felt were unfair violations of their Islamic right to education (see chapter 4 in this volume). The youth also felt despair and fear over the unforgiving nature of their environment. Some of the youth became convinced that remaining in Iran would be futile – that they were powerless against systematic blocks to their advancement. When their school was reopened after two months of closure, the youth revitalized their school newsletter called 'The Voice of Today's Generation' under a new name, 'The Heart of Asia', to reflect both their emotional response towards Afghanistan and their assertion of its value and importance regionally. Meanwhile, a quieter stream of opinion within the upsurge in nationalism among the youth admitted (privately, often requesting anonymity) that they wished they could move to a third country.

While often aware of what the more 'correct' patriotic responses were to direct questions regarding repatriation, anxiety and uncertainty often dominated the youth's everyday conversations, particularly given the likely difficulty of re-entering Iran after crossing the border into Afghanistan. Where Zetter (1999) suggests that Greek-Cypriot refugees had 'retained the conviction – to varying degrees and despite all the objective evidence – that their exile is temporary and that they will eventually return home' (1999: 4), a significant number of Afghan refugee youth appeared more reluctant to admit any eventuality to repatriation, with some declaring definitively that they would not return despite some peer pressure to show preference for repatriation.

The youth's anxieties over repatriation included concern over Afghanistan's 'lower' culture, lack of infrastructure, Westernization/degraded Islam and insecurity, as well as their own job prospect fears, perceived mismatched skill set for daily life in the country, and distress that they would lose their friends. Girls especially feared that the more traditional, conservative culture in Afghanistan would make life unbearable, prohibiting them from engaging in the cultural activities, work, study and physical mobility they enjoyed in Iran. Having grown up with Islamic codes prevalent in Iran, some girls were concerned that they would have to wear Afghanistan-style Islamic coverings, which they believed would be less morally correct than the Iranian *magna'eh* (a head-dress similar in style to a nun's habit).

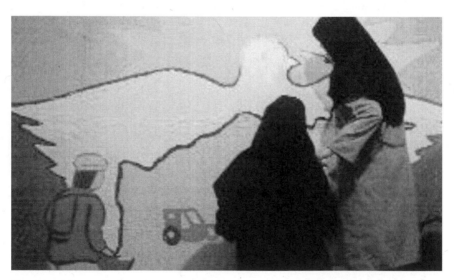

Figure 5.3: Afghan girls wearing the Iranian *magna'eh* in Tehran.

Figure 5.4: Afghan women wearing the Afghan *chador* in Kabul.

In comparison, the positive aspects of life in Afghanistan were less diverse and often expressed more poetically. The youth cited lack of discrimination, a feeling of empowerment, having the opportunity to help rebuild the country, and, quite simply, being in one's own country as advantages of repatriation. Some youth suggested that in Afghanistan they would not be able to reach their potential, whereas others felt they had to repatriate in order to be able to achieve their goals. Education was viewed as higher in quality in Iran, but more freely accessible – where facilities existed – in Afghanistan. The majority believed they would repatriate, some more out of a sense of fatalism ('we have to go back at some point') than choice, with several pointing out that they would need to spend several years adjusting to the conditions in Afghanistan. The general understanding was that the Iranian government's policies would make re-entry into Iran difficult if not impossible, and thus the perceived permanence of repatriation was a significant source of anxiety.

Their parents, meanwhile, almost all believed that living in Iran had been positive from the standpoint of education. For those that found life in Iran had drawbacks, the concerns they raised regarding their children included addiction and the negative influence of 'overly free' Iranian youth, lowered prospects in the economic sector, loss of self-esteem from discrimination, as well as loss of Afghan identity. A number of the parents pointed out the ironies their children faced, whereby they were much better educated than they would have been in Afghanistan yet were relegated to menial jobs in the economic sector; or where they had learned a great deal yet lost themselves as Afghans.

As for repatriation, around a quarter of the fifty parents we interviewed said they wanted their children to return to Afghanistan; another quarter said they wanted them to return if Afghanistan was reconstructed or secure; almost half expressed a preference for the youth remaining in Iran; while the few who expressed other opinions felt it would be better to go abroad, did not have a preference, or felt that their family was in a kind of limbo, unable to return, unable to stay.

2006 Follow-up Study Methodology

The SARC data collection period ended in December 2003. When we next heard from teachers at the school a year later, we were told that eighty per cent of the youth we had interviewed had moved to Afghanistan. I was able to contact two of the youth in particular. Nasir[4] (twenty-year old, male) and Amin (twenty-one-year old, male) were close friends who had lived all their lives in Iran as refugees before moving to Afghanistan in late 2004. I remembered them both as well-liked and respected young men in the final year of their studies, Nasir a charismatic, idealistic extrovert and Amin quieter, studious and pragmatic – seemingly an inseparable pair. I was able to arrange a meeting with them in 2005, and we worked together on research projects for six months in Kabul. Nasir subsequently migrated back to Tehran while Amin chose to remain in Afghanistan.

I contacted them both again in late 2006 for the purposes of this follow-up study. I requested that they each, as participant-researchers, interview themselves (one male) and three of their former SARC project peers (one male and two females), and send me electronic audio recordings of their interviews. Nasir was in Tehran at the time, and Amin in Kabul, so I was able to acquire four interviews of SARC youth who had remained refugees, conducted by a continuing refugee, and four of those who had repatriated, conducted by a youth who had repatriated himself.

I sent Nasir and Amin identical interview questionnaires that focused on significant life events, national affiliation, migration, home and aspirations for the future. I offered very limited instruction and training on the questionnaire, asking instead that Nasir and Amin interpret and paraphrase the questions as they saw fit and add other questions or prompts of interest to them regarding repatriation and life as forced migrants. I was interested in tracking changes in what I hoped was fairly neutral terminology in the interview schedule, asking for example about 'going' to Afghanistan rather than 'return' to see what terms the youth used in referring to repatriation. Some of my questions were rather vague and unclear; for instance, one question asked if the interviewee had travelled with his/her family, and how they had felt about any such travels. A question asking about 'travel with family', I reasoned, could mean the original migration to Iran, displacement within Iran, leisure travel, or repatriation – interviewer prompts would possibly reflect the direction of Nasir and Amin's interests in highlighting differing concerns in the refugee and returnee contexts.

My aim was thus to analyse their interviews on three levels: first, contrasting the discourses of male and female youth returnees in Kabul against those of their male and female peers left behind (or, in one case, re-migrated) in Tehran; second, evaluating all the youth's current perspectives against their SARC interviews three years earlier; and third, juxtaposing the assumptions, modifications in interview wording, and research framings of the two interviewers against one another. My own prior relationships with the youth, especially the interviewers, offered a contextualization of and check on the data collection process.

Nasir and Amin conducted their interviews in December 2006. The interviews averaged twenty-six minutes in length and were conducted in Farsi, and I transcribed and translated them. Nasir, who was conducting interviews in Tehran, was unable to find two females who had previously participated in the SARC project. He substituted two other female long-term forced migrants studying at the informal school where we had based the SARC research. Otherwise I recalled the faces, personalities and interests of the other six interviewees from 2003.

The interviewees ages ranged from 15 to 21 (average 18.9) and their ethnicities were Tajik (1), Hazara (1), Qezelbash (1), Seyyed (3) and undisclosed (2). All were Farsi-speaking and their religious backgrounds were Shi'a (5), Sunni (1) and undisclosed (2). All of the youth had received their high school diplomas, with one youth being enrolled in university. All but two had no pre forced migration memories of Afghanistan, having either been only a toddler or not born when their family first crossed into Iran. All were the most educated members in their families. The interviewees were not, nor were they meant to be, a representative sample of Afghan refugee youth in Iran. Instead, commonality of refugee context and relatively uniform age and education allowed for a somewhat less complicated analysis of the influence of return on their lives.

Attitudes towards Repatriation Choices

Life in Afghanistan was difficult in 2006. Given the resurgence of Taliban activity, the weak economy, and much lower level of development in Afghanistan relative to Iran,[5] I expected to hear dissatisfaction from the youth who had chosen to repatriate. I presumed that the youth in Tehran, meanwhile, would be thankful they had remained in the relative stability of Iran, where informal Afghan schools were still maintaining a precarious but steady existence despite official government prohibitions. In fact the reverse was true: the repatriated youth expressed happiness over their decision to move and were certain they did not want to return to Iran while the refugee youth were frustrated and concerned that they had very limited future prospects in Iran. I will now present the stories of the returnee youth, as captured by participant-researcher Amin.

The Returnees

The youth had been very close in Tehran, perhaps forced by dint of the many pressures on them to build a strong community with each other in their overcrowded school. From all the accounts I have heard, most of the youth then lost touch with each other in the struggle and confusion of repatriating. However, Amin was able to find three of his former classmates for the purposes of this study relatively quickly: Maryam (female, seventeen years old), Zekya (female, twenty years old) and Mohammad (male, twenty years old). I remembered Maryam as a highly idealistic chatterbox – precocious, academically successful and earnest. Zekya, on the other hand, was strong-willed and forthright, with flashing green eyes and a strong gravitation towards symbolism and the aesthetic. Mohammad, meanwhile, had been an energetic athlete, his mischievous smile holding the easy confidence of a popular young man.

During the SARC interviews in 2003, Maryam and Zekya said that they wanted to repatriate for ideological reasons ('it's my country/I must help rebuild'). Amin was fairly clear that he and his family's future lay in Afghanistan, as his father had already travelled several times to Kabul in search of housing and livelihoods prospects. Mohammad expressed no preference for repatriation in 2003 directly, instead suggesting that he had never considered himself Iranian despite living in Iran for fifteen years, and that he felt it was a good time to return to Afghanistan to help rebuild, even as he was concerned that external influences were corrupting Afghan society.

In 2006, Amin interviewed himself and Maryam, Zekya and Amin in Kabul regarding their repatriation experiences. He began by directing my question about 'travel with family' towards the moment of crossing the Iran-Afghanistan border and travelling through different provinces of Afghanistan towards Kabul. All four interviews at that point took on the air of an often repeated story – a lodestone of returnee experience – and were remarkably uniform. For all the returnees, crossing the border was a pivotal and highly emotional moment, where the disparity between Iran's more developed infrastructure and Afghanistan's devastation caused the youth distress, pain and anxiety, and made them think they had made a terrible mistake. In the words of Maryam:

We were very shocked, it was unbelievable that Afghanistan was so ... [interrupts herself] Nobody wanted to come to Afghanistan except me.

Day and night I would say: let's go to Afghanistan let's go to Afghanistan, we've got to build Afghanistan, and I'd had all these plans for what I would do and all of those dissolved at once. I didn't know what to do, to laugh or to cry. I was like that an entire week, neither crying nor laughing.

The adjustment process was difficult and involved much economic hardship for all the youth and their families. The two female returnees struggled in particular. Zekya described how she fought on her first day in Afghanistan with a stranger who informed her she was not allowed, as a woman, to approach a heritage site. Maryam recounted how she almost fell into a well because she did not know how to pump water – domestic chores were much more physically taxing in Afghanistan. The youth also had to adjust their behaviour and clothing to integrate with Afghan society. Shifting away from the Iranian accent[6] was particularly important, as was evident in the (in two cases, rather unsuccessful) ways in which the youth tried to adopt Dari phrases and a Kabul accent in their 2006 interviews. Maryam described a painful episode in her integration process as follows:

When I first came here it was very difficult for me, my accent was very bad, I couldn't speak Dari at all. People would all call me *Iranigak* (little Iranian), and in the streets, or in schools they called me *Iranigak*. In school the teachers seemed to have a particular grudge against us. I went to grade 12 and my algebra teacher – and I'll never forget this, this is the worst memory of my life – I was new at the school and I was wearing a black *magna'eh* and suddenly he pulled it, and he pulled it so hard that it ripped a bit, and he said 'this isn't Iran that you're wearing this, a black headscarf, you've made yourself like a crow, this is Afghanistan'. I took my bag and went home and I felt really bad, and the next day my dad went with me to school and said 'what is going on here that you treat my daughter so badly' – just think, there I was a grade 12 student, taking my dad to school! – and so the teacher did apologise, but it was the worst experience of my life.

After their initial shock and the period of adjustment, the lives of three out of the four youth improved and, more acclimatized, the youth began to feel that they had made the right choice in repatriating. In general, they reported that their families were also reasonably content. Zekya and Maryam recounted how they believed their families had moved to Afghanistan on their insistence, and how both had struggled with depression and guilt during the re-acculturation period, but how also, in time, they came to see that everyone appreciated having moved. According to Zekya, increased opportunities and access to schooling (even if the educational system in Afghanistan was not as strong) had made her family happy and thankful about the move. In Maryam's family, her older brother who was studying in

Kabul University was particularly happy about having moved. The rest of her family were less enthusiastic, with her parents maintaining they were only in Afghanistan for their children's education. Despite their complaints, however, she said that reading between the lines, one could see that they preferred repatriation as their plans for the future were always about Afghanistan.

Amin and Mohammad said that their families had both moved on their father's instigation. Apart from Amin's mother and sister, who had not wanted to move originally and continued to be unhappy with repatriation, the two families had passed through the sharp downturn of the adjustment period to a sense of preference for life in Afghanistan over life in Iran.

Of the four returnee youth, Amin (the interviewer) is now studying his preferred subject in university; Maryam is working for an international organization and hopes to be accepted to a midwifery programme at university; Zekya is a host for Radio Arman, the most popular radio station in Kabul, and plans to apply for university in the coming year; and Mohammad, whose life continues to be difficult, is working and attempting to further his education through self-learning at home. In general, the returnees demonstrate an acceptance of their situations: although their lives are not perfect, the youth have clear goals which they believe can be achieved. Despite Mohammad's family's unsatisfactory situation of having 'the power of making decisions ... more or less not with [them]', Mohammad finds comfort in having weathered the worst of his repatriation. The youth admit freely their difficulties in adjusting to life in Afghanistan and earlier unhappiness ('I cursed the fact that I am Afghan' – Maryam) but believe the adjustment was something that they – and indeed, all Afghans in Iran – would have had to pass through sooner or later. They now express contentment with their decision to return and are hopeful about and have concrete plans for the future. Indeed, in comparative terms relative to the descriptive accounts their parents gave of their difficulties in adjusting to life in Iran, the youth appeared to adjust more rapidly to their new lives in Iran.

The Continuing Refugees

In Tehran, Nasir was able to track down former SARC participant Hamed (male, twenty years old), a tall, generous, warm-hearted young man who enjoyed joking about and playing the perpetual long-suffering victim at the hands of his friends. However, the schoolteacher who had helped the SARC project identify and interact with our fifty interviewees in 2003 was unable to find any female former SARC youth in Tehran. As a result Nasir substituted Hanifa (fifteen years old) and Leila (eighteen years old), both young women who had studied at the same informal Afghan school.

In his 2003 SARC interview, Nasir did not disclose whether he wanted to repatriate to Afghanistan. I heard from his peers that he was embarrassed to admit that he did not want to return. Hamed, meanwhile, said directly that he did not like Afghanistan and felt it to be culturally inferior to Iran. There is no SARC data on the two female refugee youth, although according to their self-reporting in 2006, Hanifa and Leila had both wanted to return in 2003.

While interviewing himself and his three peers in Tehran in 2006, Nasir interpreted 'travel with family' to mean movement and displacement within Iran. He offered in his self-interview a detailed history of his family's migration from Esfahan, a city in the south of Iran, to Tehran in the north, and subsequent displacement from suburb to suburb in greater Tehran. He identified this movement as the source of much of his later suffering: he was expelled from an Iranian school he loved in the 1990s due to a new government policy regarding Afghan education which required that Afghans only study in the city in which they had been registered – in his case, Esfahan. He was too young to move from Tehran to Esfahan on his own to continue studying in an Iranian school, and thus was forced to enrol in a resource-poor informal Afghan school. While he had travelled across the Iranian border to Afghanistan in 2004, he did not offer a 'border crossing' story, but instead said briefly that he had felt good in Afghanistan since, as a man, he was not vulnerable to the kinds of harassment and beatings Afghan men can face in Iran.

Hamed described how his family had also travelled within Iran. They were forced to move from Tehran to the countryside in Kashan (central Iran) for seven months for undisclosed reasons. The move was difficult for Hamed as he lost his friends and found rural living unpleasant. He was relieved when his family returned to Tehran. Leila, meanwhile, moved to Mashad (eastern Iran, close to the Iranian-Afghan border) for two years before returning to Tehran where rent increases forced her family to move almost yearly. She saw Afghanistan as a place where her displacements and the transitory nature of her relationships could come to an end. Hanifa had not travelled while in Iran, and felt that 'travel is good' even if it meant a period of adjusting to new people and environments.

By favouring an 'internal displacement' interpretation of 'travel with family' over others, Nasir seemed to be attempting to highlight his own and others' loss and unhappiness through movement, and their lack of stability within Iran. Nasir's self-interview demonstrated clearly his frustrations with feeling Iranian but not being accepted, and his helplessness in the face of rejection. He described his unhappiness over several incidents where his Afghan nationality resulted in expulsion from educational or cultural activities in Iran. At the same time, however, he seemed to feel trapped in an 'Iranianized' identity:

I had never seen Afghanistan, I'd grown up with Iranian culture and I am like a completely Iranian individual, and I can even speak Farsi much better than many Iranians that are in the provinces, but I'd never seen Afghanistan … I grew up in Iran, my memories are Iran's, the good, bad, ugly are all Iran's. I'm 20, and only one of those years, last year, belongs to Afghanistan. The rest belong to Iran. But honestly, I don't feel calm or secure in Iran. I feel like I'm in a cage.

Nasir added numerous questions and probes to his interviews that attempted to investigate his interviewees' feelings about their identity 'beyond slogans', in his words. His questions included:

Do you think if you went to Afghanistan you would feel good or bad?

Do you think you could reach your wishes in Iran?

Sitting by yourself one day, have you ever thought to yourself: I wish I were Iranian instead of Afghan?

If they gave you Iranian citizenship, would you stay here and become Iranian or return?

Do you wish Iran and Afghanistan would become one country?

In two cases, the interviews ended with his interviewees admitting, to his evident satisfaction, a greater preference for Iran than Afghanistan. A rather striking undercurrent of anxiety and incoherence permeated the interviews of Hamed and Hanifa, who contradicted themselves, vacillating between stating that they wanted to go to Afghanistan and preferred to remain in Iran. They were often unable to define their national affiliations and loyalty, torn between a sense of filial duty towards Afghanistan and a desire to be accepted into Iranian society, no longer outsiders by birth. Hamed was particularly inconsistent – he at first stated:

Well, until 2 or 3 months ago, I really wanted to go to Afghanistan, but now it's changed and I don't want to go at all.

But then in the following exchange, he expressed a different sentiment:

With all the problems I've seen in Iran, personally I'd really like to go to Afghanistan. Go there and stay, not return. Because honestly in Iran we as Afghans are held back a lot. If in our own country we are able to get a small, suitable job with a low wage, I've been told that life can pass really well there.

Interviewer (Nasir): *I don't understand, on the one hand you say you want to go, on the other you say you don't want to go. Help me out here!*

First in our state, we can't make decisions for ourselves; our parents make decisions for us. Second, now it's winter in Afghanistan and it's also winter in Iran. For now, I don't at all want to go, but if more of our countrymen were going, that is if there was a lot of hustle and bustle and most people were going back, I would 100% go back, for example in the spring, I've sworn with members of my family that in the spring we would go check it out.

I found these inconsistencies interesting, as they had not been evident in the SARC interviews from 2003. The 2006 refugee interviews point towards some frustration over lack of agency, with decision-making being contingent on external circumstances rather than on personal choice. For instance, in the excerpt from Hamed's interview, three statements appear to indicate Hamed's powerlessness: '*personally*, I'd really like to go', 'we can't make decisions for ourselves; our parents make decisions for us', and 'if … most people were going, I would 100% go back'. Lack of agency might also have been some form of justification for the dissonance of stubbornly remaining in a country which had strongly and repeatedly made Afghan refugees unwelcome and removed many of their prospects for work and education.

Nasir had a tendency to ask somewhat leading questions, and had a beginning researcher expectation (shared by his counterpart Amin) that he would find uniformity and 'one' convergent answer to his questions. Despite his often cajoling or persistent courtroom barrister approach to questioning, not all the interviewees expressed conflict, however: as one of two youth who had memories of Afghanistan (her family migrated to Iran when she was eight years old), Leila was very stable in her Afghan nationality: 'I remember the wars with Najib[7] and the coming of the Taliban, however long I live I wouldn't ever forget my main and fundamental identity as an Afghan.' In fact, certain of the temporary nature of her stay in Iran, Leila described the conscious effort she made to maintain commitment to her activities in Iran:

Given that we would like to go to Afghanistan but can't, it's been good to realise that for now we are staying here so that we could work on all the little dreams without continually thinking that we will return today or tomorrow. We haven't been thinking: no, this goal can't be reached because we're returning to Afghanistan.

Nasir, as the only youth who had repatriated but then decided to return to refugee life in Iran, maintained that his return to Iran was not of his own choice:

Why did I come back? Because I was forced to, I couldn't not come, because I believe a person who wants to reach some things has to give something up, I fired my final bullet to go to university in Iran, with [Amin] I wandered around a lot and tried to find other countries to go to but since we weren't young we weren't able to. I never wanted to return again to Iran but I was forced to in order to continue my studies.

The remark that he was 'forced' to return to Iran is somewhat disingenuous as, clearly, Nasir did have the option of remaining in Afghanistan to study in Kabul like his friend Amin. Unfortunately, after leaving Afghanistan to try and enter a university in Iran, Nasir found that his admissions application had been blocked and, despite much effort on his part for five months, was eventually rejected. He lost most of his savings in the process, and is now living and working at a tailor's shop despite not really knowing the trade. He wants to continue his studies and is attempting to find the means to enter a university in India.

Hamed also wants to work and study but is struggling. He had set up a computer and language teaching institution in Tehran with three of his brothers, but the authorities shut down their institution two months before his interview. Left with no income and no prospects for entering university, and only allowed menial unskilled labour by Iranian law, he is finding life increasingly difficult. Both he and Nasir have the feeling that they are going through all the right motions but not getting anywhere. Hanifa and Leila, being younger and still engaged in studies and teaching, are less concerned about the future. They are also aware that they will only be able to study and work in Iran as a temporary arrangement, but appear to assume and be reconciled with the prospect that they will return to Afghanistan in the future.

Implications of Repatriation

Afghan refugee youth, often under-investigated in large-scale surveys of male or female heads of refugee households, warrant much more particularized attention than I have been able to present in this study. The diverse perspectives I have included above indicate that refugee youth are far from a monolithic category, and more research would be necessary to understand how adolescents influence and are affected by repatriation choices, especially in exploring the experiences of long-term returnees. I do suggest, however, three ways in which different long-term refugee youth in Iran may have experienced return to Afghanistan:

Repatriation as Self-reconciliation

Bash and Zezlina-Phillips (2006) suggest that transition, for refugee adolescents, is multi-faceted. Refugee youth must position themselves psychologically relative to childhood and adulthood as well as national affiliation. They suggest that the transitions of adolescence, mixed with the blurred boundaries of exile and hybrid identity, constitute a significant but not insurmountable challenge for youth in finding and defining their identities. Muggeridge and Doná (2006), meanwhile, propose that the first visit home for refugees constitutes an important milestone, causing a shift in inner equilibrium and releasing refugees from the limbo of exile, 'closing one chapter and unlocking a process of engagement with subsequent events' (2006: 424). Brought together, these propositions might suggest that for long-term refugee youth, the first visit to the unfamiliar 'home' of their family's origin enables them to shift into a different plane of engagement with life. Having gained insight into what had been the 'otherness' of their origins, returnee youth are better able to reconcile their inner conflict, anchor their sense of self, and proceed with greater confidence and direction out of adolescence.

The returnee interviews offer some evidence that repatriation enabled the youth to achieve greater coherence and self-knowledge about their place in the world:

> In Iran, it could be said that identity was something that was obscure, not only for me but for all Afghan youth who lived there. We lived there like other individuals and youth, but there was always something unknown that we always lacked, and that was our identity, if we said we didn't have Iranian residency and were Afghan our identity was something that was tread upon and wasn't given any value, which happily in Afghanistan this issue doesn't emerge much. I can say that there's one thing I'm proud of, and that is that I am Afghan. Maybe Afghanistan isn't a place that people think much of, but I am proud to be from here (Zekya, female returnee, twenty years old).

Not only had the returnees solidified their identities as definitively Afghan, but they had also put into perspective their relationship with Iran. They recognized the positive contributions of their time in Iran to their lives (awareness of a larger world, greater gender sensitivity, a strong education) while separating themselves from Iranian society. The continuing refugees (apart from Leila, who had spent close to half her life in Afghanistan) were ambivalent about their identity, desiring acceptance in Iranian society even as the government mounted pressure on Afghans to repatriate. Nasir, who had achieved his 'first visit' home but declined to stay, remained conflicted over his identity. In his case, his internalization of what Hoodfar (chapter 4 in this volume) terms the 'cultural chauvinism' of Iran may have factored in his inability to reconcile with his Afghanness and may have led to his decision to reject educational opportunities in Afghanistan and return to the 'superior' culture and educational system of Iran.

Repatriation as Rite of Passage

An alternative explanation for the greater success of returnee youth in finding a sense of self and direction is self-selection: in general the youth found their original position on repatriation validated through time. The data could support a suggestion that the returnees' conviction and desire to repatriate gave them strength to overcome adversity and work towards their goals. The returnees believed there was a difference between themselves as they were in Afghanistan and as they had been in Iran, that they had had to change in order to cope with conditions in Kabul: 'When I was in Iran, I thought Afghanistan was a place where all my dreams would come true... When I came here, I put all those dreams aside, they seemed really plastic to me. This place needs dreams that are somehow stony' (Maryam, female returnee, seventeen years old).

Monsutti (2007) suggests that economic migration by young Afghan men is a masculine rite of passage – young males migrating to Iran reached adulthood in proving their ability to be economic providers for their families in Afghanistan. Perhaps for Afghan refugee youth born in exile, enduring the suffering of return is also a rite of passage, initiating the youth into Afghan society. Their initiation includes economic distress, facing derision at being *Iranigak,* and adjusting to the customs and lack of infrastructure of Afghanistan. For all the returnees, crossing the border into Afghanistan was a painful and pivotal event, even though its repeated story was a well-worn badge of honour. Nasir, as the one failed returnee in the study, declined to share his own border-crossing story, perhaps demonstrating his rejection of the symbolism and transformative power of the event.

Acculturation stress was a commonality among the returnees and a marker differentiating their coming of age from those still in exile. Asked what they thought of the youth who had remained in Tehran, the returnees said that they were unsure what their former classmates were trying to gain – were they cowards? – by remaining in Iran, as quite simply it was hard to live in a country that was not your own. Surviving the pain of repatriation gave the youth a basis for reclaiming the stoicism of Afghan identity, expressing solidarity with those who had remained in the country, and earning the right to join the larger community in Afghanistan as insiders.

Repatriation as Moral Destination

For the returnee youth, staying in Iran had been untenable: 'In Iran we were upset about being Afghan' (Amin, male returnee, twenty-one years old); 'it was absolutely required to be 100% controlled and careful in what we did. We were forced, we had no options' (Mohammad, male returnee, twenty years old). Contrary to our expectations, the youth had a strong voice in the repatriation decision-making processes in their family, in some cases reportedly convincing their reluctant family members to repatriate against their economic best interests. Their hope for access to education in Afghanistan held great weight in the decision-making process of the family, but the youth's idealism and sense of possibility were also highly potent forces.

Given their lack of political and economic clout, the youth made Islamic obligation and morality a central platform in their analysis of Iran's coercive repatriation programme. They appropriated human rights discourse and notions of 'borderless Islam' to assert their right to access refugee education in Iran (see chapter 4 in this volume). Their analysis sat uneasily, however, alongside their sense of obligation towards their country, which they held in great esteem. As dutiful and devoted Afghans, how could they justify overstaying their welcome in Iran now that the conflict in Afghanistan was officially over and the collective task of reconstruction had begun?

Repatriation, then, was a moral imperative for the youth, at a personal rather than political level. Placing 'the spirit' in Afghanistan allowed the youth to preserve their sense of worth and dignity in the face of Iranian rebuffs, even when – as in the case of Nasir and Hamed – they chose to remain in Iran. In the final accounting, it also allowed the youth to take a moral high ground: whatever harassment the youth may have faced from Iranians, they were adamant that they would not reciprocate in treating Iranians poorly in Afghanistan. Through morality discourse the youth were able to claim one important area in which Afghanistan was more developed than Iran, and challenge or break the hold of the Iranian nationalism in which they had been immersed most of their lives.

Concluding Thoughts: from Rights to Right and Wrong

This study, based as it has been on the stories of eight Afghan youth in a very specific refugee context in Tehran, is too limited to provide any definitive findings. Furthermore, by the very nature of our participatory research, which emphasized self-expression and dialogue among the youth and quite a lot of contact with me, the sample I have studied is 'contaminated' and unlikely to represent most Afghan refugee youth in Iran. However, the youth's reactions and concerns during the crisis of repatriation decision-making do suggest some areas for further study.

Studies of Afghan migration suggest that remaining in exile can be a strategy for maximizing economic opportunities and dispersing risk (Stigter 2006) and that 'encouraging messages' on trusted radio and television programmes regarding reconstruction and livelihoods prospects in Afghanistan were likely to have been a major factor influencing many Afghans to repatriate (Turton and Marsden 2002). Economic concerns may be pivotal for migrant workers or those on subsistence lifestyles, and certainly constitute an important element in migration decision-making, but theories with an overly strong emphasis on the rational and self-determining secular individual can neglect other important forces, especially in highly community-driven societies.

As indicated by the overwhelming majority of the parents we interviewed, the education of the younger generation formed a major motivation (or in retrospect, justification) for the original migration to Afghanistan. Life in Iran may have been hard, with high medical expenses, poor economic opportunities and uncomfortable living conditions, but the educational benefits of life in Iran were never dismissed. However, where parents worried about the future prospects of their children and their potential for health, happiness and success, the youth, while also fearful of their future, also expressed concern over their duties as Afghan youth. This study suggests that ethics was an important frame through which youth viewed themselves and their actions, influencing repatriation decision-making and re-acculturation. Civic obligation was particularly important among the young women interviewed, who insisted on returning to Afghanistan despite their awareness that their lives as women in Afghanistan would be more uncomfortable and restricted.

Complex and less direct, even counter-intuitive reasoning in repatriation decision-making, such as social or familial obligation and ideology, are not always easy to understand or research in studies of forced migration. This may need to be addressed, as there are many households – whether religious or secular – in which leading an upright life may factor into and even counter economic considerations. I am not espousing greater dependence on international human rights treaties, which are legal constructs often developed in and for contexts that are far removed from the realities of many refugees – and their hosting countries. Rather, it may be beneficial to engage more deeply with the morality of repatriation as seen through local cultural values.

The refugee youth in this study were in a defining and transitional period in their lives, and questions of right and wrong were pivotal. The notions of morality that consistently seemed important to them were linked with Middle Eastern ideals of hospitality and their personal, religious and civic standards of ethics. The youth's discourse emphasized obligation – the responsibilities of the Islamic state and their duties as loyal nationalists – rather than the fulfilment of their rights as individuals. Indeed, in an environment inundated with the Islamic Republic's vaunted values, they may well have expected that their moral conduct would invite a reciprocity from the state that mirrored divine justice.

Derrida (2002, cited in Silverstone 2006) presents unconditional hospitality – welcoming the uninvited without any expectation of reciprocity – as culture in itself, as equal to ethics. Roger Silverstone concurs, calling hospitality 'a primary moment of morality' (2006: 139). Given the everyday realities of massive displacement due to catastrophe and war, the ethical responsibility to provide asylum is clear and adequately delineated in international human rights discourse. What is often less prominent is the idea that, as suggested by Derrida and Silverstone and firmly maintained by the youth in my study, the basis of hospitality (or asylum) is *relationship*. Whether in policy or theory, it may be fruitful to enlarge discussions of ethics in repatriation from what is 'provided for' forced migrants to how value systems relate to each other. In other words, in addition to incorporating local traditions into analyses of asylum and repatriation programmes, it may be helpful to look at the system of values that institutions, states and individuals bring to the asylum space, looking for points where they meet, conflict, are upheld or flouted. Such a framing may support alternative understandings of the effectiveness and implications of migration policy, suggest different solutions to refugee dilemmas, and foreground defining influences on vulnerable populations that could in some cases (such as those of refugee youth) be taken away in the longer term into the future.

Notes

1. This article is dedicated, with love, to my late Ph.D. supervisor, Roger Silverstone.
2. Please see chapter 4 in this volume for a more detailed explanation of the methodology and sample population for the SARC project in Tehran.
3. My features are sometimes mistaken as being Hazara (one of the ethnicities in Afghanistan) due to my mixed Chinese-Iranian heritage.
4. The names of all the refugee youth in this article have been changed to protect their identities.
5. For example, the 2008 UN Human Development Report (HDR) estimates life expectancy at birth in Afghanistan to be 43.2 years compared with 70.5 for Iran. The adult literacy rate, as a percentage of the population over 15 years of age, is 28.0 for Afghanistan, and 84.0 for Iran. See http://hdr.undp.org/en/media/HDI_2008_EN_Tables.pdf .
6. The Farsi spoken in Iran and Dari spoken in Afghanistan are very similar, differing only in some points of grammar, vocabulary and accent.
7. President Najibullah headed the Afghan government from 1986 until 1992, when the Northern Alliance, a coalition of mujahideen armies, overturned his regime and formed a coalition government.

References

Abbasi-Shavasi, M.J., et al. 2005. 'Return to Afghanistan? A Study of Afghans Living in Iran', Kabul: Afghanistan Research and Evaluation Unit.

Anderson, P. 2001. '"You Don't Belong Here in Germany…": On the Social Situation of Refugee Children in Germany', *Journal of Refugee Studies* 14(2).

Bakewell, O. 2000. 'Uncovering Local Perspectives on Humanitarian Assistance and its Outcomes', *Disasters* 24(2).

Bash, L. and E. Zezlina-Phillips. 2006. 'Identity, Boundary and Schooling: Perspectives on the Experiences and Perceptions of Refugee Children', *Intercultural Education* 17(1).

Bisharat, G.E. 1997. 'Exile to compatriot: transformations in the social identity of Palestinian refugees in the West Bank', in A. Gupta, J. Ferguson (eds), *Culture, Power, Place: Explorations in Critical Anthropology*. Durham, NC: Duke University Press.

Black, R. 2002. 'Conceptions of "home" and the political geography of refugee repatriation: between assumption and contested reality in Bosnia-Herzegovina', *Applied Geography* 22.

Black, R. and K. Koser 1999. *The End of the Refugee Cycle?: Refugee Repatriation and Reconstruction*, New York: Berghahn Books.

Blitz, B.K., R. Sales, et al. 2005. 'Non-Voluntary Return? The Politics of Return to Afghanistan', *Political Studies* 53.

Bradley, M. 2006. 'Return of Forced Migrants. Research Guides', *Forced Migration Online*. Downloaded on 10 December 2006 from http://www.forcedmigration.org/guides/fmo042/

Chimni, B.S. 2002. 'Refugees and Reconstruction of "Post-Conflict" Societies: A Critical Perspective', *International Peacekeeping* 9(2).

Cornish, F., K. Peltzer et al. 1999. 'Returning Strangers: Children of Malawian Refugees Come "Home"?', *Journal of Refugee Studies* 12(3).

Cruise O'Brien, R. 1972. *White Society in Black Africa: The French in Senegal.* London: Faber.

Dhruvarajan, V. 1993. 'Ethnic Cultural Retention and Transmission among First Generation Hindu Asian Indians in a Canadian Prairrie City', *Journal of Comparative Family Studies* 24.

Eisenbruch, M. 1997. 'The Cry for the Lost Placenta: Cultural Bereavement and Cultural Survival among Cambodians who Resettled, were Repatriated, or Stayed at Home', in M. van Tilburg and A. Vingerhoets (eds), *Psychological aspects of geographical moves: homesickness and acculturation stress*. Tilburg, The Netherlands: Tilburg University Press.

Gmelch, G. 1980. 'Return Migration', *Annual Review of Anthropology* 9.

Graham, M. and S. Khosravi. 1977. 'Home is Where You Make it', *Journal of Refugee Studies* 10(2).

Gupta, A. and J. Ferguson. 1997. *Culture, power, place: exploration in cultural anthropology*. Durham, NC: Duke University Press.

Hakimzadeh, S. 2006. 'Iran: A Vast Diaspora Abroad and Millions of Refugees at Home', *Migration Information Source*. Downloaded on 12 December 2006 from http://www.migrationinformation.org/Profiles/display.cfm?ID=424

Kakoli, R. 2000. 'Repatriation and De-territorialization: Meskhetian Turks' Conception of Home', *Journal of Refugee Studies* 13(4).

Khattak, S.G. 2002. 'Floating Upwards from History: Afghan women's experience of displacement', *Development* 45(1).

Kumsa, M.K. 2006. '"No! I'm Not a Refugee!" The Poetics of Be-Longing among Young Oromos in Toronto', *Journal of Refugee Studies* 19(2).

Lumpp, K. and S. Shimozawa et al. 2004. 'Voluntary repatriation to Afghanistan: key features', *Refugee Survey Quarterly* 23(3).

Malkki, L.H. 1997. 'National geographic: the rooting of peoples and the territorialization of national identity among scholars and refugees', in A. Gupta, J. Ferguson (eds), *Culture, power, place: explorations in critical anthropology.* Durham, NC: Duke University Press.

Monsutti, A. 2007. 'Migration as a rite of passage: young Afghans building masculinity and adulthood in Iran', *Iranian Studies* 40(2).

Muggeridge, H. and G. Doná. 2006. 'Back Home? Refugees' Experiences of their First Visit back to their Country of Origin', *Journal of Refugee Studies* 19(4).

Nader, L. 2006. 'Human rights and moral imperialism: a double-edged story', *Anthropology News* (September 2006). Downloaded on 21 February 2007 from http://www.lib.berkeley.edu/ANTH/deptpubs/nader.2006.47.9.pdf.

Powles, J. 2002. 'Home and Homelessness', *Journal of Refugee Studies* 15(1).

Rousseau, C. and M. Morales et al. 2001. 'Going Home: Giving Voice to Memory Strategies of Young Mayan Refugees who Returned to Guatemala as a Community', *Culture, Medicine and Psychiatry* 25.

STEIN, B. 1997. Paper presented at the 'Promoting Democracy, Human Rights, and Re-integration in Post-Conflict Societies Conference' held on October 30–31st. Downloaded from http://pdf.dec.org/pdf_docs/pnacd092.pdf on April 2007.

Silverstone, R. 2006. *Media and Morality: On the Rise of the Mediapolis.* London: Polity Press.

Stigter, E. 2006. 'Afghan Migratory Strategies', *Refugee Survey Quarterly* 25(2).

Turton, D. and P. Marsden. 2002. 'Taking Refugees for a Ride? The Politics of Refugee Return to Afghanistan'. Issues Papers Series. Afghanistan Research and Evaluation Unit.

UNHCR. 2005. Measuring Protection by Numbers.

Vargas, C.M. 1999. 'Cultural Mediation for Refugee Children: A Comparative Derived Model', *Journal of Refugee Studies* 12(3).

Warner, D. 1994. 'Voluntary Repatriation and the Meaning of Return to Home: A Critique of Liberal Mathematics', *Journal of Refugee Studies* 7(2/3).

Zetter, R. 1994. 'The Greek-Cypriot Refugees: Perceptions of Return Under Conditions of Protracted Exile', *International Migration Review* 28(2).

——— 1999. 'Reconceptualizing the Myth of Return: Continuity and Transition Amongst the Greek-Cypriot Refugees of 1974', *Journal of Refugee Studies* 12(1).

Zieck, M. 2004. 'Voluntary repatriation: paradigm, pitfalls, progress', *Refugee Survey Quarterly* 23(3).

6
Food and Identity among Young Afghans in Iran

Alessandro Monsutti

Memories of Home

It is the evening before 'id ul-fitr, *on a building site [in Tehran]. It is freezing cold in the small room where five or six young Afghan workers and I are staying. Abdullah[2] has just arrived from Afghanistan. He extracts from one of the many pockets of his coat a plastic bag with some letters and audio cassettes. He gives one to Mohammad with a* sawghât, *a gift. It is a small blue-green fabric bag with an inscription: 'from the mother of Karimi, Lukh, to be handed over to Mohammad Karimi in Iran'. 'What is it?' asks Mohammad playfully,* 'naswâr?[3]' *Laughter. He takes conspicuously the Swiss army knife I gave him and opens the bag:* khasta *(almonds of the apricot's stone) and some* kishta *(dried apricots without stones). He pours some on a small plate and keeps the rest for his workmates. The dried fruits are earthy and crunchy from the dust. Mohammad jokes: 'they come from home, from our land ... and indeed, we may feel the land!'*

Mohammad, who is in front of me, listens to the cassette with headphones. His eyes become nostalgic, his face sad. Yâ allâh, az mosâferat khasta shodom!, *'by God, I am tired of migrating![4]', he says with the loud voice of people who are listening to headphones. Sometimes, he puts the sound on: the voice of his little daughter who greets him, simple noise of home, a child who sneezes, cooking pots...* Yâ allâh, bekhi, az mosâferat khasta shodom, del-e man tang shoda!, *'by God, really, I am tired of migrating, my heart is tight!'*
[...]
After the evening meal, the guests say with a strange sad irony otâq-âbâd!, *'be your room prosperous!' in spite of the usual* khâna-âbâd!, *'be your house prosperous!' They*

comment: 'It is not a home here, it is only a room on a building site!'
(Personal field diary, Tehran, 25 November 2003)

Mohammad is no longer a young man; he is in his thirties. He spent twelve of the last eighteen years in Iran and he is the foreman of workers who are between fourteen and twenty years old and who will grow to adulthood in Iran like him. The symbolic value of the *sawghât* is strong. It is a gift conveyed by a traveller, which will bring people closer in spite of distance. That such a gift is in the form of food is not insignificant. Memories of home are brought back by the dried fruits and nuts, by the dust being crunched under the teeth, by kitchen sounds and by the voices of a toddler. The place of origin is recalled by the basic senses – taste, smell, sight and hearing – the most powerful vector for retrieving long-lost memories of the past and for symbolizing social ties.

Food, Identity and Memory

The study. of food and eating has a long history in social anthropology, covering material or economic factors as well as symbolic and structural dimensions.[5] Food is obviously essential for corporal existence but it is also a social language. As Claudia Roden writes in the foreword of a volume dedicated to the culinary cultures of the Middle East: 'There is a lot more to food than eating and cooking. Behind every dish lies a world, a culture, a history. Dishes have social meaning, they have emotional and symbolic significance. Food is about power. It is an expression of identity and ideology. It touches on issues of class, gender, race and ethnicity. It is a clue to history. It is a language' (Roden in Zubaida and Tapper 2000: vii). Food is central to identity because it is literally incorporated, blurring the boundary between the world and the self, as expressed by the famous German expression, *man ist, was man isst* ('one is what one eats').

Food was of central importance for structuralism in the 1960s and 1970s, particularly in the work of authors like Claude Lévi-Strauss or Mary Douglas, who felt it formed a cultural system of classification. In the 1980s, a more recent generation of scholars, represented among others by Pierre Bourdieu, Jack Goody and Sydney Mintz, has started to look at the social relations – including those of power and differentiation – involved in food production, distribution and exchange, and consumption.[6]

Studies on the social meaning of food and eating as identity marker are twofold: 'Like all culturally defined material substances used in the creation and maintenance of social relationships, food serves both to solidify group membership and to set groups apart' (Mintz and Du Bois 2002: 109). On one hand, commensality and food sharing may build a sense of collective belonging and solidarity. On the other hand, eating behaviour may also be a way to display wealth and social stratification. Exchange and generosity are both a means to create a feeling of group identity and of hierarchy, a way to make friends and to express competition. Foods and drinks may be seen as markers of social boundaries and differences, including religion, ethnicity, class, gender and age.[7] For example, it has been shown that class differences – as well as gender ones – are often expressed through tastes and personal preferences.

According to Fischler (2001: 62–66), the fact that human beings are omnivores implies the capacity of adaptation to a wide range of contexts, but also the possibility of choosing and the existence of social and personal differences in tastes. In spite of some transcultural tendencies – like the preference children seem to have for sweets – the main feature of human diet is its diversity and plasticity (Fischler 2001: 110). That implies on the one hand a certain freedom of choice and on the other hand a pressure linked to the necessity to diversify the food sources and to innovate permanently. What Fischler calls the paradox of the omnivore lies in a double bind, a tension between two contradictory constraints causing a fundamental anxiety: the comforting need for familiar meals and the inescapable quest for unknown foods.

Migration,[8] but also war, have been recognized as important agents of dietary change (Mintz and Du Bois 2002: 105), but the social aspects of food consumption have been insufficiently acknowledged within the field of refugee studies. Lentz (1999) notes – not very surprisingly – that modifications in agricultural production, and more generally in modes of production, have an impact on dietary patterns. New economic constraints and opportunities affect survival strategies and food habits. In changing contexts, the division of labour, the gender and generation roles are modified within the household. With another perspective, Sutton (2001) has centred his study of food among people on the move (more precisely Greek migrants) on the social construction of memory. He has showed 'the importance of the sensory in reconnecting and remembering experiences and places one has left behind for short- or long-term migration' (2001: 74). Food is a valued artefact, a way of consuming and rekindling inner sensory memory. As a crucial vector of personal and group identity, it is literally embodied with memories of the past on which identities are formed but it can also be a means to project a certain image of oneself and to mark social hierarchies. Sutton speaks of synesthesia, defined as 'the synthesis or crossing of experiences from different sensory registers' (2001: 17) – taste, smell, sight and even hearing (as illustrated by Mohammad Karimi listening to the kitchen noise of his distant home). Possibly due to the fact that taste and smell may not be described through a very elaborated vocabulary, they have the capacity to evoke the social situations with which they were originally associated.

Sutton also mentions 'the power of tangible everyday experiences to evoke the memories on which identities are formed' (2001: 74). Societies are undoubtedly structured through rituals and feasts. Ceremonial meals connect participants, sharing food reasserts social ties (Mintz and Du Bois 2002: 107). But indeed, the relevance of food does not only stem from social structures and symbolic categories but also from the fact that eating is a very mundane practice. Ordinary as well as ritual food may be vectors of memory and identity. While certain foods have a symbolic charge because they are linked to ritual contexts, many others become particularly meaningful because they are eaten or drunken every day, like bread, water or tea among Afghans. Discourses on home are thus reproduced everyday through the meals, although the first changes in food habits which are likely to take place concern foods and meals which are the least symbolically significant, in particular breakfast (Caplan 1997: 13). At the same time, '[f]requently, foods for special occasions continue to be prepared from "traditional" ingredients. By contrast, new staples (or manufactured foodstuffs purchased in order to supplement an insufficient agricultural production) seem to be quickly incorporated into the everyday diet, where considerations of taste and symbolic ranking become secondary to harsh economic realities' (Lentz 1999: 4).

In the Middle East, as elsewhere, food is a domain rich in stereotypes allowing one to class and to build group boundaries (Bromberger 1985, Centlivres 1988). It is then a fascinating but certainly not an easy task to bring together three important topics in the social sciences – migration, food and youth – and to study how young Afghan refugees and migrants have adapted to their life in Iran through food and commensality. The particular situation of young migrants stems from the fact that their sense of belonging and identity is shaped by elder generations (Chatty, Crivello and Lewando Hundt 2005: 388). Food is a valued artefact, a way of consuming and rekindling inner sensory memory. But the specificity of Afghan youth compared, for instance, to the Greek migrants studied by Sutton comes thus from the fact that many of them have never been to their homeland. Food and eating is not a mere remembering of their past. It may be both a way to reactivate and to appropriate the discourse of the older generation, and to mark their difference adopting new habits from the host society.

For young Afghans in Iran, food practices constitute an arena where identities are negotiated in their complexity. Four lines of tension may be recognized. First, at the interpersonal level, the ideal of equality implied by commensality may compete with the hierarchy inherent to hospitality. According to Mauss's conception of the gift, the host – the giver – is superior to the guest – the receiver. However, among the Afghans, this relation is euphemized. The host enhances his prestige by voluntarily demeaning himself, by putting the guest in the position of 'honour', opposite to the door, and staying himself in the 'low' place by the entrance, at the guest's service. Food consumption and preferences translate differences in power, wealth, social class, origin, gender and generation. Second, food preferences play an important role in the social construction of childhood, adulthood and inter-generational relations. Adopting new food habits, young Afghans mark their difference from older generations and express closeness to the host society; they state their autonomy as a peer-group and their longing for the modernity of Iran (including the situation of women, considered unanimously to be better than in Afghanistan) compared to the backwardness attributed to the country of their parents. Third, food also expresses – paradoxically – the ambivalent perception of the host society, oscillating between the mentioned fascination with the modernity of Iran and a bitterness caused by the attitude of the Iranian population and authorities towards the Afghan refugees and migrants who feel used and despised. Finally, migration to Iran has led to a process of urbanization and detribalization. It may foster a broader identity with reference to the Afghan nation, but concrete existence is based on narrow social ties. An abstract sense of Afghan-ness, developed in exile and symbolically embedded in emblematic dishes, coexists with an everyday life which tends to be fragmented by group of origin.

Research Methods and Population Sample

This paper is a contribution to the larger project 'Children and Adolescents in Sahrawi and Afghani Refugee Households: Living with the Effects of Prolonged Armed Conflict and Forced Migration' (hereafter referred to as the SARC project). It further builds on a previous research project with young people in Palestinian households in Lebanon, Syria, Jordan, the West Bank and the Gaza Strip. In both projects youth are situated in the context of the family group, the community, and the wider social, economic and political arena (Chatty 2007). The main objective of the overall project is to offer an alternative approach to the supposed universal model of children's social and psychological development. Here, the research is socially and culturally contextualized; it is sensitive to local conditions and looks at the strategies and narratives developed by the youth: 'Accepting the premise that young people are active in the construction of their own lives and societies, it was maintained that social relationships and perspectives are worthy of study in their own right' (Chatty, Crivello and Lewando Hundt 2005: 399).

Inspired by such a theoretical and methodological principle, the present chapter deals more specifically with the relationship between food and eating habits, memories of home, the reproduction of social ties and the construction of ideas of belonging and identity among Afghan refugee children and young people in Iran. It is complementary to the research among the Sahrawis in Algeria carried out by Nicola Cozza, who followed the same methodological approach.[9] We examined how migration has modified food practices, but also, conversely, how food processing problems may have fostered social change (Mintz and Du Bois 2002). Indeed, food and eating play a crucial role in consolidating past relationships, creating new ones, and marking out networks and groups.

For more than twenty years, Afghanistan has been torn apart by war, resulting in the largest refugee population in the world at the end of the twentieth century (more than six million in 1990 according to UNHCR). Iran is one of the main destinations: in November 2004, the Islamic Republic hosted about one million registered Afghans. It has been also estimated that more than 500,000 single male Afghan labourers live in Iran employed mainly in the agricultural and construction sectors (Abbasi Shavazi, Glazebrook et al. 2005). There are thus two distinct although connected groups of Afghans in Iran: families and labourers without their families.[10]

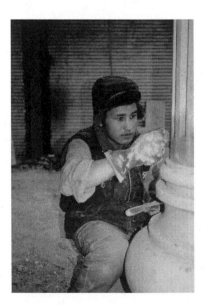

Figure 6.1: A young Afghan worker (Tehran, December 2003).

I have collected information among those two populations, meeting Afghan adolescents living with their families and going to school, and young male migrants working in groups on building sites. All interviews and informal discussions have been carried out in Persian. Several aspects have been studied: the symbolic dimension of food, especially bread and rice, mutton and chicken, water and tea, but also emblematic dishes; the reproduction of social ties through food consumption in everyday life and ceremonies (hospitality, religious festivals like *'id-e ramazân*); consumption and exchange; and gender, social construction of masculinity and generation.

Due to the rumours concerning forced repatriation by the Iranian government and increasing administrative and police pressure on Afghan refugees, people seemed rather worried to see a Western researcher going around refugee schools and asking questions. My goal was certainly not to add more trouble to the already difficult life of Afghans in Iran. I have therefore been able to carry out only a few focus group interviews in two refugee schools in Tehran and Qom. Taking into account the concern for security and this difficult context, I reactivated long-term relationships among migrants working on building sites and have spent part of my research stay in this exclusively male world with which I had been in contact during previous fieldworks. Their families were mostly living in Afghanistan, but many of them were between fourteen and twenty years old. They thus fell into the scope of the SARC project. Most of the people I met were Hazaras or Shiite *sayyed*.[11] I was able to see again people I had already met in Afghanistan, Pakistan and Iran and then, through participant observation, to have a comparative view of their food habits throughout the migratory itinerary. Technically, these people were not refugees, as they were constantly moving between Afghanistan, Pakistan and Iran, and their families (father, mother, wife, children) were living in their country of origin. Yet their displacements were often caused by the same kind of hardship which pushed refugees out of their land (violence, insecurity, poverty, drought, etc.).

The research has been carried out following various methods: participant observation while living among the Afghans; frequency of food consumption chart; weekly intakes charts (daily dietary food log); focus groups on food, social life and identity; in-depth qualitative interviews on food, social life and identity.[12]

Sixty-four weekly intakes charts have been collected in two refugee schools in Shahr-e Rey (at the southern edge of Tehran's agglomeration)[13] and in Qom (a city some 150 kilometres south of Tehran);[14] in refugee families (Qom) and among young workers (Tehran).[15] In the school in Shahr-e Rey, I was unable to meet all the youth who filled out the charts, while I met some who did not. Nevertheless, I carried out several focus groups, sitting alone in a small room with students of different ages and social backgrounds. In Qom, the discussions took place in the presence of some teachers who were sometimes interfering, a situation that influenced the interviews. However, the charts were discussed informally with a wide range of people to identify key themes in food practices, including: food habits changes; everyday life meals versus festive food (the fieldwork took place partly during the month of Ramadan); Iranian food versus Afghan food; and symbolic aspects of food, tastes and recipes.

The reliability of the qualitative data has been established by cross-checking and comparing the collected information. Their relevance has been asserted through regularity (i.e. when information is given independently by different people) and saturation (i.e. when no new information was able to be drawn from interviews or observation).

Food Consumption and Social Relations in a Migratory Context

For Afghans living in Iran, and also in Pakistan, food crystallizes discourses on the lost homeland. Cooking and eating take an emblematic value and embody personal and collective identities. A large proportion of the Afghan population in Iran was rural before war. In exile, those people have been cut off from food productive activities. In Iran and in Pakistan, Afghans do not eat what they have grown themselves. But unlike in Pakistan (Centlivres-Demont 1996), in Iran only a very small minority of Afghans live in refugee camps and receive or have received food rations. There is a difference between eating at home (families) and eating on building sites (single men). But in both cases, the migratory context may transform the traditional familial division of labour.

Richard Tapper and Nancy Tapper (1986) distinguish four domains of discourse in their study of food and commensality among the Durrani Pashtuns of Northern Afghanistan: the Quranic, the Tribal, the Humoral and the Magical. I will concentrate here on the Quranic and the Tribal, which express the tension between the fact that 'food-sharing is the key symbol of their social and political equality' and that Afghan society is very competitive and 'hospitality and feasting in particular are means by which success or failure in such competitions is assessed' (Tapper and Tapper 1986: 67–68). Egalitarian ideals are counterbalanced by relations of political and economic inequality. Communal religious ceremonies are a means to symbolically display the equality of men. But hospitality, which is a particular way of exchanging food, is also the arena where different households may struggle for social status and symbolic pre-eminence (Tapper and Tapper 1986: 74).

Everyday Life and Food Consumption

Inspired by Greek ancient medicine, food is traditionally classified in Afghanistan along four qualities, hot and cold, moist and dry, the former distinction being by far more salient in everyday life (Centlivres 1985; Tapper and Tapper 1986). In such a holistic system, also influenced by Ayurvedic conceptions, food consumption is always discussed in relation to diseases, seasons, climate, etc. In Islam, foods are classified as *hallâl* (licit), *makruh* (not recommended) or *harâm* (prohibited). For instance, according to some informants, animals with cloven-hoofs – like cows and goats – are *hallâl*, riding animals and animals with a single hoof – like horse and donkey – are *makruh*, while animals with fingers and claws – dog, fox, cat, etc. – are *harâm*. Unlike their Sunni neighbours, Afghan Shiites consider the rabbit to be *makruh*.

In rural Afghanistan, bread is the main food. In Persian, *nân* actually means 'bread', but designates food in general. It may be prepared in a clay oven (*nân-e tandur*) or cooked on a thin plate (*nân-e tâwa*). People often eat it dipped in a light meat broth (*shurwâ*). *Qoruti* (bread dunked in *qorut*, dried buttermilk, upon which boiling water is poured in order to obtain a kind of sour cream) is appreciated. Red beans (*lubiâ*), different kinds of peas (*mâsh*, *mushung*, etc.), chickpeas (*nokhod*) and lentils (*adas, dâl*) are other common meals, but not all the Afghan varieties are available in Iran.[16] Yogurt (*mâst*) is appreciated, while meat (*gusht*) and rice (*berenj*) are rare. Rice is considered a luxury and rather urban food.[17]

In Iran, there are different types of bread, generally cooked in an industrial horizontal gas oven: *nân-e lavâsh* (very thin); *nân-e taftun* (thin, but slightly larger); *nân-e barbari* (thicker); *nân-e sangak* (rather thick and crispy, cooked on small stones). Most Afghans prefer the *nân-e barbari* and the *nân-e sangak*, which are most similar to the *nân-e tandur*. However, even young Afghans who have always lived in Iran consider that Iranian bread is clean and modern but not very tasty. Although some have never tried Afghan bread, they have heard their parents and friends talking about it and unanimously consider bread to be much better in Afghanistan where it is cooked in a vertical charcoal-fired clay *tandur*. As a young student of the school in Shahr-e Rey explains: 'Iranian bread is cooked with gas. We know from what people say, it is less good than bread cooked with charcoal, because baking is less regular, you may have burnt parts and almost raw parts in the same bread.' The virtues of Afghan bread are compared to the virtues of Afghan people – tough, dense, genuine – while 'Iranians would fall sick after one month in Afghanistan, because their stomach is weak and unable to digest Afghan bread' comments another student who had left Afghanistan as a small child and had never been back since then. In order to recreate lost tastes, some families have built a *tandur* at home and may sell bread to neighbours.

As for water (*âb*), the judgement is sometimes reversed: if some young informants celebrate the water of the Afghan mountains, which is 'so pure and sweet', many consider that water is clean in Iran. They stress the fact that it is possible to drink tap water without any risk, while it is a problem to find pure water in Afghanistan, especially in urban centres. The topic can cause big discussions: 'Water is better in Afghanistan, as it comes from springs and wells, not from pipes. – Hmm! I don't agree, I heard the water was unclean in cities like Kabul, Mazar or Herat! – Sure, but in Bamyan, the water is so sweet, it comes directly from the springs!' This dialogue illustrates a tension between the reconstructed memories of the purity of homeland on the one hand and the awareness of health problems on the other.

Tea (*cây*) may be taken at any time of the day, but not while eating the main meals except for breakfast. In Hazarajat, for example, sugar is poured only in the first cup of the morning; in the daytime, one can take some sweets, but the tea itself is drunk *talkh* ('bitter'). Green tea or black tea are consumed according to personal preferences and seasons. The former, especially widespread in the North, is supposed to be cold and thirst-quenching, while the latter is considered as hot and preferred in winter. In Iran, however, green tea is rare. Black tea is prepared on a samovar and drunk in small glasses with much sugar. Afghans claim to drink more tea than Iranians but their tea uses fewer tea leaves. Tea may be an important part of every social encounter, but people stress the difference between the simple sharing of tea and sweets or of salty meals (cooked with water and salt, *âb o namak*); the former punctuates a mere interaction while the latter seals a social relation. Salt appears thus to be of more symbolic and social importance than sugar, possibly because its consumption creates a relation between the host and the women who have cooked the food in the back of the house.

Like bread, Afghan meat – and more specifically kebab (*kabâb*) – is also considered as being much better and tastier, with no need for spices like the Iranians use. It remains a rare item. The symbolic status of the *shurwâ* among Afghans in Iran is unclear. It is rather meant to be eaten by the poor (negative dimension), but it is one of the rare occasions to eat meat (positive dimension). Furthermore, it refers to a certain idea of self-control and asceticism, but also of generosity through the use of *jawâni* (from *jawân*, 'young'), a piece of meat wrapped in bread, often given by a guest to a young member of the host family doing the service, or exchanged between table companions. It is also a way to display social position: except within the close circle of relatives, women and men eat separately, and when many people are present, they group by age around the different plates. Usually, the most important person of the household or an old and respected guest divides the meat at the end of the meal. All my informants eat a lot of *shurwâ* (some young people say *âbgusht*, which is an Iranian term, see Appendix 1, Chart 1), between two and five times a week. Normally prepared with mutton in Afghanistan, it is almost always made from chicken among the Afghans living in Iran (see Appendix 1, Charts 1 and 3). People comment that they eat the animals they breed in Afghanistan; while in Iran, they must buy the meat. Mutton is too expensive and the main meat becomes then the less-valued chicken, which is considered less tasty but is also much cheaper. Although appreciated, mutton is very rarely eaten, once a month for some, even less for others. Mutton is considered hot and gives more power than chicken, which tends to be generally considered neutral or cold.[18]   The change of food habits is then interpreted as a loss of autonomy. The autarkic ideal of domestic units in Afghanistan is confronted by a more direct dependence on market prices in Iran.

Figure 6.2: A young worker dividing the chicken of the *shurwâ* in absence of any elder (Tehran, December 2003).

Qoruti is a sort of poor equivalent of the *shurwâ* – being without meat – but is seen as a typical Afghan dish and may bring back memories of the past, especially for older generations.[19] As it may be difficult to find Afghan *qorut* in Iranian cities, it may alternatively be prepared from *chaka* (coagulated buttermilk, softer than *qorut*) or from *kashk* (Iranian dried buttermilk). Genuine *dugh* (fresh buttermilk) is also difficult to find and is often prepared from yogurt.

According to many of my informants, Afghans eat spicier food than the Iranians. Such a difference is often explained by reference to the traditional classification of foods and sometimes by the colder climate of a mountainous region like Hazarajat. For some other people, Afghan food is based on genuine tastes and does not require complicated preparations as does Iranian food. Oil, tomato and salt are the secret to delicious flavours. Afghan food is more direct, less prissy, and the hit of spice, undiluted, is part of that. The Iranian palate tends towards sour foods, where Afghans can bear spicy foods. Indeed, hot food is supposed to be specially appreciated by adult men who are said to be colder than young people and women (Tapper and Tapper 1986). Coldness is linked to self-control, a supposedly male quality. Women, who are supposed to be emotive and to lack self-control, are hot. Masculinity gives the capacity – or even the requirement – to consume hot foods, while femininity has to be counterbalanced by cold foods. Spices also connote hardiness while Iranians are considered softer and to have less manly manners than Afghans.

Like all migrants, Afghans try to recreate old tastes and family recipes, but have also adopted new food. The most common seem to be spaghetti (called macaroni, *makâroni*), sausage and canned tuna (see Appendix 1, Charts 1, 2 and 3). Changes may also be seen in the culinary terminology: *âbgusht* for *shurwâ*; *khoresht* for *qorma* (see Appendix 1, Chart 1, for example). Some dialect expressions tend to be replaced by more standard ones: *eftâri* instead of *roza-wâzi* (literally 'fast opening') in Hazaragi for the evening meal during Ramadan; *sahari* for *pashaoni* (from *pas-e shab*, 'after the night') for the morning meal during Ramadan, etc.

Although food is the basic necessity of life and could not be understood without referring to economic constraints, it remains a crucial cultural marker. Yet, it is fluid and adapts to changing circumstances; some elements remain the same and others are modified. In contrast to their objective precarious situation in Iran, Afghans have a discourse of self-valorization through the quality of their food which highlights their own toughness.

Food Exchange and Emblems

Especially in an insecure social environment, rules relating to commensality play a crucial role in defining the boundaries of social groups, from households to tribal sections, ethnic groups or religious communities (Tapper and Tapper 1986: 64). For example, on building sites, Afghan and Iranian workers do not eat together. When asked if he may share a meal with an Iranian colleague, a Hazara informant violently says *ne, hech wakht, emkân nist!*, 'no, never, it is impossible!' Commensality is a way to display equality and solidarity – the Quranic domain according to Tapper and Tapper (1986) – while hospitality is also a way to express hierarchy – the Tribal domain according to Tapper and Tapper (1986). Ritual meals bring people together and connect them with their absent kith and kin; they may also reaffirm relationships of inclusion and exclusion in a tension between a sense of group belonging and competition. Indeed, rituals surrounding food can reinforce religious and ethnic boundaries, and can also reinforce hierarchy and power relations within a group.[20]

My interlocutors independently gave me a rather similar list of the emblematic dishes of Afghanistan: *âshak* (a kind of agnolotti stuffed with a type of baby leek, boiled and eaten with a sauce made of *qorut* or yoghurt) and *bolâni* (fried rissoles stuffed with leek). They eat them at home for feasts and when they have guests. They also mentioned *mantu* (a kind of steamed tortellini stuffed with meat, eaten in a sauce, chickpeas and *qorut* or yoghurt), but they do not usually eat them at home, as a special cooking-pot is necessary (it is considered rather as a bazaar snack in Afghanistan, and in Iran, they can often be found at football matches). Surprisingly, *qâbili palao* (pilaf rice with meat, carrot, raisin, and pistachios or almonds) was not mentioned systematically as an emblematic preparation, despite its status as the quintessential dish in urban Afghanistan and in the wider diaspora. In some instances, *busrâgh* (a kind of madeleine) and *kichri qorut* (a kind of risotto topped with *qorut*) were mentioned. Other ingredients or dishes that people miss are the *dumba* (fat of the sheep's tail) and the *qadid* or *landi* (dried mutton-jerky), both considered as hot food.

It must be stressed that *âshak* and *bolâni* are rather urban dishes in Afghanistan. May we make the hypothesis that exile tends to produce a more homogenous 'Afghan culture'? May we imagine that exile contributes to producing a stereotyped and folklorized conception of culture? Does life in Iran open a double process of urbanization? First, the Afghans in Iran are originally a largely rural population which have settled in cities. Secondly, the conception that the younger generations of Afghan migrants have of their home country seems to be shaped by Kabuli culture.[21]

A symbolically interesting dish was *âsh* (see Appendix 1, Chart 2). It is known in both Iran and Afghanistan, but it is prepared in different ways: it always has noodles, vegetables and beans, but in the Afghan recipe it is more liquid and accompanied with *qorut*. Seeming to express a certain frustration and searching for a kind of symbolic revenge over the Iranians, a student met in a school comments, almost shouting: *âsh-e irâni, maza na meda!*, 'Iranian *âsh* is tasteless!'

There is a succession of feasts which contribute to the reproduction of social relations: religious festivals (especially the *'id ul-fitr* or *'id-e ramazân* which concludes Ramadan; the *'id ul-kabir* or *'id-e qorbân*, which marks the period of the *hajj* and commemorates Abraham's willingness to sacrifice his son; the *'âshurâ'* when the Shiites commemorate the martyrdom of Imam Husain, the grandson of the Prophet Mohammad), the New Year (*nawruz*), engagements and weddings, charity meals, etc.

The fasting month of Ramadan is an important time in the ritual calendar. For many Afghans in Iran, the *eftâri* normally includes many items which are hardly available in rural Afghanistan, like feta cheese and dates. They often have a dinner one or two hours later with products which appear 'more Afghan': *shurwâ, qorma,* rice, chickpeas, beans or lentils. At *'id-e ramazân,* it is customary to offer alms. During the 2003 fieldwork, for example, this constituted 600 tomans for people eating bread, 3,000 tomans for those who eat rice, a practice marking the difference between the poor and the rich defined in terms of food habits.

The commemoration of the martyrdom of the Imam Husain during the first month of the Islamic lunar calendar (Moharram) by the Shiites functions as a kind of outlet for tensions and frustrations accumulated during the year. Unlike during Ramadan, the atmosphere is not festive, it is rather a mourning period. According to their means, some families take advantage of this period to organize a charity meal (a *nazr,* which actually means 'votive offering, vow, promise given to God'). A usual meal is *halim,* crushed wheat with minced mutton, beans and lentils. Several families may join their efforts to prepare it in a big pan and invite their relatives and their neighbours for a communal meal. Sometimes the Iranian owner of the house or some Iranian neighbours may be asked to come, but Iranians do not seem to be much associated with these events. These *nazr* are the occasion to read the entire Quran (*qorân-khâni*) for the death. Beside *halim,* a sweet dish of flour cooked with sugar, oil and water called *halwâ* is customarily prepared: *surkh* (red), if cooked for several hours; *zard* (yellow), if cooked for about twenty minutes. On the occasion of *nazr* or at other times, *halwâ* or *shola-zard* (rice, sugar and curcuma) is distributed to the inhabitants of the neighbourhood, including Iranians.

These invitations play an important role in the social life of migrant families. They take place in the cycle of exchange, and mutual services along the different kinds of gifts: *sawghât,* a gift brought from another place by a person arriving from a trip (very often, women send apricot stones and almonds with some raisin to their husband or son working in Iran); *shirini,* a gift delivered by hand; *yâdgari,* a gift for someone who is leaving; *jawâni,* meat and bread given to mark friendship or reconciliation when people eat the *shurwâ; nazr,* a charity meal offered to honour the family dead; and *nazri,* food brought to neighbours as a votive gift.

Practical links present in everyday life may command everyday working relations. But festivities gave rise to meetings of a more official nature, when extended family and lineage functioned as the significant level. According to Bourdieu, a distinction may be made between official kinship and practical kinship: the former, based on an abstract geographical definition of groups that legitimated a social order, came to the fore at certain highpoints of social life; the latter, arising out of everyday strategies, consisted in the relations actually deployed for the ordinary needs of existence (Bourdieu 1972: 78, 83;

1980: 279, 282–84). Unlike work relationships and employment structures, such festivities bring paternal kinship to centre stage.

Gifts and invitations which bound Afghans to Iranians were comparatively rare. Some informants have been invited home for a meal by Iranian acquaintances, some never. But it appears in any case, that the frequency of such invitations (in both directions) is very low. 'Iran is a repressive country!' commented some students at the school in Shahr-e Rey. They said that they play in the street with Iranian children, but they rarely visited their homes to drink tea, and even less to eat cooked meals. They nevertheless all claimed that Iranians love Afghan food, which is at once simple and tasty, and always try to be invited.

Between Modernity and Nostalgia

For many of the youth, born in Iran or having no recollection of their time in Afghanistan, food may be both an identity marker and a source of discomfort, in a complex expression of nostalgia for the lost homeland, fascination for the host country as well as feelings of exclusion. Afghan cuisine is one of the emblems of their country of origin to which they have easy access. With the loss of control and Afghan-ness brought about by refugee status, food is one measure of identity that is within their own power. Where they do not know their own food in the overwhelming Iranian-ness of their education, food is something that has remained theirs in the domestic sphere and inner community, rather like accent, and has nothing to do with modernity, at which the Iranians have eclipsed them.

At the same time, food is a source of shame for many young Afghans in that they have to eat like poor people. When away from home, they hate to look like they are eating poor food (lots of bread), to be looked down upon as eating like Afghans. They tend to consider bread, feta cheese and fruits as lesser food, while 'high class' food like meat or rice are highly desired. Food is thus linked to status, poverty and self-esteem, and is quite a sensitive issue in its own right.

The Afghan youth is caught in a double bind: there may be a tendency to dismiss the trappings of culture which their parents find dear; but alternatively food remains a significant tie to Afghanistan.

Coming of Age and Migration

Migration is part of the Afghan social and cultural landscape. In spite of the unprecedented wave of returns following the fall of the Taliban regime and the establishment of a government backed by the international community, multidirectional cross-border movements had not come to an end.

For many young labourers in particular, migration offers the opportunity to broaden their social networks beyond narrow kinship and neighbourhood ties. It may be conceived as a necessary stage in their existence, a rite of passage to adulthood and a step towards manhood.[22] The perilous journey may be understood as a spatial and partially social separation from family and home which contributes to cutting the links with the social period of childhood. Their stay in Iran, during which they have to prove their capacity to face hardship under the supervision of an older relative and to save money while living among itinerant and temporary working teams, represents a period of liminality. Upon their return to their village of origin, they will be reincorporated as adult marriageable men, although they will keep commuting between Afghanistan and Iran for part of their life. The young workers are supposed to develop control over their emotions and desires. They must resist the temptations of the host society (including prostitution). Indeed, manhood implies the capacity to live modestly, to save money for the family left in the village of origin in Afghanistan, then to eat little in everyday life,[23] but also to overindulge in some festive circumstances.

Figure 6.3: A foreman cooking for the younger members of his working team (Tehran, November 2003).

Migration has brought important social, cultural and economic changes. It also contributes to the blurring of the traditional sexual division of tasks. In Iran, men living apart from their families cook, do the washing and the washing-up, sew, and generally speaking assume all domestic chores.

Conversely, the reduced presence of men in their home villages allows women to modify the usual division of tasks and, in many cases, to engage in normally forbidden activities. The mobility of people and the dispersion of members of households and broader groups of solidarity are not in themselves destructuring phenomena. They are a way of life rather than merely a response to external constraints and constitute an arena where the roles of men and women, of the youth and the elderly, are constantly renegotiated.

Among labourers living away from their families, there is no sharp difference in food practices between young and older people. They all share the experience of continual movement between Afghanistan and Iran; they eat together on the building sites and have minimal interaction with the host society. Primarily motivated by an economic concern, they may nevertheless adopt new food (like canned tuna or spaghetti) and bring them back to their homeland (see figure 6.4).

The situation is different within families. Young male refugees living with their family may go through a kind of reverse rite of passage: it is most often the male youth who return to Afghanistan with their fathers to see if conditions are right for the rest of the family, while the female youth stay back and wait.[24] Unlike the labourers, they maintain food identity in the social group and do not adopt new tasks, like cooking, to the same extent. But the members of younger generations, born or raised in Iran, develop new food tastes which are different from their parents. As shown in chart 2, one evening the female adolescent ate Iranian style sausages when her parents had *qoruti*. She seems to consider the latter dish as a heritage of backwards rural life in Afghanistan, while her father complains about the loss of control over the younger generations and the pernicious influence of Iranian habits. Adopting new food can be a way for the youth to distinguish themselves from adults; the children and adolescents state their autonomy and express that they have integrated Iranian values and way of life, which are considered as more progressive than the Afghan ones. As clearly shown for the Sahrawi case,[25] food consumption and preferences play a role in the social construction of adulthood and childhood but also of inter-generational relationships.

Food and Identity, Migration and Social Change

Many observers have stressed the weakness of national identity in Afghanistan before the war. Two other levels of identity were more salient (Centlivres, Centlivres-Demont 1988: 34–35). First, there is the subnational level, the *qawm*, a multiform term that exemplifies well the complexity of Afghan society. Most often translated as 'solidarity group', it refers to a group of agnatic kinsmen, but the level to which it refers varies. According to the context, it can mean enlarged kinship, lineage, tribe or ethnic group, or even a professional or religious group. Second, there is the supranational level, the *umma*, the Islamic moral community of believers, which transcends – at least ideally – state borders and cultural boundaries.

These dimensions have evolved during war and in exile through a multiple process. First there is the development of an encompassing representation of the nation among large parts of the Afghan population (which before the war to have been present mostly among a small elite of urban people and émigrés) (Centlivres 1991, 1994). Then there is now a competing development with the rise of political discourses on ethnic groups among a new progressive elite (the process of ethnicization is particularly clear among the Hazaras since 1989).[26] Ethnicity has been manipulated by some political actors who reinforce tensions in order to mobilize a constituency, especially since the Soviet withdrawal in 1989 (Schetter 2003). A deep fragmentation of effective ties of solidarity (transnational migratory networks are based on very narrow social groups) coexists today with a rather abstract sense of Afghan-ness.

These tensions are translated in food habits and commensality among the young Afghans in Iran. On one hand, exile and migration may have a unifying effect at the level of representation and discourse, and can reinforce broad cultural references to Afghanistan. On the other hand, differences concerning food consumption between families of various social and geographical origins persist. Narrow and fragmented everyday social ties that one may observe through food practices, commensality and hospitality have not disappeared in Iran, in spite of a growing– somewhat stereotyped – discourse on the unity of the Afghan nation.

Food and eating have the particularity to internalize remembrance as well as reciprocity and debt. The consumption of food can create both real and imagined communities: 'there is an imagined community implied in the act of eating food "from home" while in exile, in the embodied knowledge that others are eating the same food. This is not to deny that real communities are created as well' (Sutton 2001: 84). The use of food appears central for the reproduction of social ties among Afghan refugees in Iran as well as among people dispersed in various countries. Hospitality and commensality organize the social life of refugee families as well as of migrant workers. The members of dispersed social groups keep in touch by the circulation of alimentary gifts, which symbolize the whole Afghan society in the etymological sense of 'putting together'.

Sutton insists on the importance of sensory experiences for remembering the places left behind by migrants. In the case of most Afghan youth in Iran, it is more a case of (re)creating a sense of belonging referring to specific foods, like dried apricots or almonds, but also recipes. Food is a mundane reminder which is efficient at different levels: national identity, region, village and family. For instance, most young refugees tend to consider *qâbili palaw*, *âshak* or *bolâni* as typical and emblematic Afghan dishes, while their parents and grand-parents were unlikely to have heard about them in the past when living in their village of origin. Young people interviewed during field research have kept the memory of regional recipes and are often surprised to learn through my questions that some of their classmates have not even heard the names of these dishes. For example, one of my young informants who has lived in Iran since his early years (see Appendix 1, Chart 1) is able to enumerate proudly a whole list of what he considers typical Hazara dishes: *leti* (flour cooked in oil with yogurt), *nân-chây* (bread dipped into tea, with sugar and butter), *nân-bota* (bread, oil and *qorut*), *nân-e patir* or simply *patir* (a kind of thick bread), *kashaw* (a kind of pancake with yogurt), *nân-e malida* (small pieces of bread dipped in oil), *khaigina* (eggs, more specifically fried eggs with tomato and onion), *dam-pukht* (rice cooked with oil and *qorut*), *pati* (beans or lentils), *pirki* (like *bolâni*, but smaller and without potato), *ârd-biro* (flour, oil and water), *maida-ogra* and *dalda-ogra* (also from flour, oil and water), *tâfa* (simple *shurwâ*), etc.

Tensions not only exist among Afghans but also in relation with the host society: the perception of the Afghan youth oscillates between a fascination for the modernity of Iran (including the situation of women, considered unanimously to be better than in Afghanistan) and a bitterness caused by the attitude of the Iranian population and authorities towards the Afghan refugees and migrants who feel rejected and despised (and even to have been politically used and betrayed by the Islamic Republic).

The changes in alimentary habits that occur in Iran are important, especially among young refugees living with their families. The modifications concern food, recipes, vocabulary and social life. For instance, the classic distinction in Afghanistan between warm and cold food and beverages did not appear in the discussion but still seemed to inform some discourses and representations.

Although the adoption of foods from Iranian urban society is a salient trend, the domestic consumption of Afghan food is like an everyday replication of difference, taken for granted and yet continually present and necessary. It is probably the easiest aspect of Afghan-ness to exhibit, given the eroding of accent and historical knowledge in the younger generation. Everyday food is heavily influenced by the Iranian cultural and social context, with for example the success of spaghetti, sausages and canned tuna, which seem to have become increasingly a globalized food found in many poor migrant diets. But dishes considered to be typically Afghan are consumed during ceremonies when the families receive guests. The symbolic valorization of Afghanistan through food and climate ('simple but good, like the people … honest and resistant') contrasts with the actual situation of the Afghan refugees in Iran, who experience social, economic and political marginality.

Food is not only an easy reference of Afghan-ness for the young migrants, which offers them a kind of symbolic compensation for the marginal place they occupy in Iranian society. In his discussion of symbolic violence, Bourdieu[27] shows how culture (including food and musical tastes, accent, etc.) is a way to mark an unequal distribution of power and wealth and to have it accepted as legitimate by the dominated people. Food is a key element of the construction of personal and group identities, childhood, adulthood, gender, etc. Discourses on bread and rice, water and tea, which are symbolic, reveal the ambivalent relations with Iranian society. Similarly, the contrast between the social and symbolic image of chicken (which seems to be increasingly consumed in exile, especially among youth) and other kinds of meat (such as mutton) refers to the difficulty in keeping their ideal of autonomy.

Figure 6.4: A young migrant back in Afghanistan having spaghetti and Iranian soft drinks with his father and uncle (Jaghori, September 2004).

The Ambivalences of Identity among Young Afghans in Iran

This chapter has brought together three important topics in the social sciences – migration, food and youth – in order to study the social practices and representations of young Afghan refugees and migrants living in Iran. It has stressed the social meaning of food and eating as an identity marker rather than material or economic factors. The consumption of food is a mundane practice repeated every day; it constantly changes and adapts to new social contexts and market supply, but it also carries a set of values and symbols which are easy to exhibit.

For the two refugee populations studied by the SARC project – as for all refugees and more generally migrants – eating and commensality constitute an arena where identities are negotiated. Practices, discourses and representations related to diet play a crucial role in the social construction of childhood and adulthood, as well as of gender and social classes. Furthermore, food is associated in both cases with the idea people may have of their autonomy, which in exile is constantly under threat. The social and political contexts are nevertheless very different. First, unlike the Sahrawis in Algeria, who live in refugee camps located in a harsh desert region and who rely on food rations provided by aid organizations, the Afghans are spread through the Iranian social fabric. Second, unlike the Sahrawis, who have set up a government-in-exile, with a president and an elected parliament and who form their own society, the Afghans are confronted by the host society on a daily basis. Finally, while many Sahrawi young children and adolescents have been able to spend some time in Europe thanks to a 'holidays abroad' programme and therefore have become familiarized with new foods, Afghan youth are not in such close contact with the West.[28]

Important differences may also be acknowledged among the Afghans in Iran. Even if their life is very hard and their diet not very diversified, young workers seem to have more resources than young refugees living with their families. The former were often more in control of their lives and had a greater support peer group. They have obviously kept stronger ties with Afghanistan and are also better able to withstand pressure from the Iranian government. For them, a stay in Iran is a way to negotiate their passage to adulthood. Migration structures the discourses on masculinity through the valorization of physical courage and generosity, hard work, self-restraint concerning spending and food consumption (indeed, a way to show self-control is to exert discipline over food habits). The latter nevertheless appear to know 'Afghan culture' better than one might have thought at first glance and they recurrently express their wish to contribute to the reconstruction of Afghanistan. Their eclectic eating style does not prevent them from having emblematic ties with their country of origin through practices and discourses related to food. Even linguistically, as they understood that their Iranian accent was difficult for me, they progressively modified their way of talking to adopt – for instance – a more dialectical Hazaragi Persian. They commented, half joking, half serious: 'At home, we speak Afghani, but outside, we speak Irani'.

Food crystallizes discourses on the self and the other. People on the move, especially children and adolescents, are important agents of social change, both in the countries of asylum and origin. Young Afghans who are in Iran, either with their families or as single migrants, have been forced by violence, insecurity or poverty to leave their homeland. They have experienced a more industrialized and urbanized way of life, and they have been cut off from the agricultural production of food. As we have seen, their food habits show multiple ambivalences: an ideal of equality implied by commensality and the hierarchy embedded in hospitality; a marker of inter-generational differences through the adoption of new food practices by the youth; a fascination for the achievements of the host society and a bitterness towards the attitude of the Iranian population and authorities; an inferiority complex and an attempt at self-valorization; an abstract feeling of Afghan-ness and a fragmentation of the effective everyday ties of solidarity.

Appendix 6.1: Examples of Weekly Intake, Daily Diet Diary

Chart 1. A male adolescent, sixteen, living in Iran for twelve years with his family; back once to Afghanistan about ten years ago. Origin: district of Shahristan

The informant has lived in Iran for a long time. His father worked outside the home during the day and his mother seemed to be ill and unable to do much housework. Being the oldest child of the family, he usually cooks at home. Having a passion for food, he knows many Afghan and Iranian recipes. This is evident in the eclectic diet of the family and the vocabulary he uses.

Time		Food / Drink	Description & preparation	Amount
Day 1	Breakfast	Tea, bread, sugar	Boiled water, tea, bread	5 cups of tea, ½ bread, one spoon of sugar
	Lunch	Rice, *khoresht*, bread	*Khoresht*: chicken liver, tomato sauce, spices, salt (ready made, sold in can) Rice boiled in water and salt for 20 minutes	Rice: 1 cup *Khoresht*: 1 cup, ¼ bread, 1 glass of water
	Dinner	Rice, *khoresht*, bread, salad	*Khoresht*: potato, red bean, meat, spices cooked together Salad: onion, tomato, cucumber, lemon, salt	Rice: ¼ cup *Khoresht*: ½ cup ½ bread 1 bowl of salad

Day 2	Breakfast	Tea, bread, sugar	Boiled water, tea, bread	Tea: 3 cups, ½ bread, one spoon of sugar
	Lunch	*Âbgusht*, bread, salt, water	*Âbgusht*: chicken, tomato sauce, spices and salt, oil	One bowl of chicken soup, ½ bread. one glass of water
	Dinner	Rice, *khoresht*, bread, salad	*Khoresht*: oil, tomato sauce, potato, red bean, chopped meat Salad: onion, tomato, cucumber, lemon	One bowl of *khoresht*, one bowl of salad, one glass of water
Day 3	Breakfast	Tea, bread, sugar		Tea: 3 cups, ½ bread, one spoon of sugar
	Lunch	Rice, *khoresht*, meat	*Khoresht*: potato, chicken, spices, tomato sauce Rice: Rice, water, salt Chopped meat	one plate of rice, one bowl of *khoresht* and meat
	Dinner	Veget able soup, bread	Soup: potato, bean, tomato sauce, water, salt	One bowl of soup, ½ bread, two glasses of water
Day 4	Breakfast	Tea, bread, sugar		Two cups of tea, ½ bread, one spoon of sugar
	Lunch	Chicken *shurwâ*, bread, cucumbe r, water	Chicken *shurwâ*: water, chicken, spice, tomato sauce, oil	One bowl of soup with a very small piece of chicken, ½ bread, one cucumber
	Dinner	Chicken *shurwâ*, water, bread	Chicken *shurwâ*: oil, water, tomato sauce, potato, onion, spices	One bowl of chicken, ½ of bread, two glasses of water

Day 5	Breakfast	Tea, bread, sugar		Two cups of tea, ½ bread, one spoon of sugar
	Lunch	Chicken *shurwâ*, bread	Chicken *shurwâ*: mutton, tomato sauce, spices, oil, onion, potato	One bowl of *shurwâ* with a very small piece of chicken, ½ bread, cucumber
	Dinner	Eggs , bread, water	Chicken soup: oil, chicken, onion, tomato sauce, spices,	Two eggs, ½ bread, two glasses of water
Day 6	Breakfast	Tea, sugar, bread, carrot marmalade		Four cups of tea, ½ bread, four spoons of marmalade, one spoon of sugar
	Lunch	Meat *shurwâ*, bread, cucumber, water	Meat *shurwâ*: meat, oil, spice, onion; bread bought from the bakery	One bowl of *shurwâ* with a small piece of meat, ½ bread, water
	Dinner	Mutton *shurwâ*, bread	Mutton *shurwâ*: mutton, onion, spice, oil, tomato sauce,	One bowl of *shurwâ*, a small quantity of meat, ½ bread, three glasses of water
Day 7	Breakfast	Tea, sugar, bread, candy		Three cups of tea, ½ bread, one spoon of sugar
	Lunch	Eggs, bread, water	Egg: Sauce, eggs, oil, salt	Two eggs, ½ bread, water
	Dinner	Spaghettis, bread, water	Boiled spaghetti served with potato, tomato sauce, oil, spices	One plate of spaghetti, ½ bread, three glasses of water

Chart 2. A female adolescent, fifteen, living in Iran with her family for three years after having spent the two previous years in Pakistan (her father has been in Iran for nine years). Origin: district of Qarabagh

The female informant was contacted through her father. The family eat dishes which are considered as typically Afghan (*âshak, kichri qorut, dugh, busrâgh,* etc.), but also new ones picked up from the Iranian host society (sausages, spaghetti, feta cheese, etc.). A generational difference may be seen, as she preferred sausages to *qoruti,* which tends to be considered as a dish for the poor in Afghanistan.

Time		Food / Drink	Description & preparation	Amount
Day 1	Breakfast	Tea, butter, marmalade, bread		One loaf of bread, 25g of butter, two cups of tea
	Lunch	Spaghetti, yoghurt, tea, water	Spaghetti, yoghurt, tea	One plate of spaghetti, five spoons of yoghurt, one glass of water, two cups of tea
	Dinner	Spinach and red beans, bread, water	Spinach, red beans, oil	
Day 2	Breakfast	Tea, feta cheese, bread		Two cups of tea, one loaf of bread, 25g of cheese
	Lunch	*Kichri qorut,* tea, water	*Kichri qorut* (typical Afghan food): a kind of risotto with soya beans topped with *qorut* (dried buttermilk) and oil	One plate of *kichri qorut,* two cups of tea
	Dinner	Bread, tea, *busrâgh*	*Busrâgh*: a sort of sweet madeleine containing floor, sugar, milk, oil, egg	Four cups of tea, one loaf of bread, *busrâgh*

Day 3	Breakfast	Tea, butter, marmalade, bread		Four cups of tea, one loaf of bread, 25g of butter and marmalade
	Lunch	*Âsh*, red beans, tea, water	*Âsh*: a kind of soup made of pasta, red beans, vegetables, oil	One bowl of *âsh*
	Dinner	*Shir berenj*, tea, water	*Shir berenj*: rice cooked with milk, oil and sugar	One plate of *shir berenj*
Day 4	Breakfast	Feta cheese, bread, tea		25g of cheese, one loaf of bread, three cups of tea
	Lunch	Rice, sausages, bread, water		One bowl of rice with sliced sausages
	Dinner	*Âshak*, *dugh*, tea	*Dugh*: a drink made of yoghurt diluted in water with salt and sometimes mint *Âshak*: a kind of agnolotti stuffed with leek and boiled	One glass of *dugh*, one plate of *âshak*
Day 5	Breakfast	Bread, feta cheese, tea		One loaf of bread, 15g of cheese, 2 cups of tea
	Lunch	Rice, yoghurt, tea, water		One plate of rice, French fries, two cups of tea, one glass of water
	Dinner	*Âshak*, yoghurt, tea		Eight *âshak* with a small quantity of yoghurt and oil, two cups of tea Breakfast

Day 6	Breakfast	Feta cheese, bread, tea	Cheese and bread bought from market	One loaf of bread, 10 g of cheese, two cups of tea
	Lunch	Rice, yoghurt, tea, water	Rice cooked at home, yoghurt and bread bought from market	One plate of rice, four spoons of yoghurt, one loaf of bread, two cups of tea
	Dinner	Sausage, yoghurt, tea (The father and the mother have eaten *qoruti*, a kind of soup of bread dipped in *qorut*)	Sausage, yoghurt and bread bought from market	One sausage, five spoons of yoghurt, one loaf of bread, two cups of tea
Day 7	Breakfast	Feta cheese, bread, tea	Cheese and bread bought from market	10 g cheese, one loaf of bread, three cups of tea
	Lunch	Rice, yoghurt, tea	Rice cooked with oil, salt and water	½ plate of rice, five spoons of yoghurt, ½ bread, two cups of tea and one glass of water
	Dinner	Spaghetti, lettuce, bread, tea		One plate of spaghettis, a small quantity of lettuce, ½ bread, one glass of water and tea

Chart 3. A young male migrant, seventeen, living on building sites with some fellow workers; in Iran for two years. Origin: district of Jaghori

The respondent was a worker living with some fellows on a building site. To save time, many lunches were eaten cold at the working place. Although he plans to go back soon to Afghanistan and will not settle down in Iran, he has picked up some new dishes (for example, canned tuna, feta cheese and sandwiches) but has not eaten what many would consider emblematic Afghan food during the week.

Time		Food / Drink	Description & preparation	Amount
Day 1	Breakfast	Tea, bread, sugar		Three cups of tea, some bread
	Lunch	Grapes, bread, water	Eaten cold at the working site	½ kg of grapes, three loaves of bread
	Dinner	Chicken *qorma*, bread	Chicken, oil, chilli, onion	Some chicken, two spoons of tomato sauce, oil, onion
Day 2	Breakfast	Tea, feta cheese, bread, sugar		Three cups of tea, two loaves of bread, two spoons of sugar
	Lunch	Red beans, chilli, bread	Red bean sauce with tomato, chilli, water	One can of red bean, three spoons of tomato sauce, one spoon of chilli
	Dinner	Chicken *qorma*, bread, candies	Chicken, tomato sauce, onion, oil, chilli, water, salt	Chicken, three spoons of tomato sauce, ½ spoon of chilli, oil, onion

Day 3	Breakfast	Bread, tea, feta cheese		2 loaves of bread, 3 cups of tea, 1 portion of cheese
	Lunch	Sandwich, cold drink	Eaten cold at the working site	One sandwich, one cold drink
	Dinner	*Shurwâ*, bread	*Shurwâ*: soup made with chicken, tomato sauce, potato, oil, onion	One bowl of *shurwâ*, bread
Day 4	Breakfast	Tea, sugar, bread, margarine, omelette	Omelette: eggs, tomato sauce, oil	Three cups of tea, one spoon of margarine
	Lunch	Bread, aubergine	Aubergine, tomato sauce, oil, onion	One loaf of bread, one aubergine
	Dinner	Sausages, bread, tea		Five sausages, three cups of tea, five loaves of bread
Day 5	Breakfast	Tea, bread, sugar		Three cups of tea, one loaf of bread
	Lunch	Feta cheese, cream, bread	Eaten cold at the working site	One portion of cheese, one packet of cream, three glasses of water
	Dinner	Eggs, juice, tea	Fried eggs with salt	Five eggs

Day 6	Breakfast	Tea, feta cheese, bread		Two cups of tea, one loaf of bread, one portion of cheese
	Lunch	Tuna, bread	Eaten cold at the working site	One can of tuna, one loaf of bread
	Dinner	*Shurwâ*, tea, cold drink	*Shurwâ*: chicken soup with tomato sauce and spices	Chicken soup, two pots of tea, nine packets of juice for guests

All the three informants seem to have a rather eclectic diet. There is no clear correlation between the length of stay and the adoption of dishes little known in Afghanistan.

Appendix 6.2: Food Glossary

Âb: water

Âbgusht (Iran): broth made with meat and some vegetable, potato, tomato sauce, and oil, boiled together; eaten with dunked bread

Âsh: soup with noodles, red beans, tomato sauce and *qorut* (the Iranian recipe is quite different)

Âshak: agnolotti stuffed with *gandana* (a kind of leek), boiled in water and topped with yoghurt, sour cream or *qorut*

Berenj: rice

Bolâni: a kind of fried rissole stuffed with leek, potato and sometimes other vegetables

Borâni: fried aubergine with tomato, served with yoghurt, sour cream or *qorut*

Busrâgh: a sort of sweet madeleine made from floor, sugar, milk, oil, eggs

Cây: tea

Chaka: coagulated buttermilk

Dalda: chopped wheat boiled in water, served with red beans and oil

Dugh: buttermilk or yoghurt diluted with water

Dumba: fat of the sheep's tail

Gusht: meat

Halim: wheat or rice, flour, chopped meat, oil

Halwâ: flour cooked with water, sugar, and oil

Kabâb: kebab, broiled meat

Khasta: almonds of the apricot's stone

Khoresht (Iran): stew of meat and vegetable with oil, onion, spices, tomato and sometimes potato

Kichri qorut: a kind of risotto with soya beans topped with *qorut* and oil

Kishta: dried apricots without stones

Leti: fried floor, sugar, oil, water that gives a sort of soup (a kind of liquid *halwâ*)

Makâroni: spaghetti

Mantu: steamed tortellini stuffed with meat, eaten in a sauce with chick peas and yoghurt, sour cream or *qorut*

Nân: bread, and by extension food in general

Nazr: charity meal (literally votive offering, vow, promise given to God)

Pirki (Hazaragi): quite similar to *bolâni*, but often smaller in size and without potato

Qâbili palaw: pilaf rice with meat, shredded carrot, raisin, almonds or pistachios

Qadid, landi: sheep's dried meat

Qorma: similar to *khoresht*

Qorut: dried buttermilk (served diluted in boiling water)

Qoruti: soup made of *qorut* diluted in boiling water, eaten with dunked bread cut in small pieces

Shir berenj: rice cooked with milk, oil and sugar

Shola-zard: a kind of sweet risotto with curcuma

Shurwâ: quite similar but often simpler than *âbgusht*; bread cut in small pieces dunked in a broth made from mutton or chicken boiled in water with onion, spices and oil; sometimes served with potato eaten at the end with the meat

Notes

1. This paper is based on fieldwork carried out for the SARC project among Afghan refugees and migrants in Iran, which took place between November and December 2003, mostly in Tehran, with some stays near Mardabad (south-west of Karaj), two trips to Qom and a short visit to the refugee camp of Shahid Naseri, near Saveh. It is also built on previous and successive researches in Afghanistan, Pakistan and Iran among Afghan refugees and migrants (Monsutti 2004, 2005). I would like to thank Dawn Chatty, Nicola Cozza, Gina Crivello, Homa Hoodfar, Sarah Kamal and Richard Tapper for the discussions on methodological and analytical issues or for their comments on previous versions of this paper.
2. All the names have been changed to protect the informants.
3. A preparation of pulverized tobacco and lime put under the tongue or between lower lip and teeth.
4. Literally: 'I am tired of travelling!'.
5. For an overview of the recent literature on food and eating, see Mintz and Du Bois (2002).
6. Among others, let us mention Lévi-Strauss (1964, 1965), Douglas (1966), Bourdieu (1979), Goody (1982), Mintz (1985).
7. For instance, according to Fischler (2001: 112), girls are generally less reluctant than boys to disclose the foods they dislike, as the latter are socially encouraged to develop a rivalry between peers and to be bolder, including in tasting new meals.
8. Studies on the relation between migration and food are dominated by a rapidly growing literature on ethnic food and the involvement of migrants in catering trade, which is not directly relevant to the present research. Let us nevertheless mention a pioneer work by Watson (1977) on the Chinese in the British catering trade and their links to their homeland.
9. See his contribution, chapter 4, in this volume.
10. For the first group, see Hoodfar and Kamal's contributions in this volume (chapters 5 and 6), and also Adelakhah and Olszewska (2007) and Tober (2007); for the second one, see Monsutti (2007).
11. The Hazaras originally dwell in central Afghanistan, a high and infertile area called Hazarajat, but many live today in cities like Kabul and Mazar-e Sharif. Unlike the majority of the Afghan population, most of them are Shiites, a fact that has deepened their political and socio-economic marginality. The *sayyed* are supposed to be descended from the Prophet Mohammed by his daughter Fatima and are present in most regions of Afghanistan.
12. The food consumption and weekly intakes charts were provided by Jeya Henry, professor of Human Nutrition, Brookes University, Oxford.
13. Thanks to Sarah Kamal and the Research Committee of the school, composed by Nasimeh Jallali, Homaira Noori, Masoomeh Moosavi, Sahar Bayat, Khadijeh Hosseini, Najibeh Hosseini, Hanifeh Azizi, Saideh Asghari, Esmat Moosavi, Mostafa Hosseini and Azizeh Karami.
14. With the help of Javed Akbari and Sarwar Hosseini.
15. See Appendix 1 for some examples. The Charts 1 and 2 are from a male and a female refugee living with their families, while the Chart 3 is from a young

worker staying on a building site with some male relatives. The charts have been translated into English by Abdul Karim Abawi.

16. Red beans remain an important part of the diet of the young Afghans interviewed, independently of their gender and of the length of their stay in Iran (see Appendix 1, Charts 1, 2 and 3).

17. Rice is a staple only in limited regions of the Middle East where it is grown and does not replace bread, which is present at every meal (Zubaida and Tapper 2000: 93–104).

18. The quality of the chicken seems, however, to vary from region to region. For example, among the Hazaras, it is not always classified within the meat category. But it is considered as the hottest meat by the Durrani Pashtuns studied by Tapper and Tapper (1986: 71).

19. See Appendix 1, Chart 2: when her parents have eaten *qoruti* one evening, the young female informant has preferred to have Iranian style sausages.

20. On food practices and consumption stereotypes as markers of social boundaries, see Bromberger (1985). Even among the Hazaras, Twelvers and Ismaelis of the region of Shibar or Kalu (Eastern Hazarajat) do not share food. More generally in Afghanistan, commensality between Shiites and Sunnites, between Hazaras and Pahstuns or Tajiks must not be taken for granted.

21. These emblematic Afghan dishes seem to be consumed by families more than by workers on the building sites (see Appendix 1, compare Charts 2 and 3).

22. I have developed these considerations elsewhere (Monsutti 2007). The rites of passage are rituals and ceremonies performed at major junctures of social life, like birth, marriage or death (see Van Gennep 1981 and Turner 1969).

23. See Appendix 1: the diet of the young worker (Chart 3) seems slightly poorer and less diversified than that of the youth living with their family (Charts 1 and 2).

24. See chapter 6 in this volume.

25. See chapter 4 in this volume.

26. See for example Harpviken (1996).

27. See Bourdieu (1979).

28. Compare with chapter 4 in this volume.

References

Abbasi-Shavarzi, M. J., D. Glazebrook, Gh. Jamshidiha, H. Mahmoudian, R. Sadeghi. 2005. *Return to Afghanistan? A Study of Afghans Living in Iran.* Kabul: Afghanistan Research and Evaluation Unit (AREU).

Adelakhah, F., Z. Olszewska. 2007. 'The Iranian Afghans', *Iranian Studies* 40(2): 137–65.

Bourdieu, P. 1972. *Esquisse d'une théorie de la pratique précédé de trois études d'ethnologie kabyle.* Geneva: Droz.

——— 1979. *La Distinction: critique sociale du jugement.* Paris: Minuit.

——— 1980. *Le Sens pratique.* Paris: Minuit.

Boyden, J., J. De Berry. 2004. *Children and Youth on the Front Line: Ethnographies, Armed Conflict and Displacement.* New York, Oxford: Berghahn Books.

Bromberger, Ch. 1985. 'Identité alimentaire et altérité culturelle dans le nord de l'Iran', in *Identité alimentaire et altérité culturelle.* Neuchâtel: Institut d'ethnologie, pp. 5–34.

Caplan, P. 1997. 'Approaches to the Study of Food, Health and Identity', in P. Caplan (ed.), *Food, Health and Identity.* London, New York: Routledge, pp. 1–31.

Centlivres, P. 1985. 'Hippocrate dans la cuisine: le chaud et le froid en Afghanistan du Nord', in *Identité alimentaire et altérité culturelle.* Neuchâtel: Institut d'ethnologie, pp. 35–57.

———1988. 'Identité et image de l'autre dans l'anthropologie populaire', in P. Centlivres, M. Centlivres-Demont (eds), *Et si on parlait de l'Afghanistan? Terrains et textes 1964–1980.* Neuchâtel: Institut d'ethnologie; Paris: Maison des sciences de l'homme, pp. 31–44.

———1988. 'L'innocence en question: les enfants afghans dans la guerre et l'exil', *Nouvelle Revue d'Ethnopsychiatrie* 12: 127–42.

———1991. 'Exil, relations interethniques et identité dans la crise afghane', *La Revue du Monde musulman et de la Méditerranée* 59–60: 70–82.

———1994. 'Les groupes ethniques et les "nationalités" dans la crise afghane', in R. Bocco, M.-R. Djalilli (eds), *Moyen-Orient: migrations, démocratisation, médiations.* Geneva: Institut universitaire des hautes études internationales; Paris: Presses universitaires de France, pp. 161–70.

Centlivres-Demont, M. 1996. 'Les réfugiés afghans au Pakistan: situation d'exil et adaptation alimentaire', in M.-C. Bataille-Benguigui, F. Cousin (eds), *Cuisines reflets des sociétés.* Paris: Sépia–Musée de l'Homme, pp. 243–55.

Chatty, D. 2007. 'Researching Refugee Youth in the Middle East: Reflections on the Importance of Comparative Research', *Journal of Refugee Studies* 20(2): 265–80.

———, G. Crivello, G. Lewando Hundt. 2005. 'Theoretical and Methodological Challenges of Studying Refugee Children in the Middle East and North Africa: young Palestinian, Afghan and Sahrawi Refugees', *Journal of Refugee Studies* 18(4): 387–409.

Douglas, M. 1966. *Purity and Danger: An Analysis of the Concepts of Pollution and Taboo.* New York, London: Routledge.

Fischler, C. 2001. *L'Homnivore: Le goût, la cuisine et le corps.* Paris: Odile Jacob.

Goody, J. 1982. *Cooking, Cuisine and Class: A Study in Comparative Sociology.* Cambridge: Cambridge University Press.

Harpviken, K. B. 1996. *Political Mobilization among the Hazara of Afghanistan: 1978–1992.* Oslo: Department of Sociology.

Lentz, C. 1999. 'Changing Food Habits: an Introduction', in C. Lentz (ed.), *Changing Food Habits: Case Studies from Africa, South America, and Eurasia.* Amsterdam: Harwood Academy, pp. 1–25.

Lévi-Strauss, C. 1964. *Mythologiques 1: Le cru et le cuit.* Paris: Plon.

––– 1965. 'Le triangle culinaire', *L'Arc* 26: 19–29.

Mintz, S. 1985. *Sweetness and Power: The Place of Sugar in Modern History.* New York: Viking.

–––, Ch. M. Du Bois. 2002. 'The Anthropology of Food and Eating', *Annual Review of Anthropology* 31: 99–119.

Monsutti, A. 2004. 'Cooperation, Remittances, and Kinship among the Hazaras', *Iranian Studies* 37(2): 219–40.

––– 2005. *War and Migration: Social Networks and Economic Strategies of the Hazaras of Afghanistan.* New York, London: Routledge.

––– 2007. 'Migration as a Rite of Passage: Young Afghans Building Masculinity and Adulthood in Iran', *Iranian Studies* 40(2): 167–85.

Saberi, H. 1991. *Noch-e Djan: la cuisine afghane.* Paris: CEREDAF.

Schetter, C. 2003. *Ethnizität und ethnische Konflikte in Afghanistan.* Berlin: Dietrich Reimer Verlag.

Sutton, D. 2001. *Remembrance of Repasts: an Anthropology of Food and Memory.* Oxford: Berg.

Tapper, R., N. Tapper. 1986. '"Eat This, it'll Do You a Power of Good": Food and Commensality Among the Durrani Pashtuns', *American Ethnologist* 13(1): 62–79.

Titus, P. 2005. 'Des vies marchandisées: les réfugiés afghans dans des réseaux de réseaux', *Ethnographiques.org* 8, http://www.ethnographiques.org/

Tober, D. 2007. '"My Body is Broken like my Country": Identity, Nation, and Repatriation among Afghan Refugees in Iran', *Iranian Studies* 40(2): 263–85.

Turner, V.W. 1969. *The Ritual Process: Structure and Anti-Structure.* London: Routledge and Kegan Paul.

Van Gennep, A. 1981 [1909]. *Les Rites de passage: étude systématique des rites.* Paris: Picard.

Watson, J.L. 1977. 'The Chinese: Hong Kong Villagers in the British Catering Trade', in J.L. Watson (ed.), *Between Two Cultures: Migrants and Minorities in Britain.* Oxford: Blackwell, pp. 181–213.

Zubaida, S., R. Tapper (eds). 2000. *A Taste of Thyme: Culinary Cultures of the Middle East.* London, New York: Tauris. [1st edn, *Culinary Cultures of the Middle East,* 1994).

Notes on Contributors

Dawn Chatty is University Reader in Anthropology and Forced Migration and Deputy Director of the Refugee Studies Centre, Queen Elizabeth house, University of Oxford, UK. She is a social anthropologist with long experience in the Middle East as a university teacher, development practitioner, and advocate for indigenous rights. She has taught at the University of California at Santa Barbara, at the State University of California at San Diego, at the American University of Beirut, at the University of Damascus, at Sultan Qaboos University and at the University of Oxford. She has worked with the regional offices of various international agencies including UNDP, UNICEF, FAO, IFAD and USAID. Her research interests include nomadic pastoralism and conservation, gender and development, health, illness and culture, and coping strategies of children and adolescents in prolonged conflict and forced migration. Her most recent books include *Conservation and Mobile Peoples: Displacement, Forced Settlement and Sustainable Development* (edited with Marcus Colchester), Berghahn Press, 2002; *Children of Palestine: Experiencing Forced Migration in the Middle East* (edited with Gillian Lewando-Hundt), Berghahn Press, 2005; and *Handbook on Nomads in the Middle East and North Africa* (ed.) Brill, 2006.

Nicola Cozza completed his doctoral research in 2004 at the Refugee Studies Centre, University of Oxford. His thesis explored the economy of Sahrawi refugees in Algeria and Mauritania with particular focus on its political and social implications. A political economist, he also completed postgraduate studies in International Cooperation (Universidad Complutense de Madrid) and Development Studies (London School of Economics). He has lived in several countries including United Kingdom, Switzerland, Spain, Mauritania and Liberia. He worked with UNHCR in Geneva and WFP in Liberia, where he developed new tools for the monitoring and evaluation of food-aid humanitarian operations, including web-based databases. He was the editor of three national evaluations of humanitarian programmes for the Government of Liberia, conducted between 2006 and 2007. His research interests include the political economy of armed conflicts, humanitarian assistance and gift, public health and agricultural economics.

Gina Crivello has a Ph.D. in Anthropology (2003) from the University of California, Riverside. Her research interests focus on processes of gender and generation in relation to youth transitions and migration, particularly in transnational and developing country contexts. She joined the Department of International Development (Queen Elizabeth House), University of Oxford, in 2002 to work as project coordinator of the Sahrawi and Afghan Refugee Children (SARC) study. In 2006 she joined Young Lives, also based at the Department of International Development, where she is a Child Research Coordinator for the qualitative component of the project.

Elena Fiddian-Qasmiyeh completed her ESRC-funded doctoral studies at Queen Elizabeth House, University of Oxford (UK) in April 2009. She is currently Senior Teaching Fellow in Development Studies at the School of Oriental and African Studies, University of London, UK. She holds degrees in Social and Political Sciences (Cambridge University), Gender and Development (London School of Economics), International Relations (University of New South Wales), and Conflict Resolution and Mediation (Universidad Abierta de Cataluña). Her doctoral thesis traces the significance of gendered identity politics in national, international and transnational dimensions of the protracted Sahrawi refugee situation, and is based on research conducted in Algeria, Syria, Cuba, Spain and South Africa between 2002 and 2007. Beyond her doctorate, Elena's multidisciplinary academic work covers a range of geopolitical settings, including the Middle East and North Africa, Sub-Saharan Africa, the Caribbean and Europe, with particular focus on issues pertaining to immigration and forced migration, Islam and gender studies, colonial histories and legacies, and transnational education networks. Her recent publications are based on research conducted with Sub-Saharan African asylum-seekers and refugees in Cairo (Egypt); Palestinian and Kurdish refugees living in the United Kingdom; and Palestinian, Syrian, Yemeni and Sahrawi university students based in Havana (Cuba). She has published in *Interventions: International Journal of Postcolonial Studies, Forced Migration Review, Journal of Refugee Studies, Anthropology News, and the Journal of North African Studies*.

Homa Hoodfar received her Ph.D. from the University of Kent at Canterbury. She is currently .professor of Social Anthropology at the University of McGill. Dr. Hoodfar has conducted field research on development and social change issues in Egypt and Iran, with an emphasis on gender, households, work and international migration in the Middle East. Further key research areas are women and Islam, and codification of Muslim family laws in the Middle East, Muslim dress code in diaspora, and the impact of long-term forced migration on family structure and gender relations on Afghan refugees in Iran and Pakistan. She has authored or edited, and co-edited a series of books: *Between Marriage and the Market: Intimate Politics and Survival in Cairo; The Muslim Veil in North America: issues and debates* (co-edited with Sajida Alvi and Sheila McDonough); *Building Civil Societies: A Guide for Social and Political Participation* (with Nelofer Pazira).

Sarah Kamal is a media specialist who has conducted independent research in Afghanistan since the summer of 2001. Her areas of interest include gender relations, development communications, and post-conflict media reconstruction. She has worked in development practice, policy and research in Canada, Nicaragua, Uganda, India, Iran and Afghanistan, consulting for international development organizations, the United Nations and the Afghan government. She was the chief editor of the National Action Plan for the Women of Afghanistan, a ten-year policy platform for the Afghan Ministry of Women's Affairs to improve the status of Afghan women, and is currently a Trudeau Scholar engaged in doctoral studies in the Department of Media and Communications at the London School of Economics, UK.

Alessandro Monsutti received his Ph.D. from the University of Neuchâtel (2002) before going to teach at the Graduate Institute of International and Development Studies, Geneva. He is currently based at the MacMillan Center for International and area Studies, Yale University. He has completed several periods of fieldwork in Afghanistan, Pakistan and Iran since 1993, and more recently in Western countries among Afghan refugees and migrants thanks to a grant given by the MacArthur Foundation, Chicago (2004–2006). His main publications include: *War and Migration: Social Networks and Economic Strategies of the Hazaras of Afghanistan*, Routledge, 2005; *Entre ordre et subversion: logiques plurielles, alternatives, écarts, paradoxes* (edited with Suzanne Chappaz-Wirthner and Olivier Schinz), Karthala, 2007; *The Other Shiites: From the Mediterranean to Central Asia* (edited with Silvia Naef and Farian Sabahi), Peter Lang, 2007; *Le Monde turco-iranien en question* (edited with Mohammad-Reza Djalili and Anna Neubauer), Karthala, 2008.

Index